Political Behavior of
the American Electorate

Political Behavior of the American Electorate
Eleventh Edition

William H. Flanigan
University of Minnesota

and

Nancy H. Zingale
University of St. Thomas

CQ PRESS

A Division of Congressional Quarterly Inc.
Washington, D.C.

CQ Press
1255 22nd Street, NW, Suite 400
Washington, DC 20037

Phone: 202-729-1900; toll-free, 1-866-427-7737 (1-866-4CQ-PRESS)

Web: www.cqpress.com

Cover design: McGaughy Design

⊚ The paper used in this publication exceeds the requirements of the American National Standard for Information Sciences— Permanence of Paper for Printed Library Materials, ANSI Z39.48-1992.

Printed and bound in the United States of America

09   08   07   06   05   1   2   3   4   5

Library of Congress Cataloging-in-Publication Data

Flanigan, William H.
    Political behavior of the American electorate / William H. Flanigan and Nancy H. Zingale.—11th ed.
        p. cm.
    Includes bibliographical references and index.
    ISBN 1-933116-67-6 (pbk. : alk. paper)
  1. Voting—United States. I. Zingale, Nancy H. II. Title

JK1967.F38 2006
324.973—dc22

                                                                2005032699

To the memory of
Ruth M. Flanigan
Edwin N. Flanigan
Amy K. Hill
James S. Hill

Contents

c h a p t e r   s e v e n

Political Communication and the Mass Media   161

c h a p t e r   e i g h t

Vote Choice and Electoral Decisions   197

Tables and Figures

Tables

Figures

Acknowledgments

U NTIL 1960 ANALYSES of the research findings and data collected by social scientists were limited to an examination of published tables, but significant changes have since occurred. The data from the major studies of American public opinion and voting behavior are now accessible to scholars throughout the world for further examination and analysis.

These developments in political analysis resulted from the cooperation of many individuals, but the efforts of two men formerly associated with the Institute for Social Research at the University of Michigan deserve special mention. Angus Campbell first opened the archives of the Survey Research Center to outside scholars. Warren Miller of the Center for Political Studies directed the organization and further expanded its archival activities through the creation of the Inter-university Consortium for Political and Social Research (ICPSR). The ICPSR, composed of more than five hundred academic and research institutions, has made available to an extensive clientele not only the archives of the Survey Research Center but also thousands of other major data collections. Scholars in the field of political behavior have benefited in incalculable ways from this work.

This book relies heavily on the ICPSR in two ways. First, we base our analyses primarily on the large quantities of material collected by the National Election Studies (NES) in the high-quality biennial election surveys conducted by the Survey Research Center, and the ICPSR Historical Archive. The ICPSR maintains and distributes the studies and the archive. Second, several generations of scholars whose work we cite have similarly benefited from the availability of these resources. We are pleased to acknowledge our great debt to the individuals involved in both the ICPSR and the NES who have contributed to the establishment of these resources and services. We must hasten to add that they bear no responsibility for the analysis and interpretation presented here. We can only hope that any weaknesses of this work will not reflect upon the general worthiness and excellence of the open archives that the ICPSR and the NES provide.

We also wish to thank our editors at CQ Press, past and present—Brenda Carter, Shana Wagger, Charisse Kiino, Kerry Kern, Tracy Villano, Ann O'Malley, Debbie Hardin, Christopher Karlsten, Talia Greenberg, Colleen McGuiness, and Jennifer Campi—for their shepherding of the last five editions of this book to publication. It is a pleasure to work with such competent and pleasant people.

W. H. F.
N. H. Z.

Introduction

THE PRESIDENTIAL ELECTION of 2004 took place amid concerns about global terrorism, with an ongoing war in Iraq that many believed ill-conceived, and an economy barely recovering from a three-year slump. The electorate appeared closely divided and polarized, with those on the left and right highly energized, working feverishly to turn out their supporters on election day, with armies of lawyers poised to challenge any wrongdoing at the polls by their opponents. The re-election of George W. Bush was narrow, but decisive, and was accompanied by Republican net gains of four seats in the U.S. Senate and five seats in the House of Representatives. Significantly, turnout was the highest it has been in forty-five years, with 58 percent of the adult population voting.

To understand and appreciate the intensity of the 2004 presidential campaign, the election of 2000, one of the most unusual in the nation's history, needs to be examined. The presidential contest between Vice President Al Gore and Bush was the closest in more than a hundred years. More remarkable, the election remained undecided for more than a month because of the uncertainty of the outcome in Florida. Not since 1876 had a presidential election remained undecided for more than a few hours after the polls closed. In Florida the voting was extremely close, and an alarming number of irregular procedures and events occurred both before and after the election that called into question the validity of many votes. An unprecedented series of political and legal steps eventually led to a five-to-four U.S. Supreme Court decision that ended the recount then in progress and effectively gave a narrow electoral college victory to Bush. The legal maneuvering, the claims and counterclaims, and the actions of officials in Florida and Washington, D.C., made those on both sides worry about the sanctity of the American electoral process. The ultimate result caused many on the Democratic side to feel that an election had been stolen from them.

Other electoral oddities abounded in 2000. For the first time since 1888 the popular vote winner was not the electoral college winner. Gore was the popular vote winner by a margin of more than 500,000 votes, but he lost the electoral college by four votes. Ralph Nader, a minor party candidate with a small percentage of the popular vote, denied the presidency to a candidate who would have otherwise won. This had not happened since 1912.

Dead heats were not limited to the presidential election. The results of the 2000 election left the U.S. Senate evenly divided between the Democrats and Republicans, with the vice president holding the tie-breaking vote. The Senate was to witness yet another unprecedented event in the late spring. Sen. James M. Jeffords of Vermont switched from Republican to independent and denied the Republicans control of the Senate. So in June following the election the Democrats reorganized the Senate. It was the first time that party control of the Senate had changed during a session.

Against this backdrop of close partisan division and lingering resentment over the election results, the horrific events of September 11, 2001, took place. The immediate political impact of the attack on the World Trade Center in New York City and the Pentagon in Washington, D.C., was for the nation and its political leadership to unite behind President Bush to face and fight the threat of terrorism. Bush's approval ratings in public opinion polls went from 57 percent (fairly low for a president still in his honeymoon period after his initial election) to 86 percent after September 11. (As discussed in Chapter 6, this "rally 'round the flag" phenomenon is common in the midst of foreign policy crises.) The war in Afghanistan, undertaken in the following months, and an array of homeland security measures were widely accepted by Congress and the public as necessary steps to take.

For many people, the terrorist attacks on American soil "changed everything" (as we ourselves said in the last edition of this book that went to press just weeks after September 11). That may or may not turn out to be an exaggeration, but one thing that has surely changed is the debut of terrorism as a powerful new symbol in American politics. Political leaders have a new and frightening symbol to use in political appeals and discussions. This would be amply illustrated in the presidential campaign of 2004.

One might also have expected that the awfulness of the attack and the outburst of patriotism that followed would have some lasting impact on the political divisions in the country. At this writing it has not. One of the most noteworthy features of the elections of 2004 is how little altered was the partisan division in the nation from what it was in 2000. Polarized in 2000, it remained so in the congressional elections of 2002 and in 2004. Resentment over the disputed outcome of the election of 2000 and a continuing weak economy had their impact. Within a few months after the September 11 attacks, Bush's presidential approval ratings had fallen to more normal ratings. By September 2002, only 68 percent approved of his performance as president.

A crucial variable in solidifying these divisions was the Bush administration's decision to go to war in Iraq. Suspicions about the veracity of intelligence reports that Iraqi leader Saddam Hussein possessed weapons of mass destruction and concerns that Iraq was a distraction from the "real" war on terrorism in Afghanistan followed existing partisan divisions among the public.

In this highly charged political atmosphere entering the 2004 election cycle, the task of the Democratic Party was to choose a candidate to challenge President Bush. The first candidate to gain visibility was Howard Dean, former governor of Vermont and a vociferous opponent of the war in Iraq. Dean raised huge amounts of money via the Internet and his grassroots Web-based campaign, featuring such innovations as Web-advertised "meet-ups." He was enormously successful in energizing hundreds of supporters throughout the country, despite concerns that as a candidate, Dean might be too liberal, too inexperienced, and too much of a loose cannon to be elected.

Concerns about electability eventually undermined the candidacy of Dean. The intensity of the negative feelings toward Bush was perhaps best illustrated by the unusually high level of commitment of rank-and-file Democrats, Democratic activists, and elected officials to choose someone as their nominee who could beat Bush. In the "up-close-and-personal" electioneering in the Democratic precinct caucuses of Iowa—by tradition the first venue for choosing delegates to the Democratic national nominating convention—Dean's standing collapsed and Massachusetts senator John Kerry surged to victory in the final days before the caucuses. Democratic hunger for a winner was so great that other early states fell in line behind the front-runner and Kerry had virtually wrapped up the nomination by winning five of seven primaries held on February 4, 2004—an unprecedented early date.

The campaign for the presidency in 2004 was fought primarily in the so-called battleground states—the dozen or so states where the outcome was close enough in 2000 to give the other side hope of victory. Florida and Ohio, and a number of other states to a lesser extent, were treated to a barrage of TV advertising throughout 2004. The rest of the states, considered safely in one camp or the other, were largely spared. Republican themes focused on President Bush's leadership in the war on terror and pointed to Kerry's alleged flip-flops on issues. A subtheme, supported by independent advertising by the Swift Boat Veterans for Truth and never disavowed by the Bush camp, questioned Kerry's record of heroism in the Vietnam War. On the domestic front, Bush promised to shore up Social Security by diverting a portion of the payroll tax to private stock accounts. The Democrats, in turn, focused on criticism of the Bush administration's handling of the war in Iraq—dishonesty in making the case for going to war, continued poor planning in carrying it out, and responsibility for providing the impetus for a new wave of terrorism—along with traditional Democratic economic themes. The Massachusetts Supreme Court made gay marriage a campaign issue by declaring it a constitutional right in Kerry's home state. Although Kerry's position was that state legislatures, not the courts, should decide such matters, the issue energized and brought to the polls anti-gay marriage activists in many states where gay marriage bans were on the ballot.

Both Republican and Democratic supporters mobilized to get out the vote. "Independent" groups, affiliated with one or the other party, mobilized activists to register new voters, to get them to the polls on election day, and to assist them in withstanding challenges to their right to vote—or, on the other side, to make such challenges. In a departure from conventional campaign strategy, Bush strategist Karl Rove spent considerable resources mobilizing Christian conservatives in safe states. Although extra Republican votes in these states might be "wasted" in terms of the electoral college, they would serve to provide President Bush a popular vote victory—something he had been denied in 2000.

The outcome in 2004 was close—but not as close as 2000. Bush won the popular vote by almost three million, versus a loss by over a half million votes in 2000. The electoral college was a close copy of 2000, with only Iowa, New Mexico, and New Hampshire changing columns. (A reallocation of electoral votes, following the 2000 census, accounts for a net switch of seven votes, as population—and thus electoral votes—shifted from "blue" to "red" states.) In 2004 a slight change in voting in Ohio would have given Ohio to Kerry, making him the winner of the electoral college while losing the popular vote nationwide. Thus two elections in a row have been extremely close in popular voting and in the electoral college, with the possibility or actuality of the popular vote and the electoral college vote diverging. Few elections in American history have been as close as 2000 and 2004.

The first edition of this book was published in 1967. The plan of the book then, as now, was to present basic analysis and generalizations about the political behavior of Americans. What was unknowable at the time was that a decade of political trauma was beginning for the American polity in the late 1960s. Not only would some basic changes in political life take place, but these changes would call into question some of the things political scientists thought they knew about the way Americans behave politically. The years since then have seen their quiet periods and their moments of political upheaval. Much has changed in the political landscape—the impeachment and forced resignation of pres- idents, the dismantling of the welfare state under Ronald Reagan, the Republican "revolution" in the House of Representatives in 1994, the fo- cus on homeland security in the post–September 11 world. Over the years since that first edition, however, we have been impressed with the overall continuity in the behavior of the electorate, even in the midst of significant changes in the political environment.

In this eleventh edition we continue to focus attention on the ma- jor concepts and characteristics that shape Americans' responses to pol- itics: Are Americans committed to upholding basic democratic values? Who votes and why? How does partisanship affect political behavior? How and why does partisanship change? How do economic and social characteristics influence individuals' politics? How much influence do the mass media have on the electorate's attitudes and political choices? How do party loyalties, candidates' personalities, and issues influence voters' choices among candidates?

Throughout the book we place the answers to these and other ques- tions in the context of the changes that have occurred in American po- litical behavior over the past fifty years. Wherever possible, we put these recent trends in the broader context of political change over the two hundred years of the Republic. Specifically, we are concerned with the decline in voter turnout, the loss of trust in government that many citi- zens have expressed, and the drop in voter attachment to political parties coupled with an increasing polarization of political activists and elites. These trends, and their implications for American democracy, have been the subject of much discussion by political analysts and commentators.

A second major focus of this book is to illustrate and document these trends in American political behavior with the best longitudinal data available. We rely heavily, although not exclusively, on data from surveys conducted by the National Election Study (NES). The NES sur- veys, covering a broad range of political topics and offering the best time-series data available, have been conducted during the fall of every election year since 1952. Unless otherwise noted, the data come from this extraordinarily rich series of studies. We hope that the numerous tables and figures contained in this book will be used not only for doc- umenting the points made in the book but also for learning to read and interpret data. Students can also explore a much wider range of data from the NES on its Web site at www.umich.edu/~nes. The data from the NES and other studies are available for classroom use through the Inter-university Consortium for Political and Social Research (ICPSR). (To see the full range of political studies available to the academic com- munity, visit the Web site of the ICPSR at www.icpsr.umich.edu.) One of our purposes is to provide an impetus for obtaining high-quality data to answer questions prompted, but not answered, by this book.

Political Culture and American Democracy

SUCCESSFUL DEMOCRACIES rest on the consent of the governed and widespread public support. In representative democracies, regular, free, and fair elections are held to choose political leaders and, when necessary, to turn these leaders out of office. A democratic system of government, at a minimum, affords its citizens the opportunity to organize, to speak freely, and to select its leaders.

Beyond this simple, widely agreed on view, which assumes a crucial role for the people in choosing their representatives and emphasizes the individual as an autonomous actor with inherent political rights, less consensus exists on what is required of citizens. On the one hand is the vision of a well-informed electorate making decisions based on rational calculations of its own best interest or, possibly, a public good. On the other hand is the picture, drawn by some critics, of a deluded public, manipulated by political elites to hold views and support policies that are in the interests of the elites instead of the people. Somewhere in between is the view that the electorate responds to generalized policy promises and symbolic issues in selecting its leaders, setting broad and vague outer limits on decision makers. Specific policies, however, are negotiated between public officials and subsets of the attentive public who are unrepresentative of the general public, both in terms of their degree of interest in a particular policy and in the political resources available to them with which to exert influence. In the chapters that follow, you will have the opportunity to judge for yourself the level of information and capacity for rational decision making that the American public displays.

In this chapter we consider two topics. First, we examine an issue brought starkly into focus by the presidential elections of 2000 and 2004.

What are the requirements for fair and free elections in a democracy and how closely does the U.S. system come to meeting that standard? Second, we look at the cultural and attitudinal requirements for instituting and sustaining a democratic system and examine the extent to which those requirements are met in the United States. How widespread is support for the political system in the United States and for the democratic values on which it is based? How confident are Americans that a democratic system is the best route to satisfactory policy outcomes?

How confident are they that their government is playing by democratic rules? What expectations do citizens have about their own roles in a democratic system? How are democratic values and appropriate citizen roles learned and transmitted from generation to generation?

Fair, Free, and Competitive Elections

Elections are a basic component of a democratic political system. They are the formal mechanism by which the people maintain or alter the existing political leadership. At regular intervals, competitive elections give ordinary citizens the power to choose their leaders and, just as important, to throw them out of office. Although the choices available to voters in a general election may not be numerous or even particularly dissimilar, democratic systems must provide for competition, usually by means of political parties, in presenting alternative candidates.

If elections are to be competitive, political leaders and organizations must be able to compete for the support of voters, and voters should have leaders competing for their support. (If some voters have no leaders competing for their support, the system must be open to the entry of new leaders who will seek the support of these unrepresented voters.)

Competitive elections require that all citizens must be free to participate fully in campaign activities before the election itself. Such campaign activities include the freedom to express one's views and the freedom to organize with others during the nominating phase and the campaign to make preferences known and to persuade others. Implicit in this is the freedom to receive information about the choices before the voters.

Citizens must be free to vote, and the right to vote should not be undermined by substantial economic or administrative barriers. No physical or social intimidation should take place. Citizens legally eligible to vote should have full and convenient access to polling places. The right to vote and the right to express one's choices freely require a secret ballot. In fair elections the ballots cast should reflect the intention of the voters, and the votes should be counted accurately. Votes should be weighted equally in translating votes into representation.

Requirements for Free and Fair Elections

A democratic system requires political leaders to compete for public support in fair and free elections. For elections to be fair and free, they must meet the following conditions.

- Freedom of citizens to form or join organizations in support of candidates
- Freedom to express preferences
- Alternative sources of information
- Ability of new leaders to enter the system and compete for support
- Right to vote without administrative barriers or intimidation
- Votes counted fairly
- Votes translated into representation fairly
- Due process and equal protection under the law

Finally, the requirements of free and fair elections should be established in law and be enforceable through the judicial system. Both citizens and leaders must enjoy equal treatment under the law.

Recent presidential elections provide an opportunity to reassess the extent to which the requirements for being fair and free have been met.

The presidential elections in 2000 and 2004 were close and intensely contested. An impressive array of independent, nonparty groups formed in support of specific candidates. While some such groups were "letterhead organizations," and others not truly independent of the parties or candidates, the number and vigor of groups, such as ACT (Americans Coming Together), MoveOn.org, and the 72-Hour Program, were noteworthy, particularly in 2004. The availability of the Internet as a place for groups to "meet" has facilitated the ability to join with like-minded people in support of one's preferred candidate.

Freedom of political expression is guaranteed by the First Amendment to the U.S. Constitution, and few legal limits are placed on what can be said about a political opponent. Local and state ordinances and ethics commissions keep outright falsehoods from the candidates and their campaigns in check, but citizens, supporters, and talk-show hosts generally can and do get away with expressing all manner of opinions regarding current and potential officeholders. The most critical issue with freedom of expression in the age of television is the imbalance in resources available to get one's views to a wide audience. Although the two major political parties are well funded, candidates seeking the presidential nomination through the primaries, minor-party candidates, and citizens with views not represented by the major parties may find themselves unable to get a hearing.

Given the vast amounts of money spent on political advertising in presidential election campaigns, much of it highly negative, the focus has often been on how to place limits on it. For years the U.S. Supreme Court has ruled that issue advocacy by individuals or independent groups is protected by First Amendment guarantees, and the Court and Congress have wrestled with the problem of placing limits on it. The bigger problem for a democracy such as the United States is reconciling freedom of expression with the disparity of resources that allows some groups to get a hearing for their views and others not.

Concerns have been raised in recent years about the concentration of ownership of mass media outlets in fewer hands. Although this has certainly happened, it is probably more than offset by the proliferation of new sources of information from the Internet and cable and satellite television. The problem likely is not whether alternative information sources exist, but whether consumers can sort through them to find credible sources and whether they will avail themselves of varied and competing views.

Despite the tight competition between the two major-party candidates, the barriers to entry into the competition by other candidates are severe. Although other candidates—Pat Buchanan and Ralph Nader in 2000 and Nader in 2004—were on the ballot in virtually every state, and Buchanan had access to public financing, the obstacles to effectively competing are serious. Both these candidates were denied a place in the nationally televised debates, and the electoral college arrangements encourage voters to see a vote for such candidates as a wasted vote. Many of the rules governing elections in the United States are designed to weed out nuisance candidates and to limit attention to those with some degree of public support. Public financing, participation in the debates, and place on the ballot all require demonstration of some minimum level of support. On an informal level, coverage of a candidate's campaign by the mass media also requires such a demonstration. Unfortunately, minor candidates are faced with a chicken-and-egg dilemma. They cannot gain access to these important resources unless they are competitive, but they cannot become competitive unless they have access to these resources.

Registering to vote has become easier in most states in recent years, and, in fact, registration has increased. (We will treat the topic of voter registration and turnout more fully in Chapter 2.) Efforts also are evident in some states to make it easier for registered voters to vote by allowing vote by mail or easing restrictions on the use of absentee ballots. Administrative problems remain, however, and fall unevenly on the citizenry. In many states, officials have been slow to process new registrations, so that individuals who have correctly followed registration procedures find themselves not registered when they get to the polling place. This problem can rarely be solved in a timely fashion by the election judges at the polling place.

The Help American Vote Act (HAVA) of 2002 was fashioned to deal with some of these problems. One provision, in effect for the election of 2004, was to allow voters who thought they were registered but did not appear on the registration lists to cast a provisional ballot that would be sealed and held, but not counted until the voter's eligibility to vote had been established. Another provision of HAVA was to mandate establishment of a statewide electronic database so problems of verifying registration can be resolved more quickly.

Nevertheless, as the competition between the two major parties has become closer and more intense, the willingness to use measures to restrict participation (or discourage fraud or both) has increased. These tendencies were at work in the presidential election in Florida in 2000 and Ohio in 2004, both hotly contested states.

An unusual registration problem in Florida in 2000 received a considerable amount of attention from the U.S. Commission on Civil Rights.[1] Because significant fraud came to light in some recent Florida elections, before the 2000 election the state legislature enacted legislation to purge the registration lists of ineligible voters (such as the dead or otherwise departed). The state contracted with a private firm to purge from the registration lists felons, who are not eligible to vote in Florida. This was done by computer-matching lists of felons from Florida and elsewhere with the voter registration lists. The procedure led many nonfelons to be removed from the lists because the lists were inaccurate and the computer match did not have to be perfect—the computer purged names if there was a 90 percent match of letters. Some people were informed that they had been purged before the election, but the procedures for reinstatement were confusing. Others were not informed beforehand and arrived at their polling place only to be told that they were ineligible to vote.

The Civil Rights Commission also heard testimony of black citizens in Florida who reported being stopped by state police on the way to the polls. If such obstruction was intentional and systematic, it would be a denial of fair access to a polling place.

Simple administrative bungling can have the same effect—for example, providing incorrect or conflicting information to would-be voters. In Ohio in 2004, voting equipment was reallocated to precincts on the basis of turnout in previous elections, not on the basis of number of registered voters. This usually meant sending voting equipment from central city areas to suburban areas. When turnout increased dramatically in 2004, voters in Cleveland and Columbus (areas with high Democratic concentrations) stood in line, reportedly, for hours waiting to vote. Doubtless some voters did not stick it out. Also, the Republican secretary of state, Kenneth Blackwell, ruled that provisional ballots, provided under the Help America Vote Act, would be counted only if they were cast in the precinct in which the voter lived. This was a permissible ruling, according to the Federal Election Assistance Commission, but nonetheless was the kind of restrictive interpretation that serves to decrease participation in elections.

Because so much information is available on the vote-counting process in Florida in the aftermath of the 2000 election, it can be used as a test of the requirement that votes be counted accurately. (Focusing on Florida may create unfairly the impression that everywhere else elections are trouble-free. That is certainly not the case. We simply have little information on most other states.)

The 2000 election in Florida demonstrated that voting procedures themselves can deny voters their vote. Voting devices fail to record votes in various ways. On punch-hole ballots the paper chad may not be dislodged and, therefore, would not be counted; on scanned ballots the choices may not be detected; and on most voting devices the voter can inadvertently void the ballot by various kinds of inappropriate marking. (In party primary elections, in which voters are required to vote in only one party's races but the ballot form allows voting in more than one party primary, large percentages of the ballots are invalidated for this reason.)[2] Voting machines do exist that detect such errors and give the voter another chance to cast a ballot correctly, but the machines are relatively expensive and not widely used. Another provision of the Help American Vote Act, which goes into effect in 2006, is to require that states give voters an opportunity to check and correct their ballots before the ballot is cast.

The marked ballot should accurately reflect the voter's intention. In 2004 in Broward County, Florida, for example, the butterfly ballot, which was enlarged to help elderly voters read it better, seems to have resulted in a considerable number of voters mistakenly casting their votes for Buchanan when they intended to vote for Al Gore. Election officials in different counties used different rules for determining the voter's intent on flawed ballots during the various phases of the recount. Some officials allowed votes to be counted if the voter's intention could be reasonably inferred from the marks or punches on the ballot. In other counties, even ballots with a clear declaration of intent—such as that of the frustrated voter who wrote "I want to vote for Gore" on the ballot—were disallowed.

The counting of votes is overseen by representatives of the competing political parties, and they are expected to keep each other honest. Even so, standardizing procedures in different election districts is difficult.* For example, in Florida in 2000 the counting of the overseas ballots attracted a great deal of attention. Many months after the election, the Republican Party was revealed to have pursued a two-part strategy: In Republican counties, it insisted that all ballots be counted even if the ballots were flawed in various ways. In Democratic counties, Republican officials followed the strict letter of the law to disallow identically flawed ballots.

Although never a major theme in democratic theory, a fair election must allow for a thorough and accurate recount to ensure that the official results faithfully reflect the voters' choices. All vote-counting procedures are susceptible to error and fraud, so the occasional authentication of official returns is crucial to maintaining the legitimacy of elections in general. Typically in the United States recounts have uncovered a certain amount of clerical error and little fraud. As a consequence, the failure to have a full recount in Florida fueled questions about the legitimacy of the election. In 2004 Democratic presidential candidate John Kerry's campaign insisted that all the provisional ballots cast in Ohio be evaluated and, if valid, counted as part of a statewide recount. The stated purpose was not to challenge the results of the election, but to assert the importance of every vote being counted.

The election of 2000, in which the popular vote winner did not win in the electoral college and did not become president, puts in stark relief the problem of translating votes into representation. How can votes be considered equal if the state in which they are cast determines how much influence they have in determining the winner? The rationale lies in the nature of a federal system. States, as well as individual citizens, are actors in such a system and their role was preserved in the electoral college as a part of the price of establishing the Union. It is one of many ways in which the American system departs from a purely representative democracy. Electoral outcomes such as 2000 are rare, however. The only other presidential elections that have resulted in a popular vote loser winning the electoral college were 1876 and 1888.[3] If one wants to consider a far more perverse case of bad translation of votes into representation, one should look at the U.S. Senate, where the votes of 16 percent of the population can elect a majority of that body.

---

*Following the Florida election controversy, a consortium of eight news organizations was formed to recount the presidential vote for the entire state. They used a number of different rules for counting disputed ballots. They found that systematically following the rules advocated by the Gore advisers would have led to a George W. Bush victory and following the rules preferred by the Bush organization would have produced a Gore victory. All major newspapers, including the *New York Times* and the *Washington Post,* carried stories on the recount project on November 9, 2001.

Finally, in 2000 the partisan overtones to the involvement of the Florida Supreme Court (which ruled to benefit the Democrat) and the U.S. Supreme Court (which ruled to benefit the Republican) in deciding the election raise questions about the extent to which elections in the United States are subject to the rule of law. The election of 2000 tested the confidence of the public in the fairness of the American electoral system. The tight competitiveness of the contest led both sides to campaign aggressively for every possible vote—and, in the confused aftermath of the election, to use every conceivable tactic to gain an advantage for their side. The challenge in a democratic electoral system is to be highly competitive without compromising the integrity of the election process. It is hard to say to what degree the election of 2000 undermined confidence in the legitimacy of the electoral process. A few months after his inauguration in 2001, only half the public reported believing that George W. Bush "won fair and square."[4] By 2004, little had changed in these feelings. Fifty percent thought the 2000 election was "fair," whereas 49 percent thought it was not—and most on both sides felt strongly. Nonetheless, most people thought the election of 2004 had been fair. Only about 15 percent thought it was unfair.[5] A postelection survey by the Pew Research Center for the People and the Press found that about half of all voters were "very confident" that votes across the country were counted accurately.[6] After the 2004 election, 77 percent of the public said they were very or fairly satisfied with the way U.S. democracy works. This was about the same percentage as in 1996 and 2000.

Political Culture as a Foundation for Democracy

Political culture is the set of values and beliefs that support (or sometimes undermine) political processes and institutions. In democracy theory, much depends upon those beliefs and values. Citizens need to accept the idea of rule by the majority and, equally, to believe that the rights of the minority should be respected. They should have some sense of their rights and obligations to participate in the political process, at a minimum through exercising the right to vote. The political elite—those who hold elected or appointed office and those involved in putting them there—need to be willing to play by the democratic rules of the game and respect the will of the majority, even when it means the loss of their positions. In the remainder of this chapter we will examine the content of American political culture and assess it as a foundation for the maintenance of democracy. We will of necessity focus attention on the values of the dominant national culture, though you should keep in mind that political subcultures exist that may support contrary values and attitudes.

System Support

Governments, whether democratic or nondemocratic, require some level of support from the public to stay in power. Their holding of power must be seen, in some sense, as *legitimate*. The source of that legitimacy could be the divine right of kings (in hereditary monarchies of the past) or from religious authority (as with the imams of present-day Iran) or from the consent of the people (in modern democracies). An important element in maintaining legitimacy is the belief that officeholders gained their position through the appropriate means (through fair and free elections in the case of democracies) and exercise their power according to prescribed procedures and within prescribed limits. In a simplified scenario, if the public in a democratic system believes in democratic values it will support leaders who come to office through democratic elections and govern according to democratic procedures. Furthermore, it would withdraw support from any leader or would-be leader who attempts to gain office or govern by undemocratic means.

A complicating factor in the consideration of system support is the impact of governmental *effectiveness* on public perceptions of legitimacy. A tyrannical government that makes the trains run on time may gain some measure of legitimacy, despite abuse of persons and procedures. Conversely, a democratically elected government that governs by democratic procedures but is chronically unable to solve its nation's problems may lose its legitimacy. Its citizens might lose faith in democracy as a workable form of government and demand a different system. Support for a political system is thus a combination of belief in the rightness of a system of government and satisfaction with the way that system is working.

On a relatively superficial level, Americans express a strong pride in their country. In response to questions in public opinion polls, 96 percent say that they are proud to be American; 89 percent say they are very patriotic; 89 percent characterize their love of America as "very strong" or "extremely strong"; and 79 percent say their feelings about the flag are "very good" or "extremely good."[7]

When people are asked about their pride in the United States, they tend to offer political factors as examples. In other countries people are much more likely to give nonpolitical reasons for their pride: their country's economy, culture, or physical beauty. They are not nearly so likely to say they are proud of their political system.[8] Americans not only give political reasons for their pride in the United States but also cite "freedom" or "liberty" as the aspect of their political system that makes them proud. Thus, not only is there strong patriotic pride in the nation, but a central democratic value also is a prominent feature of that sentiment.

Pride in the nation and its democratic form of government translates into high levels of political system support. Of the respondents to a national survey 85 percent agree that, "whatever its faults, the United States still has the best system of government in the world." More than half of the public "would not change anything" in the American political system.[9]

Vague principles may be widely endorsed even though, at the same time, specific applications may be opposed. So it should not be surprising that respondents will agree to vague statements of system support while they endorse contradictory specifics. For example, 80 percent of the public say that the Constitution should not be amended.[10] However, majorities also believe that the Constitution should be changed to abolish the electoral college or mandate a balanced budget. Almost certainly none of these answers reveals how people would behave if faced with real choices on amending the Constitution.

Democratic Beliefs and Values

The beliefs and values supporting the American political system are variously referred to as the *American creed,* the *American consensus,* and the *American ethos.*[11] Among the most important values making up this creed are beliefs in *freedom, equality,* and *individualism.*

Social and political theorists make a distinction between the economic system and the political system. Most would say that the United States has, as an ideal, a democratic political system and a capitalist or free-market economic system. Ordinary citizens are more likely to mix the two and view freedom as a basic value in both. The freedom to own property, fundamental to a capitalist economic system, is considered by ordinary citizens of the United States to be as important as the right to vote, for example.

Although highly valued in American culture, freedom is not considered an absolute. People accept all kinds of limitations on their freedom. For example, when given a choice between government intervention and a wholly free market, the American public is clearly in favor of strong government activity. In the 2004 National Election Study, by a ratio of more than two to one, the public preferred strong government intervention to handle economic problems rather than depending solely on free-market operations. Similarly, majorities of the public support limiting the freedom to read pornography, to own guns, and to smoke cigarettes.

The widespread belief in equality similarly needs to be qualified. Americans believe in "equality before the law" and in "equal opportunity" but are largely uninterested in using government to promote economic and social equality. For example, the public agrees overwhelmingly with the proposition that "our society should do whatever is necessary to make sure that everyone has an equal opportunity to succeed."[12] But a substantial minority of the public believes "we have gone too far in pushing equal rights in this country."[13] In many respects, the value placed on individualism undermines the commitment to equality. Most social groups exhibit widespread support for the idea that people can and should get ahead by virtue of their own hard work.

Belief in Democratic Procedures

A distinction often is made between democratic *goals,* such as equality and individual freedom, and democratic *procedures,* such as majority rule; protection of the political rights of freedom of speech, press, and assembly; and due process of law. The distinction is an important one when the extent to which these ideals are supported in the political culture of a system is under consideration, because democratic goals can be pursued through undemocratic means or democratic procedures can be used for antidemocratic ends. Likewise, mass support may exist for democratic goals but not for democratic procedures or vice versa.

A widely held and perfectly plausible expectation is that the American public supports both these kinds of democratic values. At an abstract level this is true enough. American citizens overwhelmingly subscribe to the basic rules and goals of democracy when the commitment is kept vague. But, as discussed above, the near unanimous support for the democratic goals of freedom and equality disappear when specific applications of these concepts are considered. The same has been true for specific applications of democratic procedures, such as protection of free speech. Majorities historically have been happy to infringe on the right to speak, to organize, and to run for office of unpopular groups such as atheists, Communists, and the Ku Klux Klan.

Rising educational levels in the United States brought an increased willingness on the part of the public to allow free speech on unpopular points of view and permit books with distasteful perspectives to remain in public libraries. Numerous studies document the shift in attitudes occurring from the mid-1950s to the 1970s, and without exception they find a strong relationship between increased tolerance and higher levels of education.[14]

Some important qualifications are in order. First, the electorate's responses are attitudes that may have little meaning for it and are not measures of its behavior or of its attitudes under crisis or threat to democratic principles. Second, people may not be more tolerant but the focus of their intolerance may have shifted. People now tolerate speeches by Marxists but object to those of fascists or racists.[15] More broadly, the desire for censorship may have shifted from political speech to other forms of expression, such as art and music, particularly when sexual or sacrilegious themes are involved.

Since the September 11, 2001, attacks, much speculation has arisen about how willing Americans would be to sacrifice rights and freedoms in waging the war on terrorism. Generally, the public is not supportive of provisions of the Patriot Act directed at ordinary citizens but is supportive of activities directed at "terrorists."[16] For example, 71 percent disapprove of federal agents searching a U.S. citizen's home without informing the person, yet majorities support a range of similar activities when the target is "terrorists." Between a quarter and a third of the public believe the Patriot Act "goes too far" in restricting people's civil liberties, whereas equal numbers think it does not go far enough.[17]

When considering public support for civil liberties and other democratic values, it is essential to keep in mind the distinction between mass attitudes and those of the political, social, and economic leaders in American society who consistently support democratic principles more strongly than the general public. Support among leaders is usually so high that it is possible to conclude that the leaders in society defend and maintain democratic procedures. Consensus among leaders on democratic rights and values makes the weakness of the general public's support less crucial.

Table 1-1 compares the responses of samples of the public with those of "political influentials" to questions about support for the "democratic rules of the game" in the 1960s and in 2004. In both cases, the political influentials were consistently more likely to support maintaining civil liberties and democratic processes than a sample of the electorate.

Presumably, leaders are recruited and educated in such a way that they come prepared with, or develop, agreement on democratic procedures. Leaders apparently make decisions that maintain democratic practices, even without widespread public support. A somewhat less comforting possibility is that political elites are simply sophisticated enough to understand what the "correct" answer is to attitude questions dealing with democratic beliefs. The seemingly greater adherence to these values by the politically active would attest to the prominence of such norms in the mass political culture but would not necessarily suggest any great commitment or willingness to abide by these values. A third possibility exists such that political leaders, like ordinary citizens, are willing to violate the rights of groups and individuals whom they particularly dislike or fear. Enough incidents of undemocratic behavior by public officials have occurred in recent decades—harassment of dissidents during the Vietnam War, "dirty tricks" to undermine the electoral process in 1972, surreptitious aiding of the Nicaraguan contras in violation of the law in the 1980s—to suggest no great depth of appreciation of democratic principles on the part of elites of either political party. The increasing incivility in Congress and the mass media that has ac-

TABLE 1-1   Political Influentials versus the Electorate, Responses to Items
Expressing Belief in Democratic Values

Item	Percentage agreeing with item	
	Political influentials	General electorate
There are times when it almost seems better for people to take the law into their own hands rather than wait for the machinery of government to act. (1964)	13	27
The majority has the right to abolish minorities if it wants to. (1964)	7	28
I don't mind a politician's methods if he manages to get the right things done. (1964)	26	42
Almost any unfairness or brutality may have to be justified when some great purpose is being carried out. (1964)	13	33
People ought to be allowed to vote even if they can't do so intelligently. (1964)	66	48
The true American way of life is disappearing so fast that we may have to use force to save it. (1964)	13	35
Favor using torture to extract information from suspected terrorists. (2004)	8	27
Favor restricting immigration into the United States to fight terrorism. (2004)	36	76

Source: The 1964 data were adapted from Herbert McClosky, "Consensus and Ideology in American Politics," *American Political Science Review* 58 (June 1964): 365, Table 1. There were 3,020 influentials and 1,484 in the public sample for 1964. The 2004 data were taken from *Global Views 2004: American Public Opinion and Foreign Policy* (Chicago: Chicago Council on Foreign Relations, 2004). See www.ccrf.org/globalviews2004. There were 450 influentials, including 100 members of Congress or their senior staff, and 1,195 in the public sample for 2004.

Note: Because respondents were forced to make a choice on each item, the number of omitted or "don't know" responses was, on the average, fewer than 1 percent and thus has little influence on the direction or magnitude of the results reported in the table.

companied the increased polarization of the society along political lines suggests that the democratic virtue of tolerance of one's opponent's views is in short supply among political elites today.

The 2000 election appears to offer examples of elites adhering to the rules of the game in some instances and abandoning the rules in others. Evidence exists of pressure from some members of the elite to abide by the result of the election (whatever that might be) and the rule of law (however interpreted) and a desire to be seen as following democratic rules. At other times, the operating principle seemed to be "do whatever you can get away with."

To take another example, reaction to the Supreme Court's decisions on flag burning illustrates several aspects of the role of political elites in supporting democratic values. Political dissidents have occasionally burned the American flag to protest policies or governmental actions with which they disagree. In retaliation, Congress and some state legislatures have passed laws making it a crime to desecrate the flag. The Supreme Court has consistently ruled these laws to be an unconstitutional infringement on free speech—classifying flag burning as "symbolic speech" and therefore protected by the First Amendment. Inevitably, such decisions provoke a public outcry and calls to amend the Constitution as a means to circumvent the Court's rulings and punish those who would burn the flag. In these circumstances, various political elites—the Court itself and some congressional leaders—support democratic values by resisting the popular passion for punishing flag burners. At the same time, other political leaders see an opportunity to exploit an issue that plays well among the public, because polls consistently show the public believes, by majorities of three or four to one, that there should be no right to burn or deface the U.S. flag.[18] In the past, proposed constitutional amendments to ban flag burning have been defeated once the issue became rephrased as "tampering with the Bill of Rights," thus demonstrating the generalized, if vague, support the public has for democratic values and the critical nature of elite leadership. The fact that legislative action to ban flag burning is once again percolating in Congress illustrates the temptations inherent in the superficial public support for civil liberties.

The widespread interest of political analysts in public opinion and democratic beliefs has been based partly on a somewhat mistaken impression. Stable democratic political systems have been assumed to rest on a nearly universal commitment to fundamental principles and their application, but the evidence is inconclusive. A democratic system cannot long survive widespread, intense hostility to democratic values, but positive belief in particular operating procedures among the public is probably unnecessary. Hostility to democratic procedures is fatal, whether among the leaders or the public, but support of specific procedures may prove essential only among leaders. Perhaps the public need not agree on basic principles so long as it does not demand disruptive policies and procedures.

Declining Trust in Government

In general, the public has considerable confidence in the *institutions* of government but not much confidence in the *individuals* charged with operating these institutions. Thus, virtually no popular support is found for abolishing the presidency or the Supreme Court or Congress, although disenchantment is widespread with the way the nation's political leadership is performing in the major branches of government. By early 2005, a little more than 10 percent of the public had "a great deal" of confidence in Congress, and roughly one quarter had "a great deal" of confidence in the presidency and the Supreme Court.[19] Such low levels of confidence, with some variations, have existed since the early 1970s and represent a noticeable drop from the levels of confidence characteristic of earlier years.

John Hibbing and Elizabeth Theiss-Morse argue, in their book *Congress as Public Enemy*, that it is the very openness to public scrutiny of congressional activities that generates distaste.[20] This may explain the higher level of confidence in the more secretive executive and Supreme Court decision making. In short, when the people see democracy in action, they do not like it very much.

Figure 1-1 shows another indicator of declining public confidence in the political system. For years, the National Election Studies have asked respondents whether they thought "the government in Washing-

FIGURE 1-1   Attitudes toward Politics and the Political System, 1952–2004

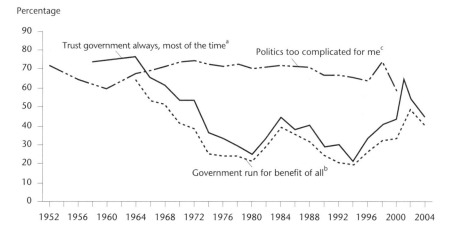

Source: National Election Studies, available at www.umich.edu/~nes.

External efficacy
[a]"How much of the time do you think you can trust the government in Washington to do what is right—just about always, most of the time or only some of the time?"
[b]"Would you say the government is pretty much run by a few big interests looking out for themselves or that it is run for the benefit of all the people?"
Internal efficacy
[c]Agree with the statement: "Sometimes politics and government seems so complicated that a person like me can't really understand what's going on."

ton could be trusted to do the right thing." Figure 1-1 shows an overall decline from high levels in the 1950s and early 1960s to the point in the early 1990s where only a third of the public believed the government will do what is right "all of the time" or "most of the time." Short-term reversals in this downward trend have been associated with policy successes or popular incumbents. President Ronald Reagan created an upbeat mood in the 1980s that translated into a modest restoration of confidence in government, as did the booming economy in the mid-1990s. After the terrorist attacks on the World Trade Center and Pentagon on September 11, a *Washington Post* poll reported an upward spike in the level of trust in government, shown at the right on Figure 1-1. Of the people questioned, 64 percent of the public said they trusted the government all or most of the time.[21] This level had not been seen since the 1960s. The unusually high level of trust began to fall almost immediately. Commercial polls show that a month later the percentage had dropped from 64 percent to 55 percent.[22] Further decline was seen over the next year or so. By January 2005, a *Los Angeles Times* poll showed the same low level of trust as one of its earlier polls in March 2001.[23]

Because the steepest decline in trust in government officials occurred between 1964 and 1976, it is easy to blame the Vietnam War and the Watergate scandal. Although no doubt contributing factors, the decline in trust had already begun before Vietnam became an issue and continued after Richard M. Nixon's resignation from office. Furthermore, the pattern of declining trust extends to many nongovernmental institutions, such as the news media, schools, the professions, and to people in general. It is paralleled by similar trends outside the United States in many of the developed nations of the world.

The Role of the Citizen

Measures such as the "trust in government" indicator or agreement that "government is run for the benefit of all," both shown in Figure 1-1, are sometimes referred to as measuring *external political efficacy*, or the extent to which citizens believe that their government is working the way it should—which, in a democratic system, involves responding to the will of the people. In contrast, the concept of *internal political efficacy* refers to the degree to which individuals see themselves as capable of influencing the political process because of their own abilities and competence. The two may sometimes be difficult to disentangle in practice, but in theory they are distinct. A person may think, "I'm a capable, knowledgeable person, but the system is so corrupt that I don't get a fair hearing" (high internal efficacy but low external efficacy). Another person might have the opposite set of feelings: "This is the greatest country in the world; if only I had an education I could run for office, too" (high external efficacy but low internal efficacy). A democratic system requires confidence in its institutions and processes. It also requires citizens who feel competent to involve themselves in politics.

A measure of internal political efficacy, the percentage of respondents over the years who agreed with the statement "Politics and government is too complicated for people like me to understand," is also included in Figure 1-1. A high proportion of the sample has agreed with the statement over the years, suggesting low internal political efficacy, although different measures would produce different results. Internal political efficacy is highly related to education, so increases in education probably account for the slight downward trend in Figure 1-1 (or upward trend in internal political efficacy) in recent years.

Despite apparent misgivings about their own political competence and the willingness of officeholders to listen, most Americans understand the basic obligations of citizens in a democracy. About 90 percent of all adults believe that good citizens have a duty to vote in elections, although many of them do not act on that commitment at every election. Although Americans also believe in the importance of informing themselves about political and governmental affairs, they readily concede that in most cases they personally are not as well informed as they should be.

The most common form of political participation is exercising the right to vote. (We will discuss voter turnout in Chapter 2, including the impact of declining levels of trust on citizens' willingness to participate.) Maintaining a representative democracy involves more than voting, however. Because the message or mandate of an election is seldom clear, specific policy concerns must be communicated to one's elected representatives. Organizing with like-minded individuals increases the chances that one's interests will be heard. Participation in voluntary associations—political and nonpolitical—has long been noted as an important contributor to democratic politics. Alexis de Tocqueville, writing in the nineteenth century, commented on Americans' proclivity toward joining organizations of all sorts. Not only do participants in voluntary associations learn useful political skills, but the existence of many organizations with overlapping memberships also tends to moderate conflict. People whose interests conflict on one set of issues may find themselves working together as allies on some other set of issues. Membership in organizations links people to each other and to their communities. In a study of Italian states, Robert D. Putnam showed that the most significant difference between those with effective democratic politics and those without was the existence of a strong associational life.[24]

Putnam has recently raised the alarm over what he refers to as the "declining social capital" in the United States. Americans, he argues, are now less likely to join organizations of all kinds—from bowling leagues to labor unions to political parties. This he attributes to women in the workforce, increased residential mobility, and technological innovations, such as television, the personal computer, and the video cassette recorder, all of which allow individuals to work and play in isolation.[25]

In a major study of political participation in the United States, Sidney Verba, Kay L. Schlozman, and Henry E. Brady seem to counter Putnam's claim, finding organizational participation in America "lively and varied."[26] In a comparison with a similar study in 1967, they find a decline in some forms of political activity, such as voting and membership in political clubs, but similar levels of participation in community activities and sizable increases in political contributions and contacting public officials about issues. Putnam would agree with the last contention, also noting increases in the membership in tertiary—or mass membership—organizations. Such organizations, however, usually do not involve the face-to-face interaction that fosters cooperation and builds community.

Verba, Schlozman, and Brady also conclude that the pattern of participation in America distorts the voice of the people. Those with education and money participate; the poor and uneducated do not. As a consequence, the interests of the affluent are well represented in government, and those of the less advantaged are not. Participation in religious institutions does not have this social class bias, and Verba, Schlozman, and Brady conclude that religious organizations are an important mechanism for developing political skills among the less advantaged citizenry.[27]

More intense forms of political activity, such as working on political campaigns, have remained much the same over this time period—although the levels of involvement have never been high. Many individuals who contribute financially to campaigns are not involved in any other way. When all forms of campaign activity, including financial contributions, are counted, somewhat more than 10 percent of the electorate is involved in some way.

Childhood Socialization

Most social groups, particularly those with distinctive sets of norms and values, make some effort to teach appropriate attitudes and expected behaviors to their new members. In a democracy, this would include teaching beliefs and values supportive of majority rule, tolerance for diverse opinions, and an understanding of the role of citizens as participants in the political process.

In most societies the process of socialization is focused primarily on the largest group of new members: children. Through the process of political socialization the political culture of a society is transmitted from one generation to the next, but this socialization is also an important mechanism through which change in the political culture can take place.

In societies in which most learning about politics occurs in the home, the prevailing political culture probably changes no faster than the attitudes of the adult population as a whole, in response to varied personal experiences and changing circumstances in the environment. In modern societies other agents of political socialization also are involved, particularly the educational system and, increasingly, the mass media. To the extent that these institutions instill a different set of values and norms compared with those held by the adult population as a whole, an opportunity exists for changing the political culture. Under the Communist regimes in the People's Republic of China and, formerly, the Union of Soviet Socialist Republics, the official ideology dominated both the schools and the mass communications system. Massive changes in values took place within the span of a generation. (The fact that contrary attitudes survived the indoctrination attests to the multiplicity of agents of socialization, even in totalitarian states.) More diversity in views is permitted in the United States, but the prevalence of middle-class values among both teachers and the media guarantees that these orientations will continue to be widespread in the population as a whole.

Given the importance of the socialization process in the transmission of the fundamental beliefs and values of the political culture, it is surprising that socialization studies have not paid more attention to the development of attitudes supportive of democratic goals and procedures. Data collected in the 1950s by David Easton, Robert D. Hess, and others show that children develop an affective attachment to the term *democracy* early (by about the third grade), but the concept acquires meaning much more slowly.[28] The progress of learning from the fourth grade to the eighth grade is shown for several concepts in Figure 1-2. Perhaps the most interesting aspect of the data in the figure is the high level of disagreement among teachers over the correctness of including the right of dissent in the meaning of democracy.

In 1999 an elaborate cross-national Civic Education Study directed by Judith Torney explored attitudes toward democratic culture among teenagers in twenty-eight countries. The data in Table 1-2 display knowledge of the concept of democracy among American ninth graders. The top of Table 1-2 shows one-sided agreement that it is very good for democracy "when everyone has the right to express their opinions freely" and "when citizens have the right to elect political leaders freely." Fifty-five percent believe the first item is "very good for democracy," only 2 percent think it is "very bad for democracy." (When the "very good" and "somewhat good" responses are added together, the total is 83 percent, as shown in parentheses in the table.)

FIGURE 1-2   Children's and Teachers' Understanding of the Concept of
Democracy

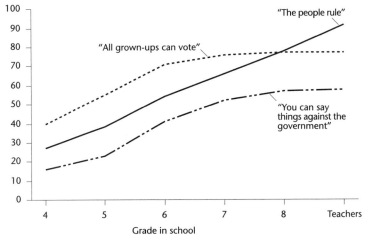

Source: Adapted from Robert D. Hess and Judith V. Torney, *The Development of Political Attitudes in Children* (New York: Anchor Books, 1968), 75, Table 13.

Collectively, ninth graders are not nearly so sure of other tenets of democracy listed in Table 1-2. For example, only 24 percent believe it is very good for democracy for political parties to have different positions on issues or for newspapers to be free of government control. Young people may absorb the ambivalence that many adults, especially their teachers, feel toward political parties and a free press, a situation also reflected in the Easton and Hess studies forty years before. (In the 1999 study, teachers divided half and half in thinking participation in political parties was a good idea in a democracy.) Ninth graders were fairly evenly divided on preventing newspapers from printing stories that might offend ethnic groups. They were even less supportive of the idea that the separation of church and state is a good idea in a democracy. All of this suggests the schools are stronger in teaching some principles of democracy than others.

The development of the child's thinking about the institutions of government and about his or her own role as a citizen has also been studied. The child's first view of government and governmental leaders casts the leaders as all-powerful and benevolent, undoubtedly the result of the twin objectives of parents and teachers to instill an acceptance of authority and to shield young children from the harsher realities of political life. Gradually, the child acquires a more realistic and more cyni-

TABLE 1-2   Ninth Graders' Views on What Is Good and Bad for Democracy,
1999

	Percentage saying	
	Very bad for democracy	Very good for democracy
When everyone has the right to express their opinions freely	2 (9)	55 (83)
When citizens have the right to elect political leaders freely	5 (12)	61 (81)
When political parties have different positions on important issues	6 (25)	24 (59)
When newspapers are free of all government control	10 (37)	24 (51)
When people participate in political parties in order to influence government	10 (29)	22 (55)
When newspapers are forbidden to publish stories that might offend ethnic groups	19 (38)	27 (50)
When there is a separation between the church and the state	24 (49)	15 (32)

Source: U.S. Department of Education, National Center for Education Statistics, Civic Education Study, 1999. See www.wam.umd.edu/~iea.

Note: The percentages in parentheses combine "very bad for democracy" responses with the "somewhat bad" and the "very good" with the "somewhat good."

cal view of the world. Children also begin with a personalized view of government. Government means the president or, for some, the police officer. In time these images are replaced or supplemented with more abstract ideas about Congress and the election process.[29]

During the elementary grades, children develop a set of attitudes toward their own roles as citizens. Initially, the emphasis is on obedience: The good citizen obeys the law, just as good children obey their parents. In the American socialization process, this is gradually replaced by a view of oneself as a more active participant in the political system: The good citizen is one who votes. Still later, the child adds the notion that the government can be influenced through the voting process.

As with other attitudes, the development of confidence in one's own ability to influence government is related to social class and intelligence among children, just as it is related to social class and education in adults. Some other aspects of the view of the citizen's role that children develop in the later elementary years might conceivably hinder their effectiveness or willingness to participate in the real world of politics later. The role of the individual in influencing government is stressed; the role of organized group activity in politics is downgraded. In the same way, American children develop a low tolerance for conflict, believing, for example, that it hurts the country when the political parties disagree.

In the past, the youngest voters were typically the most trusting of government, a tendency one would expect, given their recent exposure to an educational process that tries to build support for the system. In the 1950s and early 1960s, when most of the major socialization studies were undertaken, young people entered adulthood with strong affective feeling toward the government and a positive orientation toward themselves as participants in it.

A study of high school seniors and their parents, carried out in 1965 by M. Kent Jennings, showed that trust and confidence in government were fairly high among the students.[30] As learning continues into adulthood, substantial modification of attitudes can occur through a variety of personal experiences with politics, new group membership, and the like. The original students in the Jennings study have been reinterviewed at intervals over the years. Their level of trust in government declined from 93 percent in 1965, to 67 percent in 1973, 51 percent in 1982, and 49 percent in 1997.

Maintaining a Democracy

Belief in democratic ideals is essential to the preservation of a democratic system, both because such beliefs inhibit citizens from undemocratic actions and because the public will demand proper behavior on the part of political leaders. Belief that the system and its leaders meet democratic expectations in adhering to democratic procedures and responding to the wishes of the public is also important. A third factor is perhaps less obvious. A democratic system must meet some standard for effectiveness in solving societal problems. If not, the public may conclude that democracy does not work, that some other form of government—such as a dictatorship—is needed to maintain order, fend off an enemy, or provide economic well-being.

When expectations are not met in the behavior of political leaders or in the experiences individuals have in the political process, disappointment, cynicism, or hostility may result. Americans come to hold high expectations for the political system and, as a consequence, are subject to considerable disenchantment with the performance of government and their own role in politics. Although no direct evidence on this point is available, nothing has been found to suggest that the value Americans place on the ideals of democracy, majority rule, or the importance of participation in politics has declined. Instead, events over the past thirty years have led to a larger perceived discrepancy between the specific American political institutions (and their incumbents) and the ideal.

Ideals, combined with the generally high expectations Americans hold for the political system, can lead to cynicism and mistrust of political leadership when scandals occur or policies appear not to work. But another form of disenchantment operates at the individual level. The American ethos and the content of the political culture lead individuals to expect a wide range of conditions and values. They expect to enjoy freedom, justice, and equality; they expect to enjoy personal economic success; and they expect to be safe from violence.

If individuals find that what is happening to them is far different from these expectations, they may react with resentment. Many individuals, to be sure, respond to adversity in personal terms and do not view their problems from a collective or political perspective. Others, however, may engage in disruptive political activities. In a society such as the United States, the people who suffer economic hardship or are victims of social injustice are oftentimes minorities that are isolated by race, ethnicity, sexual orientation, or some other identifiable characteristic. Under these circumstances such a group may develop a set of subcultural values that is different from the values of the dominant culture. The group may passively withdraw from political activity or it may become actively disruptive of the system. The bombing of the federal building in Oklahoma City in 1995 or the anthrax attacks in 2001 illustrate that a disruptive, antisystem sentiment can emerge. The rioting in Seattle, Washington, at the World Trade Organization meetings in 2000 may represent a new capacity to mobilize large numbers of people with different agendas. The Internet has created an unprecedented opportunity for communication and mobilization of individuals who would not have been so well connected in the past.

Public opinion polls indicate considerable variation in Americans' assessment of their society. One general question that has been used for many years asks whether the country is going in the "right direction" or has gotten on the "wrong track." For most of the last three decades, the public has been more dissatisfied than satisfied with the way the country is going. In the fall of 2004, 38 percent of the public said the country was going in the "right direction" and 59 percent said the country was on the "wrong track," a relatively negative assessment by historical standards.[31] At the same time, when asked to agree or disagree with the statement, "Whatever its faults, the United States still has the best system of government in the world," 89 percent agreed—and most of those agreed strongly.[32]

Given the lack of sophistication in the public's understanding of democratic values and procedures, along with the declining levels of trust in government and its leaders, some uneasiness emerges about public support for American democracy—and perhaps for any democratic regime. The United States can be seen as a democratic system that has survived without a strong democratic political culture because governmental policies have gained continual, widespread acceptance. If that satisfaction erodes, however, the public has no deep commitment to democratic values and processes that will inhibit support of antidemocratic leaders or disruptive activities.

Democratic theory implies that the public should demand values and procedures embodying democratic principles. The hope or expectation is that the public in a democratic society will insist on certain values and processes. A mass public demanding democratic values and procedures would provide strong support for a democratic regime. However, a democratic system could survive with much lower levels of support, given other conditions.

In our view, a distinction should be made between the factors necessary for establishing a democracy and those contributing to maintaining one. The example of contemporary Russia, to mention only one case, suggests that stronger public support probably is required for the successful launching of a democracy than it is for maintaining an already established democracy. Possibly, preserving a regime simply requires that no substantial proportion of the society be actively hostile to the regime and engage in disruptive activities. In other words, absence of disruptive acts, not the presence of supportive attitudes, is crucial.

However, leaders' positive support for a political system is essential to its existence. If some leaders are willing to oppose the system, it is crucial that there be no substantial number of followers to which such leaders can appeal. The followers' attitudes, as opposed to their willingness to act themselves, may provide a base of support for antisystem behavior by leaders. In this sense, unanimous public support for democratic principles would be a firmer basis for a democratic system.

The high levels of dissatisfaction, accompanied by a lack of strong commitment to democratic values in the American public, appear to create some potential for public support of undemocratic leaders. As shown in subsequent chapters, many Americans feel an attachment to one or the other of the established political parties, an attachment that inhibits their embracing new political leaders. The parties and the public's attachment to them are often seen as preventing political change. They can also be seen as encouraging stability and preserving a democratic system by lessening the likelihood of a demagogue's rise to power.

Notes

1. U.S. Commission on Civil Rights, "Voting Irregularities in Florida during the 2000 Presidential Election," available at www.usccr.gov/vote2000/stdraft1/main.htm. See especially chap. 5.
2. In party primary elections voting in both primaries invalidates up to one-third of the ballots.
3. Arguably, 1960 is another case. See note to Figure 2-1.
4. Gallup Poll, April 20–22, 2001, Roper Center of the University of Connecticut, accession number 0381385.
5. 2004 National Election Study, available at www.umich.edu/~nes.
6. Pew Research Center for the People and the Press, www.people-press.org.
7. "Opinion Roundup," *Public Perspective* 3 (May/June 1992): 7–9; and 2004 National Election Study.
8. Gabriel Almond and Sidney Verba, *The Civic Culture* (Princeton: Princeton University Press, 1963). These patterns have been evident in cross-national public opinion polls since Almond and Verba first recorded them in 1963.
9. ABC News/*Washington Post* Poll, December 14–15, 2000, Roper Center of the University of Connecticut, accession number 0375554.
10. ABC News/*Washington Post* Poll, December 14–15, 2000.
11. For a major effort to capture this fundamental aspect of political culture, see Herbert McClosky and John Zaller, *The American Ethos* (Cambridge, Mass.: Harvard University Press, 1984).
12. 2004 National Election Study.
13. 2004 National Election Study.
14. For the major study of the 1950s, see Samuel Stouffer, *Communism, Conformity, and Civil Liberties* (Garden City, N.Y.: Doubleday, 1955). For a more recent work, see C. Z. Nunn, H. J. Crockett, and J. A. Williams, *Tolerance for Nonconformity* (San Francisco: Jossey-Bass, 1978).
15. John L. Sullivan, James Piereson, and George E. Marcus, *Political Tolerance and American Democracy* (Chicago: University of Chicago Press, 1982); and George E. Marcus, John L. Sullivan, Elizabeth Theiss-Morse, and Sandra L. Wood, *With Malice toward Some* (Cambridge, England: Cambridge University Press, 1995).
16. Gallup, CNN, *USA Today* Polls, February 2004, Roper Center of the University of Connecticut, accession number 0449108, 0449109, and 0449110, respectively.
17. Gallup Poll, November 2003, Roper Center of the University of Connecticut, accession number 1600423.
18. In April 2000 the Freedom Forum found 25 percent agreed that "people should be allowed to burn or deface the American flag as a political statement" and 74 percent disagreed. The public was evenly divided on amending the Constitution to prohibit desecration of the flag. See Roper Center of the University of Connecticut, accession numbers 0367822 and 0367832.
19. Harris Poll, February 2005, Roper Center of the University of Connecticut, accession numbers 1619470 and 1619479.
20. John Hibbing and Elizabeth Theiss-Morse, *Congress as Public Enemy* (Cambridge, England: Cambridge University Press, 1995), chap. 3.
21. Stephen Barr, "Trust in Government Surges during Crisis," *Washington Post,* September 30, 2001, C02.
22. CBS News/*New York Times* Poll, October 25–28, 2001, Roper Center of the University of Connecticut, accession number 0390700.
23. *Los Angeles Times* Poll, January 2005, Roper Center of the University of Connecticut, accession number 1614922.

24. Robert D. Putnam, *Making Democracy Work: Civic Traditions in Modern Italy* (Princeton: Princeton University Press, 1993).
25. Robert D. Putnam, "Bowling Alone: America's Declining Social Capital," *Journal of Democracy* 6 (January 1995): 65–78.
26. Sidney Verba, Kay L. Schlozman, and Henry E. Brady, *Voice and Equality: Civic Voluntarism in American Politics* (Cambridge, Mass.: Harvard University Press, 1995), 509.
27. Verba, Schlozman, and Brady, *Voice and Equality,* chap. 17.
28. The results of this study have been reported in several articles and in Robert D. Hess and Judith V. Torney, *The Development of Political Attitudes in Children* (New York: Anchor Books, 1968); and David Easton and Jack Dennis, *Children in the Political System: Origins of Political Legitimacy* (New York: McGraw-Hill, 1969).
29. David Easton and Jack Dennis, "The Child's Image of Government," in *Socialization to Politics: A Reader,* ed. Jack Dennis (New York: Wiley, 1973), 67.
30. The findings of this study are most extensively reported in M. Kent Jennings and Richard G. Niemi, *The Political Character of Adolescence: The Influence of Families and Schools* (Princeton: Princeton University Press, 1974); and M. Kent Jennings and Richard G. Niemi, *Generations and Politics* (Princeton: Princeton University Press, 1981).
31. 2004 National Election Study.
32. ABC News/*Washington Post* Poll, December 14–15, 2000, Roper Center of the University of Connecticut, accession number 0375554.

Suggested Readings

Almond, Gabriel, and Sidney Verba. *The Civic Culture.* Princeton: Princeton University Press, 1963. A classic study of political culture in five nations, including the United States.

Hibbing, John R., and Elizabeth Theiss-Morse. *Stealth Democracy: Americans' Beliefs about How Government Should Work.* Cambridge, England: Cambridge University Press, 2002. A provocative analysis of the public's attitudes toward American political processes.

Marcus, George E., John L. Sullivan, Elizabeth Theiss-Morse, and Sandra L. Wood. *With Malice toward Some.* Cambridge, England: Cambridge University Press, 1995. An innovative study of the public's tolerance of unpopular groups.

McClosky, Herbert, and John Zaller. *The American Ethos.* Cambridge, Mass.: Harvard University Press, 1984. An analysis of the public's attitudes toward democracy and capitalism.

Putnam, Robert D. *Bowling Alone: The Collapse and Revival of American Community.* New York: Simon and Schuster, 2000. An analysis of the decline of participation in civic affairs.

Rosenstone, Steven J., and John Mark Hansen. *Mobilization, Participation, and Democracy in America.* New York: Macmillan, 1993. An analysis of the interaction between the strategic choices of political elites and the choices of citizens to participate in politics.

Skocpol, Theda, and Morris P. Fiorina, eds. *Civic Engagement in American Democracy.* Washington, D.C.: Brookings Institution, 1999. A collection of readings on civic engagement in historical perspective.

Verba, Sidney, Kay L. Schlozman, and Henry E. Brady. *Voice and Equality: Civic Voluntarism in American Politics.* Cambridge, England: Cambridge University Press,

1995. A survey of various forms of political participation, their determinants, and the impact on representative democracy.

Internet Resources

The Web site of the National Election Studies, www.umich.edu/~nes, offers extensive data on topics covered in this chapter. Click on "Support for the Political System." Some of the attitudinal data cover 1952 to the present. For all items, additional information is presented on numerous social groupings in each election year.

If you have access to LexisNexis through your school, click on "Academic Universe," then "Reference," and then "Polls and Surveys." This will give you access to the Roper Center for Public Opinion Research, which has a keyword search capability. Hundreds, perhaps thousands, of items related to political culture can be found there from surveys taken from the 1930s to the present.

For a rich collection of data on American ninth graders, see the Civic Education Study at www.wam.umd.edu/~iea.

c h a p t e r   t w o

Suffrage and Turnout

IN 2004 THE OFFICIAL VOTING turnout rate in the presidential election was 58 percent, one of the highest in fifty years and up 8 percentage points from 2000. Turnout had been in a steady decline over the last four decades, from a high of more than 60 percent in the 1960s, interrupted only by a jump to 55 percent in the three-candidate contest of 1992.

The decline in the voting turnout rate since 1960 was accompanied by a great deal of commentary and concern about the future of American democracy. The decline in turnout appeared paradoxical, because it occurred at a time when the legal impediments to voting have been eliminated or eased and the education levels of American citizens are reaching all-time highs. Despite greater opportunities to vote, Americans seemed to be doing so less frequently. A favorite theme of editorial writers focused on the declining turnout rate as a symbol of the growing disenchantment of voters with the political system.

Whether 2004 represents a reversal in the overall decline in turnout is too soon to tell. In this chapter, we will put the downward trend in turnout—along with the reversals in 1992 and 2004—into a broader historical context. We will look at the factors that make some individuals more likely to vote than others and examine how changes in the political environment can affect whether people vote. We will also look at the way in which voting turnout is estimated and, in doing so, raise some questions about whether the concern over declining turnout is justified.

Extensions of Suffrage

Suffrage, or the *franchise,* means the right to vote. Originally, the U.S. Constitution gave the determination of who should have the right to vote entirely to the states. Later, amendments were added to the Constitution that restricted the states' abilities to deny the right to vote on the basis of such characteristics as race, gender, or age. However, the basic constitutional provision that gives states the right to set the qualifications for voting remains, and over the years states have used such things as the ownership of property, literacy, and length of residency as criteria for granting or withholding the right to vote.

During the colonial period and the early years of the Republic, suffrage was commonly restricted to white males possessing varying amounts of property. In effect, only a small proportion of the adult population was eligible to vote. The severity of the impact of property requirements varied from state to state, and their enforcement differed perhaps even more. Gradually, the required amount of property held or the amount of taxes paid to obtain suffrage was reduced. Sometimes these changes were hard-won reforms enacted by state legislatures or by state constitutional amendment; at other times practical considerations led to substantial reforms. For example, delays in acquiring final title to land holdings in the western frontier areas during the 1800s made establishing property requirements for suffrage impractical. Often during the early years of American history, candidates in local elections would simply agree among themselves that all white males could vote instead of trying to impose complicated restrictions on the electorate. Only in more settled communities could complex restrictions on suffrage be effectively enforced. In sections of the East, however, wealthy landlords sometimes supported the enfranchisement of their poorer tenants with the expectation of controlling their votes.[1]

After the eventual granting of suffrage to all white males, the next major change was the enfranchisement of black males by constitutional amendment following the Civil War. Even though the change was part of a set of issues so divisive that it had led to war, the numerical impact of adding black males was slight in the nation as a whole. However, unlike other changes in suffrage, it had a geographical bias: The impact of enfranchising black males was felt almost entirely in the South. (Their subsequent disfranchisement in the South will be discussed later.) The next major constitutional extension of voting rights was suffrage for women in 1920. It created by far the most dramatic increase in the number of eligible voters, roughly doubling the size of the potential electorate. In the early 1970s, through a combination of federal statutory law and state laws followed by constitutional amendment, the definition of citizenship for purposes of voting was lowered to age eighteen, accomplishing another major extension of suffrage.

These extensions of suffrage, which have not been easy or inevitable, may be explained by the existence of certain political forces. In stable political systems such as the United States, the extension of suffrage will result from (1) a widely shared commitment to moral principles that entail further grants of suffrage and (2) the expectation among political leaders that the newly franchised will support the political preferences of the leaders.

As discussed in Chapter 1, the political culture and political rhetoric of America carries strong themes of individualism and equality. These values are reinforced in the educational system, in the media, and throughout popular culture. As a result, the commitment most Americans have to equality, individualism, and democracy has provided a basis for supporting extensions of voting rights.

But more than idealism contributed to the expansion of the electorate. In the two most dramatic extensions of suffrage, to blacks and to women, political leaders expected the newly enfranchised to support certain policies. Republicans—the party of abolition—anticipated that black voters in the South after the Civil War would help to secure Republican domination of the southern states. Perhaps most southern states passed through a period during which at least some chance existed of combining the votes of blacks and poor whites into a governing majority. The intense prejudice of whites and the difficulty in maintaining the enfranchisement of blacks kept the strategy from working under most circumstances, but a significant element in Republican enthusiasm for black suffrage was the knowledge that Republican voters were being added to the rolls.

The same mixture of idealism and self-interest that was behind the efforts to enfranchise blacks appears to have supported suffrage for women as well. Women were expected to clean up politics once they had the vote. They were seen optimistically as the cure for corruption in government, as unwavering opponents of alcohol, and as champions of virtue in the electorate. Reformers of all sorts encouraged the enfranchisement of women as a means of promoting their own goals.

No doubt similar factors were at work in the most recent extension of suffrage to eighteen- to twenty-year-olds. But perhaps more important was the widespread feeling that a system drafting young people to fight in the unpopular Vietnam War ought to extend to them the right to participate in the electoral process.

A unique aspect of the extension of suffrage in the United States was the addition of states in the frontier expansion across the continent. During the decades immediately preceding the Civil War, the politics of slavery dominated political decisions about additions of states, with accompanying expectations about the policy impact of expansion. Here, too, the question of the enlargement of the electorate was dominated mostly by concern over the political persuasion of the newly enfranchised voters.

Because throughout American history different state and local election practices have existed, no single set of eligibility requirements can be used as a basis for deciding who belonged to the electorate at any one time. For example, individual states had granted suffrage to blacks, women, and young voters, either in law or in practice, before these groups' nationwide enfranchisement. In some states, women had previously been allowed to vote in local and school elections but not in statewide or federal contests. Thus, many different eligible electorates existed with different characteristics.

Restrictions on Suffrage

Under the provisions of the U.S. Constitution, the states set the qualifications for voters. The three extensions of suffrage by constitutional amendment did not alter this but prohibited the states from using certain criteria (race, gender, or age) to deny the right to vote. Because states retained the right to impose other restrictions, they have at times used these restrictions to prevent whole classes of people from voting. The most notorious of these efforts was the effective disfranchisement of blacks in the southern states during the late nineteenth and early twentieth centuries.

Several techniques for disfranchising blacks have been used during the past century in the South, and from time to time some of these techniques were applied in the North on a more limited basis to restrict the electoral participation of immigrants. The most common methods included white primaries, the poll tax, literacy tests, discriminatory administrative procedures, and intimidation. In some southern states only whites were allowed to vote in party primaries (the crucial election in one-party states), under the rationale that primaries to nominate candidates were internal functions of a private organization. The U.S. Supreme Court ruled such white primaries unconstitutional in 1944 on the grounds that the selection of candidates for election is a public function in which discrimination on the basis of race is prohibited. The now illegal poll tax, whereby each individual was charged a flat fee as a prerequisite for registration to vote, was used for years and no doubt disfranchised both poor blacks and poor whites. In some states the effect was cumulative, because poll taxes had to be paid for all previous years in which the individual had not voted. The poll tax eventually became unpopular with the white voters who had to pay it whereas the blacks, disfranchised by other means, did not. The literacy test gave local officials a device that could be administered in a selective way to permit registration of whites and practically prohibit the registration of blacks. The standards of literacy applied to blacks in some cases—for example, reading and interpreting the state constitution to the satisfaction of the white registrar—made it impossible for even highly educated blacks to register, whereas whites might be required to know only how to sign their names. To remain effective over long periods of time, these and other similar administrative devices probably depended on intimidation or the use of violence against blacks. Detailed analysis by Jerrold D. Rusk and John J. Stucker of the impact of the poll tax and literacy tests from 1876 to 1916 suggests that the poll tax was the more effective device, and its efficacy was greatest where the tax rate was highest and its application most cumulative.[2]

A study of black registration in 1958 by Donald R. Matthews and James W. Prothro indicated that southern states using poll taxes and literacy tests still inhibited black voter registration after World War II.[3] The poll tax has since been outlawed by amendment to the U.S. Constitution, and the use of federal voting registrars in the South under the terms of the Voting Rights Act of 1965 has eliminated the worst excesses in the application of literacy tests. Registration rates in the South for whites and blacks were approximately equal by 1980, and turnout rates have concurrently increased to the point that little difference in turnout is evident now between the North and South in presidential voting.

The outlawing of the poll tax through constitutional amendment and the suspension of literacy tests by the Voting Rights Act of 1965 and its extensions have eliminated two important restrictions on the right to vote. Other state restrictions on suffrage remain, although there is great variation from state to state. In all but four states, prison inmates cannot vote. In many states, convicted felons cannot vote until they have served their entire sentence—in other words, completed probation or parole; in some, a felony conviction entails a permanent forfeiture of voting rights. With the prison population growing, this amounts to a sizable restriction of the franchise. Because of longer sentences and higher rates of incarceration among blacks, the restriction falls more heavily on the black population. A recent study by the Sentencing Project estimates that 13 percent of black males are disfranchised under these requirements.[4]

Residency requirements are another common restriction on suffrage. In the past such requirements were often highly restrictive. Some states mandated up to two years of residence in the state before one was eligible to vote. Highly mobile segments of the population were thus often disfranchised intermittently as each move required a reestablishment of residence. In the 1970s the Middle Atlantic states, with their mobile populations and traditionally rigorous residency requirements, had as high a rate of unregistered citizens as did the states of the former Confederacy with their legacy of racial discrimination.

In 1972 the Supreme Court linked the imposition of a residency requirement to the length of time needed to prepare lists of registered voters before an election, suggesting that thirty days was sufficient to do this. Since then the Court has allowed state laws requiring fifty days to stand.

By the early 1990s the legal barriers to voting had been reduced, for the most part, to the requirement that voters be registered to vote in advance of an election. The inconvenience of administrative arrangements for voter registration and the frequent need to reregister have offered greater obstacles to voting than has the imposition of other eligibility standards. Some states have moved toward same-day registration and vote by mail in an effort to remove impediments to voting and to increase electoral turnout. The Help American Vote Act of 2002 provided a federal mandate to the states to adopt a system of provisional ballots and a statewide electronic database of registered voters in an effort to overcome glitches in registration procedures.

Nevertheless, as was discussed in Chapter 1, the close presidential elections of 2000 and 2004 showed that at least as many forces are at work trying to use suppression of turnout for partisan advantage as there are efforts to increase turnout. The presidential election in Florida in 2000 and, to a lesser extent, Ohio in 2004 revealed an impressive array of means whereby voters were denied the right to vote. After its investigation following the election in Florida, the U.S. Commission on Civil Rights wrote that its "findings make one thing clear: widespread voter disenfranchisement—not the dead-heat contest—was the extraordinary feature in the Florida election."[5]

Turnout in American Elections Historically

One of the most persistent complaints about the current American electoral system is its failure to achieve the high rates of voter turnout found in other countries and common in the United States in the nineteenth century. U.S. voter turnout was close to 80 percent before 1900 (see Figure 2-1); modern democracies around the world frequently record similarly high levels. Turnout in the United States since the start of the twentieth century, in contrast, has exceeded 60 percent only in presidential elections, and in recent years the figure has often fallen below 50 percent.

These unfavorable comparisons are somewhat misleading. The *voting turnout rate* is the percentage of the eligible population that votes in a particular election. It is ideally calculated as the number of votes cast divided by the total number of eligible adult citizens. The definition of *eligible adult* takes into account the historical changes in eligibility occasioned by the extension of suffrage to blacks, women, and eighteen-year-olds, but it does not take into account state restrictions on eligibility, such as residency requirements. As discussed, these restrictions may be substantial. Thus, some of those included in the eligible population are not legally able to vote; the turnout rate, when calculated in this

FIGURE 2-1   Estimated Turnout of Eligible Voters in Presidential Elections in the South, Non-South, and the Nation, 1860–2004

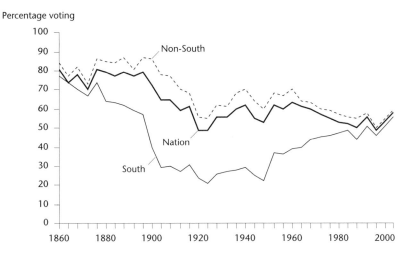

Percentage voting

Source: Robert Lane, *Political Life* (New York: Free Press, 1965), 20; Walter Dean Burnham, "The Changing Shape of the American Political Universe," *American Political Science Review 59* (March 1965): 11, Figure 1; U.S. Bureau of the Census, *Historical Statistics of the United States, Colonial Times to 1970,* bicentennial ed. (Washington, D.C.: U.S. Government Printing Office, 1975), 1078–1080; U.S. Bureau of the Census, *Statistical Abstract of the United States, 1996,* 116th ed. (Washington, D.C.: U.S. Government Printing Office, 1996), 287; and www.census.gov.

manner, appears lower than it actually is. And in some states, blacks, women, and eighteen-year-olds were given the right to vote before suffrage was extended to them by amendment to the U.S. Constitution. Not including them in the denominator makes the turnout rate in earlier years appear higher than it actually was.

Even today in the United States, the calculation of the voting turnout rate is difficult. The total number of ballots cast throughout the country is unknown; only the total vote for particular races is reported. For example, not included are the people who went to the polls but skipped the presidential race. And the numbers who inadvertently invalidated their ballots are not counted. Even worse, no official count exists of citizens, because the decennial census no longer asks about citizenship. Thus, all noncitizens are counted as if they were eligible to vote. An analysis by Ruy A. Teixeira suggests an underestimate of turnout of about 4 percent in 1988.[6] Recently, the U.S. Bureau of the Census has published recalculated estimates of the turnout rate since 1978, using citizenship and reported vote from its Current Population Survey. The estimates are considerably higher than the "official rate," in part because they are based on reported vote—which may be inflated because individuals are reluctant to admit they did not vote—and in part because they are able to exclude noncitizens, who are ineligible to vote, in the denominator. (The Census Bureau estimates the number of noncitizens at eighteen million.) According to the Census Bureau estimate, turnout in 2004 was 63.8 percent. For 1992, the estimate is even higher—67.7 percent. Estimates in presidential elections since 1980 are in the high 50 percent to mid-60 percent range.[7]

Nevertheless, the data in Figure 2-1 show some dramatic changes occurred historically in the rate of voter turnout. Each major extension of suffrage—in 1868, 1920, and 1971—was marked by a drop in the proportion of the electorate voting. Perhaps this is not surprising, because the newly eligible voters might be expected to take some time to acquire the habit of exercising their right to vote. Furthermore, the drop in the turnout rate occasioned by the extension of suffrage was, in each case, the continuation of a downward trend.

During the nineteenth century, national turnout appears to have been extremely high—always more than 70 percent. The decline in national turnout from shortly before 1900 to 1916 is in part attributable to the restriction of black voting in the South. This decline in voting in the South also resulted from the increasing one-party domination of the region. In many southern states the real election was the Democratic primary, with the Republicans offering only token opposition, or none at all, in the general election. Turnout was often extremely low in the general election—far lower than can be accounted for simply by the disfranchisement of blacks.

Explaining the voting record shown in Figure 2-1 for the northern states presents a more difficult problem. Turnout declined substantially in the first two decades of the twentieth century and has not returned to its previous levels. The disfranchisement of blacks and whites in the South cannot account for northern nonvoting.

Two different explanations have been offered for the decline in voting in the North that commenced in the late 1890s. A persuasive set of arguments has been made by E. E. Schattschneider and Walter Dean Burnham in their individual studies of this period.[8] They contend that a high level of party loyalty and political involvement during the last quarter of the nineteenth century caused high turnout and great partisan stability. Then, during the 1890s, electoral patterns shifted in such a way that the South became safely Democratic, and most of the rest of the nation came under the domination of the Republican Party. Schattschneider's analysis emphasizes the extent to which this alignment enabled conservatives in both regions to dominate American politics for many years. According to this line of argument, one consequence of declining competition and greater conservatism throughout the electoral system was a loss of interest in politics accompanied by lower turnout and less partisan loyalty in the early twentieth century. Burnham emphasizes the disintegration of party voting with more ticket-splitting and lower turnout in off-year elections.

Some elements of this account are undeniably accurate. Electoral patterns did change somewhat around the turn of the century, with many regions of the nation changing from competitive to one-party areas. Throughout areas previously characterized by high turnout, straight-ticket voting, and stable voting patterns, turnout and partisan stability suffered greater fluctuations.

An alternative set of arguments gives these patterns a different interpretation.[9] The high rate of turnout in the nineteenth century may not have resulted from political involvement by an interested, well-informed electorate. On the contrary, it may have been possible only because of low levels of information and interest. During the last half of the nineteenth century, a largely uninformed electorate was aroused to vote by means of extreme and emotional political appeals. Presumably, in the absence of more general awareness of the political situation, these alarmist arguments produced firm commitments to vote. By and large, the parties manipulated the electorate—a manipulation possible because the electorate was not well informed.

Furthermore, proponents of this argument allege that the party organizations "delivered" or "voted" substantial numbers of voters during this period, by party loyalists casting multiple votes, "voting tombstones," or buying votes. Thus the remarkable stability of party voting may be a testimony to the corruption of the party organizations. The decline of stable party voting in the early twentieth century coincides with attacks on political corruption and party machines. The resultant weakening of party machines and increased honesty in electoral activities could have reduced turnout. In fact, the apparent hostility of the electorate to the parties throughout this period seems inconsistent with strong party loyalty. A study by Jerrold D. Rusk shows dramatic changes in voting patterns associated with electoral reform laws, especially the introduction of the Australian ballot.[10] Before the introduction of electoral reforms, voting was often not secret. Distinctively colored ballots prepared by the political parties and limited to one party were distributed to voters, marked, and openly placed in the ballot box. The Australian ballot provided for secret voting and an official ballot with all candidates' names appearing on it.

Another of the reforms instituted during the early twentieth century to combat corruption was the imposition of a system of voter registration. Besides limiting the opportunity for fraudulent voting, registration requirements created an additional barrier to the act of voting that had the effect of causing the least motivated potential voters to drop out of the electorate. Many states introduced permanent or semipermanent forms of registration that involved only a one-time effort by the voter. However, in others, such as New York, where annual registration was required in many cities, the barrier to voting could be formidable.

After reaching an all-time low in the early 1920s, turnout in national elections increased steadily until 1940. A substantial, though temporary, drop in turnout occurred during World War II and its aftermath, and since 1960 there has been a gradual decline. Great differences in turnout among the states are concealed within these national data. Rates of voting in the South, as shown in Figure 2-1, were consistently low until recently when they nearly converge with northern turnout. Regional differences in turnout in presidential voting have almost disappeared. State variation within regions, however, is still considerable.

High- and Low-Stimulus Elections

Elections vary in the amount of interest and attention they generate in the electorate. As can be seen in Figure 2-2, presidential elections draw

FIGURE 2-2   Turnout of Eligible Voters in Presidential and Congressional Elections, 1868–2004

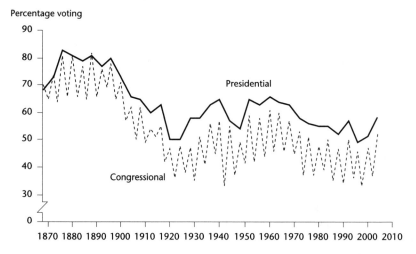

Source: Inter-university Consortium for Political and Social Research, Historical Data Archive; U.S. Bureau of the Census, *Historical Statistics of the United States, 1973,* 94th ed. (Washington, D.C.: U.S. Government Printing Office, 1973), 379; U.S. Bureau of the Census, *Statistical Abstract of the United States, 1996,* 116th ed. (Washington, D.C.: U.S. Government Printing Office, 1996), 287; U.S. House of Representatives, Office of the Clerk, clerk.house.gov; and www.census.gov.

higher turnout, whereas off-year congressional elections are characterized by lower levels of turnout. Even in a presidential election year, fewer people vote in congressional elections than vote for president. The most dramatic decline in turnout is the 10 to 20 percent drop in voting experienced in off-year elections. Primaries and local elections elicit still lower turnout. Most of these differences in turnout can be accounted for by the lower visibility of the latter elections. When less information about an election is available to the voter, a lower level of interest is produced.

The differences in level of interest from presidential elections to congressional elections to local elections can be viewed as a result of five factors.

1. Differences in media coverage given the election
2. Significance attached by voters to the office
3. Importance of issues raised in the campaign
4. Attractiveness of the candidates
5. Competitiveness of the contest

Variation in these factors leads to what Angus Campbell called *high-stimulus* and *low-stimulus elections.*[11]

Newspapers and television give far more coverage to the activities and speeches of presidential candidates than to those of congressional candidates. Even the most indifferent citizen comes to possess impressions and some information about presidential candidates and their campaigns. Such bombardment through the mass media awakens the relatively uninterested and often provides them with some reason to vote. This is not nearly so likely to happen in other election campaigns, where only the motivated citizens will become informed and concerned to any degree. Even so, a week or so after the election, a substantial proportion of the voters will not recall the name of the congressional candidate for whom they voted.

The factors of media coverage, the significance of the office, and the importance of the issues do a better job of explaining the differences in the levels of turnout in presidential elections versus other kinds of elections than they do among presidential elections themselves. None of these factors can account for the decline in turnout in presidential voting over the past four decades. Media coverage and campaigning through the media have increased; no evidence suggests that the significance attached to the presidency has declined; and critical issues have been intensely debated, such as civil rights and the Vietnam War in 1968, the Vietnam War again in 1972, and the Iranian hostage crisis and inflation in 1980. Yet a steady erosion in turnout occurred throughout these years.

The lack of attractiveness of the presidential candidates has often been cited as a possible explanation, contrasting the enormously popular Dwight D. Eisenhower in 1952 and 1956 with the lesser-of-two-evils contests of later years. Certainly low-turnout elections have taken place in which both candidates were viewed unfavorably (the Michael S. Dukakis–George Bush contest in 1988 and the 1996 match-up between Bill Clinton and Bob Dole, for example). But a candidate viewed very negatively by a portion of the electorate may also increase turnout by bringing large numbers of voters to the polls to vote in opposition. George W. Bush seems to have had that effect in 2004. His polarizing presidency had the effect of motivating both supporters and opponents, resulting in higher than usual turnout.

Something a bit different appears to have happened in 1992. Although none of the three candidates, the senior Bush, Clinton, or Ross Perot, was viewed particularly favorably in personal terms by the electorate, the fact that there were three alternatives brought more people to the polls. If some people do not vote because they do not like either of the candidates, then having more candidates in the race increases the chances that one candidate will be deemed worthy of a vote.

Another factor often thought to raise the level of turnout in an election, perhaps by increasing the level of interest, is the degree of competition between the parties. Presumably, the closer and more uncertain the outcome, the more people will see their vote as potentially decisive. Undeniably, the virtual absence of party competition in the South during the period of black disfranchisement was associated with extremely low levels of turnout, even among white voters. Both turnout and competition in the South have increased since blacks joined the electorate.

However, the elections of 1968, 1976, 1980, and 1988 suggest that the expectation of a close race does not invariably lead to heightened turnout, whereas the 1984 election that reelected the popular Ronald Reagan shows that the expectation of a landslide does not necessarily depress turnout. Conversely, the expectation that Clinton would easily win in 1996 is widely interpreted as having depressed turnout in that election.

The high turnout in 2004 surely resulted in part from the competitiveness of the race nationwide. It probably resulted also from the sense of urgency that people had, on both sides, about the war in Iraq and the threat of terrorism, and the sense on the part of Bush's opponents that the 2000 election had been unjustly taken from them. An unprecedented effort was made on the part of the political parties and many other organizations to get out the vote in 2004. Most organizations concentrated their efforts in the so-called battleground states where both sides had a chance to win. The Republican Party, however, also made a big effort to turn out supporters in safe Republican states. The strategy was so successful that safe southern states—some of which had their highest turnout ever—were the engine behind the popular vote victory for Bush. Without this boost in turnout from safe southern states, Bush would have once again won the electoral college vote while losing the popular vote, an outcome he wanted to avoid.

Another aspect of competitiveness also has a relationship to the level of turnout, especially in congressional and state elections. The decision to allow a race to remain uncontested or to offer only a "sacrificial lamb" can dramatically reduce turnout. In contrast, a hotly contested race with strenuous activity by party organizations is likely to get more voters to the polls on election day, even though the final outcome may not be particularly close.

Voters and Nonvoters

All but a small proportion of the eligible electorate vote at least occasionally, but individuals vary in the regularity with which they cast their ballots. Individual interest in politics is one factor creating such differences. In the previous section, the level of interest in a campaign was treated as a characteristic of the political environment, generated by the importance of the office at stake, the amount of media coverage, and so on. But interest and involvement in politics are also characteristics of individuals, and individuals vary substantially in the attention they pay to politics, their involvement in politics, and the amount of information about candidates and issues they acquire. As one would expect, the probability of voting increases at each level of expressed interest and involvement in political campaigns. This relationship is illustrated in Figure 2-3. The highly interested, involved, and informed citizens (a combination of characteristics highly valued in the belief system of a democratic society) turn out to cast their ballots on election day, whereas the apathetic, uninvolved, and ill-informed stay at home.

Two deviant cases that run contrary to the expected pattern can also be seen in Figure 2-3. The first deviant condition, *alienation*, de-

FIGURE 2-3   Relationship between Electoral Participation and Interest, Involvement, and Information

		Low	High
Level of interest, involvement, and information	High	Alienation or intimidation	Model citizenship
	Low	Apathy	Manipulation

Likelihood of voting

scribes voters characterized by high interest and low turnout. The situation may be one of voluntary alienation in which individuals withdraw from political participation purposefully. Their high level of interest and information implies some reason for their withdrawal. They are dissatisfied with, or offended by, the political system. *Nonvoluntary alienation* refers to situations in which interested potential voters are prevented from participating, perhaps through intimidation. Both situations are dangerous to the political system because highly interested and informed citizens who do not participate have the potential for extremely disruptive activities. Alienation in this form is thought to be uncommon in American politics. In the United States, the interested and informed are consistently the most likely to participate even though they are somewhat more cynical about the political system. Furthermore, a study focusing primarily on the causes of nonvoting in the 1976 election found voters and nonvoters to be similar in their levels of alienation and cynicism toward politics. For only 6 percent of the nonvoters was rejection of politics the main explanation of their nonvoting.[12] Studies have consistently shown no relationship between cynicism or alienation and nonvoting in elections.

The second deviant case, *manipulation,* describes voters characterized by low interest and high turnout. It refers to a situation in which individuals with little information or interest become involved in voting. Presumably, this manipulation is achieved by getting individuals to vote either through coercion or by highly stimulating and arousing appeals. Coercive methods for ensuring turnout may range from police-state orders to fines for failure to vote. More common in the American political system are exceptionally moving or alarming appeals, bringing to the polls people so unsophisticated that they are easily swayed. Very high levels of turnout can be inspired by emotional, inflammatory appeals— which offer one possible explanation for the high turnout levels in the United States for many years after the Civil War. Campaigns were marked by extreme appeals, and, because education levels were low, it is reasonable to suspect that there were lower levels of interest, involvement, and information than during the campaigns of the twentieth century.

Even though interest in politics is strongly correlated with voting, about half of those who say they have hardly any interest do vote in presidential elections, suggesting that still other factors are also at work. One of these is a sense of civic duty—the attitude that a good citizen has an obligation to vote, that voting is important, regardless of the expected impact on the outcome. Because such feelings are usually a prime focus of the political socialization fostered by the American educational system, turnout is the highest among those with the longest exposure to this system. Length of education is one of the best predictors of an individual's likelihood of voting.

Because education is so closely associated with relative affluence and social status, people who vote are usually slightly better off in socioeconomic terms than the population as a whole. This bias is likely to increase in low-stimulus elections as greater numbers of occasional voters drop out of the electorate, leaving the field to the better educated and more affluent who rarely miss an election. In analyzing voting in presidential primaries, Barbara Norrander found voters in the 1988 Super Tuesday primaries to be older, better educated, and wealthier than their counterparts who did not vote. However, the common assumption that this leads to drastic political differences between primary voters and the general electorate is unfounded. In studying the 1980 presidential primaries, she discovered no substantial ideological or issue differences between primary voters and general election voters.[13]

Another important factor contributing to nonvoting is age. A relatively large proportion of young people pass up their first opportunities to vote. This situation has been magnified in presidential elections since 1972. The extension of the franchise to eighteen-year-olds enlarged the pool of eligible voters, yet since then turnout has, on average, declined. Figure 2-4, based on survey data from the 2004 presidential election, shows that the likelihood of voting increases from young adulthood through middle age.* In most presidential years, including 2004, a slight decline in turnout was evident among the most elderly portion of the population.

The tendency of young people not to vote is partially offset by their generally higher levels of education. Although the turnout of middle-aged people is higher at each educational level than that of young adults, the gap narrows among the better educated (see Figure 2-5).

Reported turnout increased in all age groups, except the oldest, in 2004. The increase was most impressive among the youngest group of eighteen- to twenty-five-year-olds whose turnout increased from 48 percent in 2000 to 60 percent in 2004. College-educated young people were almost as likely to vote as their elders in 2004. In his assessment of turnout in 2004, Thomas E. Patterson notes that voters under thirty-five were much more likely to say that they "really disliked" one of the candidates, lending support to the hypothesis that the *un*attractiveness of the candidates may be an incentive to turn out to vote.[14]

---

*The reported vote obtained in surveys, including surveys by the Bureau of the Census, is consistently higher than that of official statistics. Validation studies suggest that more than 10 percent of the respondents claim to have voted when they did not. Bias in survey samples—that is, interviewing disproportionate numbers of voters—is also a factor contributing to the difference. See U.S. Bureau of the Census, "Current Population Reports," *Studies in the Measurement of Voter Turnout,* Series P-23, No. 168 (Washington, D.C.: U.S. Government Printing Office, 1990).

FIGURE 2-4   Percentage of the Electorate Reporting Having Registered and
Voted in the 2004 Presidential Election by Age

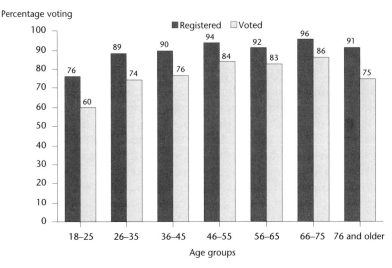

Source: 2004 National Election Study, available at www.umich.edu/~nes.

Much of the nonvoting among young people may be attributed to
the unsettled circumstances of this age group rather than to simple dis-
interest in politics, although young people are slightly less interested
than older people of similar educational levels. Military service, being
away at college, geographic mobility with the possible failure to meet
residence requirements, and the additional hurdle of initial registration
all create barriers to voting for young citizens that are less likely to affect
older ones. Efforts to promote voter registration have affected the
young, with about three-fourths of the youngest members of the electorate having registered to vote. But registering is not the same as turning out to vote. As can be seen in Figure 2-4, on election day in November 2004 young people who were registered were more likely not to vote
than older people who were registered.

By age thirty-five, most people have joined the voting population at
least on an occasional basis. A small proportion of the middle-aged and
older group remains outside the voting public. These habitual nonvoters,
who have passed up several opportunities to vote, are less than 5 percent
of the total electorate, according to current survey research estimates.**

** This "best estimate" of individuals outside the political system is unquestionably
low. First, a disproportionately large number of people outside the political system
would not even be included in the population of households from which the sample
is drawn. Second, many of those in the sample who were never contacted or who refused to be interviewed would probably be classified as outside the political system.

FIGURE 2-5   Turnout in the 2004 Presidential Election by Age and
Education

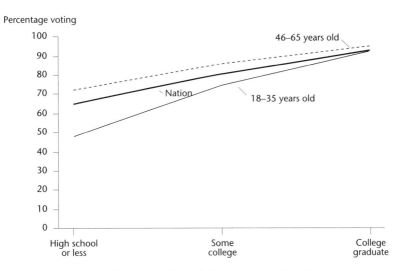

Source: 2004 National Election Study, available at www.umich.edu/~nes.

This group has steadily decreased in size, and the social forces that brought about the decrease will likely reduce it still further. In the past, habitual nonvoters were disproportionately southern, black, and female. Restrictions against black suffrage, coupled with a traditional culture that worked against active participation of women in civic life, meant that fifty years ago in the South large proportions of blacks of both genders, as well as white women, had never voted in a presidential election. Figure 2-6 shows the historic changes that took place as a result of the civil rights movement of the 1950s and 1960s. In 1952 large percentages of black women and men and, to a lesser extent, white women in the South had never voted. These percentages fell dramatically in the next two decades. By the late twentieth century, turnout patterns were similar in the North and South.

Registration as a Barrier to Voting

Registration requirements are the last major legal impediment to voting. Registration poses barriers to voting in several ways. In most parts of the country, an unregistered citizen must go to the courthouse several weeks before the election, during working hours, and fill out a form. Although not a horrendous burden, it does take time and some ability to deal with a governmental bureaucracy. Regulations also typi-

FIGURE 2-6   Percentage of Adults Who Have Never Voted by Race and
Gender for the South and Non-South, 1952–1980

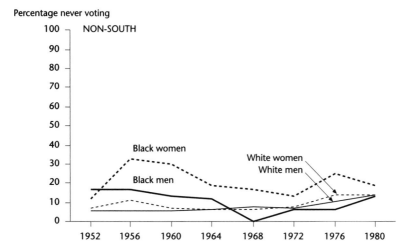

Source: National Election Studies, available at www.umich.edu/~nes.

Note: The states in the South are Alabama, Arkansas, Florida, Georgia, Kentucky, Louisiana, Maryland, Mississippi, North Carolina, Oklahoma, South Carolina, Tennessee, Texas, Virginia, and West Virginia. The remainder are the states in the non-South.

cally cancel the registration of people who fail to vote in a few consecutive elections. In addition, residential mobility annually relocates millions of citizens in new precincts in which they must reregister. All of these circumstances raise the costs of political involvement, costs that a significant number of citizens will choose not to assume. Furthermore, voter registration is not always purely an electoral matter: An unknown number of Americans prefer to remain off registration lists to avoid jury duty or bill collectors or a former spouse.

Not surprisingly, individuals with little or no interest in politics lack the motivation to overcome registration barriers on their own. Voter registration drives, in which volunteers go door to door or register voters at shopping malls and on college campuses, capture many politically uninvolved people. A certain proportion of these people will not have the interest or incentive to bear the additional costs of getting to the polls on election day. The Census Bureau reported that 72 percent of all citizens were registered to vote in the 2004 election. About one out of nine failed to vote.[15]

Table 2-1 illustrates differences between unregistered citizens, registered nonvoters, and registered voters in terms of their level of interest in the election campaign and their partisanship. The registered nonvoters generally fall between the two other groups. In 2004 a clear partisan impact can be seen in the failure of large numbers of potential voters to vote. Whereas Democrats narrowly outnumber Republicans in the electorate as a whole, Republicans outnumber Democrats among those who voted. Democrats far outnumber Republicans among those who registered but did not make it to the polls on election day.

In recent years, various plans have been introduced to reduce the difficulty in registration as a way to boost voter turnout. Some state gov-

TABLE 2-1   Interest and Partisanship of Registered Voters and Nonvoters and Unregistered Citizens, 2004

		Registered	
	Unregistered	Nonvoters	Voters
Very much interested	10%	22%	48%
Somewhat interested	49	46	43
Not interested at all	41	32	10
Total	100%	100%	101%
Strong Democrat	4%	17%	18%
Weak Democrat	11	22	14
Independent Democrat	26	16	16
Independent	24	17	6
Independent Republican	17	12	11
Weak Republican	7	10	14
Strong Republican	4	5	21
Other, don't know, apolitical	7	1	1
Total	100%	100%	101%
(N)	(111)	(136)	(812)

Source: 2004 National Election Study, available at www.umich.edu/~nes.

ernments have implemented same-day registration, whereby individuals can register at the polls on election day. Most notably, in 1993 Congress passed, and President Clinton signed into law, the "motor voter" bill, which provides that registration forms will be available at a variety of governmental agencies that citizens visit for other purposes. These include agencies where motor vehicles are registered and driver's licenses are obtained, though, because of a Republican-sponsored amendment, states are not required to provide them at unemployment and welfare offices. The purpose of the bill is clearly to make it easier for all citizens to exercise their right to vote, but Democratic support and Republican concerns point to a potential side effect. Because the unregistered tend to be poorer and less well educated, Democrats, who traditionally represent such groups, hope (and Republicans fear) that reducing registration obstacles will increase the number of Democratic voters.

Many of the same political considerations were at play in the passage of the Help American Vote Act of 2002, which mandated that states provide provisional ballots for those citizens who believe they are registered to vote but whose names are not on the registration rolls. Much of the debate in Congress involved the form of identification that voters seeking to cast provisional ballots would need to produce at the polls. Republican legislators sought more rigid standards to prevent voter fraud; Democrats generally argued for keeping the barriers to a minimum.[16] As in the historical extensions of the suffrage, these efforts to facilitate voter registration mix philosophical concerns with political motivations.

Registration requirements are one reason that the United States has significantly lower turnout rates than other western democracies, where governments take responsibility for maintaining registration lists instead of placing the burden of registration on the individual.[17] Reducing registration requirements is a logical and fairly easy means to increase the turnout rate, but it should not be expected to have an astounding effect. The best estimate of the impact of reducing registration barriers suggests it will increase turnout about 8 percentage points.[18] Although this is significant, the resulting turnout rate would still be substantially below that of other industrialized nations. Similarly, the Federal Election Commission estimates that the 1993 motor voter law resulted in an increase of less than 2 percent in registration in 1996 over 1992.[19] In part, the impact was so small because many states had already implemented aspects of the law so their practices and procedures did not change. During 1995 and 1996, almost one-third of all registrations were by mail and one-third came through some form of motor voter program. Public assistance offices were the source of a little more than 6 percent of the registrations, even though not all states provided registration forms in these offices.

Despite Republican fears that easing registration requirements would bring more Democrats to the polls, the main impact of making it easier to register seems to have been a decline in the proportion of the officially registered who vote. Failure to register prohibits voting, but registering does not ensure turnout. More of those only casually interested in politics and government register—because it is so easy. But when election day arrives, it takes the same amount of energy to get to the polling place as it always did.

The minimal impact of lessening registration requirements has led some states to experiment with easing the act of voting itself—by mailing ballots to registered voters and allowing them to vote by mail. Other states have loosened the conditions under which voters can request absentee ballots. Oregon has pursued these possibilities most aggressively, with the entire electorate receiving mail-in ballots in the 2004 election. Interest in using absentee ballots rose in many states in 2004, in part because of fears of long lines, concern about the absence of a paper trail with electronic ballot arrangements, and other issues. About 20 percent of the eventual voters nationwide cast their ballots before election day, with most of these voting by absentee ballot more than a week before election day. Although an unprecedented number of early ballots were cast in 2004, the procedure apparently was more a convenience or safeguard for voters who would have voted anyway than a means to draw the marginal voter to the polls.

Is the Level of Turnout in the United States a Cause for Concern?

A great deal of editorial ink has been spilled to lament, and academic analysis undertaken to explain, the generally low level of turnout in the United States in recent decades. The spikes in turnout in 1992 and again in 2004 offer food for thought but no clear indication whether these are aberrations or the possible reversal of a trend. In this section we will look at some of the explanations that have been offered for the overall decline in turnout and then suggest some alternative ways of looking at the issue.

Part of the difficulty analysts have had in understanding the overall decline in turnout over the past forty years is that it has happened at the same time that legal restrictions on voting have eased and education levels have increased. These circumstances should be expected to increase turnout. One explanation for the decline in the face of these factors has focused on the expansion of the electorate in 1971 to include eighteen-year-olds. Because young people are less likely to vote than older people, their inclusion in the electorate would be expected to decrease turnout, other things being equal. However, this can account for only a small portion of the decline.

Another possibility, raised by political commentators in 1972, 1980, and 1984, is that calling the election early in the evening, before the polls have closed in all states, especially western states, reduces turnout. Once potential voters learn that a television network has declared a winner in the race for president, the argument goes, they will no longer be interested in voting for president or any other office. However, the 1976 and 2000 elections were so close that the winner was not known until long after the polls had closed in all fifty states, and no appreciable impact was seen on turnout. Public concern about calling the election too early, together with congressional threats of regulation, led the networks to restrict their reporting voluntarily in 1988 and thereafter. However, if public opinion polls before the election all point to a clear winner, as they did in 1996, the impact on turnout may be the same. Persuasive as the idea is, the evidence on this matter is inconclusive, and no one has clearly demonstrated that these factors have influenced turnout in a significant way.[20]

A somewhat more sweeping form of this argument—and one harder to test—suggests that the style of media coverage of campaigns has turned elections into a spectator sport that voters watch with varying degrees of interest but feel no need to engage in. The prediction of the winners in polls, the focus in presidential debates on who "won" instead of on substance, the attention to the "horse-race" aspects of the primary campaigns, and the networks' competition to call the election first are all alleged factors in the withdrawal of the voter from active participation.

In a major study of nonvoting, Ruy Teixeira offers two general explanations for the decline in turnout since 1960.[21] First, he cites a set of circumstances that he calls *social connectedness*—that is, the extent to which individuals are socially integrated into their community. This is similar to Putnam's idea of *social capital,* which was discussed in Chapter 1. Older people, married people, those who attend church and are settled in the community are more socially connected than young, single, mobile people who do not belong to community organizations. Over the past few decades, the proportion of socially unconnected people has increased. Teixeira estimates that about one-third of the decline in turnout is associated with the decline in social connectedness.

The second factor is the extent of *political connectedness*—that is, the degree to which people feel interested and involved in government and believe government is concerned and responsive to them. The decline in political connectedness over the past three decades is manifested in a loss of trust in government, a lower sense of political efficacy, a decline in interest in politics, and a diminished sense of civic duty, many of the same trends noted in Chapter 1. These changing attitudes toward government and politics account for more than half of the decline in turnout, according to Teixeira's estimates.

Turnout rose sharply in 1992, and examining the possible reasons for it would be worthwhile. The presence of Ross Perot in the 1992 presidential race contributed to the higher turnout. An atypically high level of turnout emerged among voters most attracted to Perot's candidacy: the young, the nonpartisan, and those disenchanted with government and political leadership. These groups, in fact, are the socially and politically disconnected whose increased numbers, Teixeira argues, have been responsible for the recent declines in turnout. Perhaps Perot's candidacy gave these voters an alternative that allowed them to connect with the political world. By 1996 Perot looked less like the outsider who could fix the system and he drew fewer of the unconnected into the electorate.

Beyond this, the 1992 campaigns of Perot, Clinton, and, to a lesser degree, George Bush used new means for reaching the voters. Talk-show appearances, Perot's infomercials, town meetings, and MTV's Rock the Vote initiative were all efforts to establish connections with the public in the age of cable television. In subsequent elections, this trend continued, with candidates making multiple appearances on the talk shows hosted by Jay Leno, David Letterman, and Oprah Winfrey. Presidential candidates clearly differ in how well they come across in these venues, but none can now avoid them. In a book on electoral participation, Steven J. Rosenstone and John Mark Hansen make the point that another aspect of participation is *mobilization*.[22] If candidates and parties fail to mobilize potential voters—or fail to find appropriate means to reach them—then it is not surprising that people do not vote. The declining turnout rate may have been a failure of party elites rather than a fault of citizens. The mobilization efforts of both parties as well as other organizations in 2004 surely contributed to the sharp increase in turnout in that election.

Throughout the discussion of turnout, we have implied the need for an explanation of nonvoting. We have assumed voting is normal or to be expected. However, the topic could be approached differently. The question could be asked, "Why do people bother to vote?"—as if nonvoting were the natural pattern or expected behavior and voting required explanation. The answer that one vote can determine the outcome of an election and that most people vote anticipating that their vote may be crucial is not reasonable, even after an extremely close election such as in 2000. One vote rarely decides an election, although many races are close; no voter should expect to cast the deciding vote in an election. However, "votes count" in an election in another sense—as an expression of preference for a candidate or for a party, regardless of whether that candidate ultimately wins or loses. Elections are more than simply a mechanism for selecting public officials; they are also a means for communicating, albeit somewhat dimly, a set of attitudes to the government. For most Americans, voting remains the only means of influence regularly used. Many see it as the only avenue open to ordinary citizens to make the government listen to their needs. The desire to be counted on one side of the fence or the other and the feeling that one ought to be so counted are perhaps the greatest spurs to voting. If this is true, then perhaps the most disturbing lesson that comes from examining electoral procedures in Florida in 2000 was the realization that your vote may not even get counted—let alone make a difference.

Our discussion—and most such discussions—also assumes that a high level of turnout is a good thing, and declining turnout is something to be concerned about. Exercising one's right to vote is seen as support for the political system, embracing of one's role as a citizen, and willingness to endorse one or another of the candidates. Failure to vote is taken as alienation from politics or apathy about the fate of the nation. Over the years, a few commentators have pointed out another possibility. Some people may not vote because of basic satisfaction with the way things are going or a feeling that things will be all right no matter which of the candidates is elected. While hardly model citizens, such people do not pose much of a problem for the political system. But then suppose that these people begin to feel that the outcome of the election will impact their lives, that one of the candidates will take the country in a direction they do not want to go. With their comfortable existence being threatened, they might decide to vote. If enough people felt this way, turnout would go up.

Something like this may have happened in 2004. The issues facing the country are urgent, but just as important, significant portions of the politically active public take a polarized view of politics. They distrust and dislike those with whom they disagree on a variety of issues. They do not want to see government in the hands of their opponents. They worked hard to mobilize like-minded people to get them to the polls to prevent the other side from winning. Turnout went up.

The point is twofold. Rising turnout is not an unmixed blessing. Although more engaged citizens may be good from a civics perspective, it can also mean that people are angry, worried, or threatened by events or by the prospect of one or another candidate holding office. Second, whether turnout remains elevated in the future or settles back to its recent levels will depend in great part on whether the current deep division in the politically active segment of the society remains.

Notes

1. Chilton Williamson, *American Suffrage from Property to Democracy: 1760–1860* (Princeton: Princeton University Press, 1960), especially 131–181.

2. Jerrold D. Rusk and John J. Stucker, "The Effect of the Southern System of Election Laws on Voting Participation," in *The History of American Electoral Behavior,* ed. Joel Silbey, Allan Bogue, and William Flanigan (Princeton: Princeton University Press, 1978). For a treatment of these and many additional topics, see also J. Morgan Kousser, *The Shaping of Southern Politics* (New Haven: Yale University Press, 1974).

3. Donald R. Matthews and James W. Prothro, "Political Factors and Negro Voter Registration in the South," *American Political Science Review* 57 (June 1963): 355–367.

4. "Losing the Vote: The Impact of Felony Disenfranchisement Laws in the United States," Sentencing Project, October 1998, available at www.sentencingproject.org.

5. U.S. Commission on Civil Rights, "Executive Summary," in "Voting Irregularities in Florida during the 2000 Presidential Election," available at www.usccr.gov/vote2000/stdraft1/exsum.htm.

6. Ruy A. Teixeira, *The Disappearing American Voter* (Washington, D.C.: Brookings Institution, 1992), 10.

7. U.S. Bureau of the Census, www.census.gov/population/www/socdemo/voting.html#hist.

8. E. E. Schattschneider, *The Semisovereign People* (New York: Holt, Rinehart, and Winston, 1960), especially chap. 5; and Walter Dean Burnham, "The Changing Shape of the American Political Universe," *American Political Science Review* 59 (March 1965): 7–28.

9. The most general statement of this argument is found in Philip E. Converse, "Change in the American Electorate," in *The Human Meaning of Social Change,* ed. Angus Campbell and Philip E. Converse (New York: Russell Sage Foundation, 1972), 263–337. For an analysis that alters the estimates of turnout, see Ray M. Shortridge, "Estimating Voter Participation," in *Analyzing Electoral History,* ed. Jerome M. Clubb, William H. Flanigan, and Nancy H. Zingale (Beverly Hills, Calif.: Sage Publications, 1981), 137–152.

10. Jerrold D. Rusk, "The Effect of the Australian Ballot Reform on Split Ticket Voting: 1876–1908," *American Political Science Review* 64 (December 1970): 1220–1238.

11. Angus Campbell, Philip E. Converse, Warren E. Miller, and Donald E. Stokes, eds., *Elections and the Political Order* (New York: Wiley, 1966), 40–62.

12. Arthur T. Hadley, *The Empty Polling Booth* (Englewood Cliffs, N.J.: Prentice-Hall, 1978), 20, 41.

13. Barbara Norrander, *Super Tuesday: Regional Politics and Presidential Primaries* (Lexington: University of Kentucky Press, 1992); and Barbara Norrander, "Ideological Representativeness of Presidential Primaries," *American Journal of Political Science* 33 (August 1989): 570–587.

14. Thomas E. Patterson, "Young Voters and the 2004 Election," *The Vanishing Voter Project,* press releases, 2004, available at www.vanishingvoter.org.

15. U.S. Bureau of the Census, www.census.gov/population/www/socdemo/voting.html.

16. *CQ Almanac Plus 2002* (Washington, D.C.: Congressional Quarterly Inc., 2003), 143.

17. G. Bingham Powell Jr., "American Voter Turnout in Comparative Perspective," *American Political Science Review* 80 (March 1986): 17–44.

18. Teixeira, *The Disappearing American Voter,* chap. 4.

19. "Executive Summary of the Federal Election Commission's Report to the Congress on the Impact of the National Voter Registration Act of 1993 on the Administration of Federal Elections," available at www.fec.gov/votregis/nvrasum.htm.

20. See Laurily K. Epstein and Gerald Strom, "Election Night Projections and West Coast Turnout," *American Politics Quarterly* 9 (October 1981): 479–491; and Raymond Wolfinger and Peter Linquiti, "Tuning In and Turning Out," *Public Opinion* (February–March 1981): 56–60.
21. Teixeira, *The Disappearing American Voter.*
22. Steven J. Rosenstone and John Mark Hansen, *Mobilization, Participation, and Democracy in America* (New York: Macmillan, 1993).

Suggested Readings

Conway, M. Margaret. *Political Participation in the United States,* 3d ed. Washington, D.C.: CQ Press, 2000. A good introduction to the study of turnout and other forms of political participation.

Patterson, Thomas E. *The Vanishing Voter: Public Involvement in an Age of Uncertainty.* New York: Alfred A. Knopf, 2002. An analysis of political participation based on a huge, yearlong survey in 2000.

Powell, G. Bingham, Jr. "American Voter Turnout in Comparative Perspective." *American Political Science Review* 80 (March 1986): 17–44. A careful analysis of the institutional and attitudinal factors that depress American turnout rates compared with those of other industrialized democracies.

Rosenstone, Steven J., and John Mark Hansen. *Mobilization, Participation, and Democracy in America.* New York: Macmillan, 1993. An analysis of the interaction between the strategic choices of political elites and the choices of citizens to participate in politics.

Rusk, Jerrold D., and John J. Stucker. "The Effect of the Southern System of Election Laws on Voting Participation." In *The History of American Electoral Behavior,* edited by Joel Silbey, Allan Bogue, and William Flanigan. Princeton: Princeton University Press, 1978. A sophisticated analysis of the disfranchisement of voters in the South in the nineteenth century.

Teixeira, Ruy A. *The Disappearing American Voter.* Washington, D.C.: Brookings Institution, 1992. A sophisticated and thorough analysis of the factors that have contributed to the decline in turnout in the United States and a discussion of the impact of proposed reforms.

U.S. Bureau of the Census. *Voting and Registration in the Election of November 1992.* Series P-20, No. 466. Washington, D.C.: U.S. Government Printing Office, April 1993. A report of findings on turnout and registration based on a huge survey that allows complex analysis of many subgroups within the U.S. population.

Internet Resources

The Web site of the National Election Studies, www.umich.edu/~nes, offers data on turnout in both presidential and off-year elections since 1952. Click on "Political Involvement and Participation in Politics." You also can examine on the Web site turnout of numerous social groups from 1952 to the present.

Turnout and registration data for the nation and the states are available at the U.S. Census Bureau Web site, www.census.gov. Click on "V" under the subject headings and then find "Voting."

For large quantities of data and commentary on the 2000 and 2004 elections, visit www.vanishingvoter.org. This is the best Web site for the analysis of current levels of turnout.

Partisanship

THE DIVISION OF POWER between the political parties in the United States is currently very close. George W. Bush won in 2004 with a margin of victory that was narrow for an incumbent president seeking reelection—the narrowest margin since Woodrow Wilson won a second term in 1916. However, it was still an improvement over his showing in 2000 when he lost the popular vote and won the electoral college by four votes. At the beginning of the 109th Congress in 2005, the Republicans held a reasonably comfortable majority in the House of Representatives (231, with 202 Democrats, 1 Independent who caucused with the Democrats, and 1 vacancy). The Republicans held 55 Senate seats; the Democrats held 44; and 1 Independent caucused with the Democrats. The majority was up from the 51–49 edge that Republicans held after the 2002 midterm elections, though not a large enough majority to prevent the Democrats from blocking legislation through the use of the filibuster. As a result of the 2002 elections, the Republicans had control of both houses of Congress as well as the presidency. Republicans held unified control of government for the first time since the 1950s, setting aside the six months at the beginning of 2001 before Vermont senator James M. Jeffords switched from Republican to Independent. Besides being narrow, the partisan division between the two political parties is contentious. After the 2003 session, Congressional Quarterly reported that its measure of party polarization was the highest since 1960.[1]

This situation reflects *partisanship*—the sense of attachment or belonging that an individual feels for a political party. In this and the next two chapters we will explore the concept of partisanship and its implications for political behavior. In this chapter we will discuss the meaning of partisanship and how the partisanship of Americans has changed over the course of the country's political history. In Chapter 4 we will examine the impact of partisanship on the way people act politically and how partisanship changes over the lifetime of the individual and between generations. In Chapter 5 we will consider the social characteristics of partisans and independents.

FIGURE 3-1   Partisan Division of the Presidential Vote in the Nation, 1824–2004

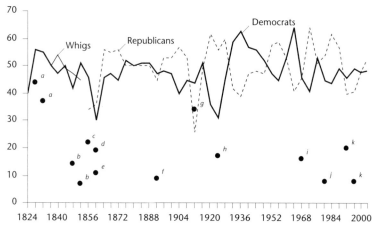

Percentage of the vote

Source: Inter-university Consortium for Political and Social Research, Historical Data Archive; and U.S. House of Representatives, Office of the Clerk, clerk.house.gov.

Note: In presenting these data, we have not drawn attention to the wide range of errors that may exist. Errors are made in collecting and recording data, as well as in computation. The presidential election of 1960 provides an illustration of another form of uncertainty that enters into these data—choices made among alternative ways of presenting the data. The popular vote is customarily listed in such a way that John F. Kennedy appears a narrow winner over Richard M. Nixon in 1960. To reach this distribution of the total vote, the Kennedy vote from Alabama must be exaggerated, because uncommitted electors were on the slate of Democratic electors in Alabama. Eventually six of the uncommitted electors voted for Harry F. Byrd; five electors voted for Kennedy. If the Kennedy popular vote in Alabama is reduced to a proportion, say five-elevenths in this case, of the vote for Democratic electors and if only this reduced popular vote is added to his national total, then Nixon, not Kennedy, has the larger popular vote total nationally in 1960. In percentages these are negligible changes, but symbolically such differences can become important. In our tables and figures we have followed the usual practice of presenting the augmented Kennedy total.

Other parties gaining at least 5 percent of the vote: [a]National Republican; [b]Free Soil; [c]American; [d]Southern Democratic; [e]Constitutional Union; [f]People's; [g]Bull Moose; [h]Progressive; [i]American Independent; [j]Anderson Independent Candidacy; [k]Perot Independent Candidacy, Reform Party. Ralph Nader's 2.7 percent in 2000 falls below this minimum and is not shown.

Party Loyalty

For almost a century and a half the U.S. electorate has supported a two-party system in national politics. Such remarkable stability is unknown in other democracies. Within this stable party system, however, voter support for Republicans and Democrats has fluctuated widely, and significant numbers of voters occasionally, as in 1992, abandon the traditional parties to support third-party or independent candidates. The aggregate vote totals for presidential elections, shown in Figure 3-1, reveal a wide range of party fortunes, even in elections close together in time. Some of the more dramatic fluctuations have involved the appearance of strong third-party candidates, such as Theodore Roosevelt in 1912, George C. Wallace in 1968, and Ross Perot in 1992 and, to a lesser degree, 1996. Perot's 1992 showing of 19 percent was the largest percentage won by a third-party candidate since 1912. Although Ralph Nader can accurately be seen as denying the presidency to Al Gore in 2000, his 2.7 percent of the popular vote was an unimpressive figure for a third-party candidate in recent years.

Despite these variations in election outcomes and despite the demonstrated capacity of American voters for highly selective and differentiated support for candidates offered them by the political parties, most voters have a basic and stable loyalty to one party or the other. This tendency of most individuals to be loyal to one political party makes the idea of partisanship, or *party identification* as it is often called, one of the most useful concepts for understanding the political behavior of individuals. After good survey data became available in the late 1940s, party identification assumed a central role in all voting behavior analysis.[2]

Party Identification

Party identification is a relatively uncomplicated measure determined by responses to the following questions.

- Generally speaking, do you usually think of yourself as a Republican, a Democrat, an independent, or what?

- (If Republican or Democrat) Would you call yourself a strong (Republican), (Democrat), or a not very strong (Republican) (Democrat)?

- (If independent) Do you think of yourself as closer to the Republican Party or to the Democratic Party?

Leaving aside for the moment the people who do not or cannot respond to such questions, this yields seven categories of participants in the electorate according to intensity of partisanship.

Strong Democrats	Weak Democrats	Independent Democrats	Independents	Independent Republicans	Weak Republicans	Strong Republicans

Partisanship

Because this self-identification measure of party loyalty is the best indicator of partisanship, political analysts commonly refer to *partisanship* and *party identification* interchangeably. Partisanship is the single most important influence on political opinions and voting behavior. Many other influences are at work on voters in U.S. society, and partisanship varies in its importance in different types of elections and in different time periods. Nevertheless, no single factor compares in significance with partisanship.

Partisanship represents the feeling of sympathy for and loyalty to a political party that an individual acquires—sometimes during childhood—and holds through life, often with increasing intensity. This self-image as a Democrat or a Republican is useful to the individual in a special way. For example, individuals who think of themselves as Republicans or Democrats respond to political information partially by using party identification to orient themselves, reacting to new information in such a way that it fits in with the ideals and feelings they already have. A Republican who hears a Republican Party leader advocate a policy has a basis in party loyalty for supporting that policy, apart from other considerations. A Democrat may feel favorably inclined toward a candidate for office because that candidate bears the Democratic label. Partisanship orients individuals in their political environment, although it may also distort their picture of reality.

This underlying partisanship is also interesting to political analysts because it provides a base against which to measure deviations in particular elections. In other words, the individual voter's long-standing loyalty to one party means that, "other things being equal," or in the absence of disrupting forces, he or she can be expected to vote for candidates of that party. However, voters are responsive to a great variety of other influences that can either strengthen or weaken their tendency to support their usual party. Variations occur from election to election in such factors as the attractiveness of the candidates, the impact of foreign and domestic policy issues, and purely local circumstances. These current factors, often called *short-term forces*, may move voters away from their usual party choices.

The concepts of partisanship and short-term forces can also be used in understanding the behavior of the electorate as a whole. If the political predispositions of all the individuals in the electorate were added up, the result would be an "expected vote" or "normal vote."[3] This is the electoral outcome that would be expected if all voters voted their party identification. Departures from this expected vote in elections represent the impact of short-term forces, such as issues or candidates.

In assessing the partisanship of the American electorate historically, we will not be able to add up individual party identifications to find an expected vote. Survey data of this type have been available only for the past seventy years or so. For the period from 1824 to 1968, we base our estimates on the only available data—election returns for aggregate units.[4] These data cannot reveal voting patterns of individuals, but they do allow one to make assessments of party loyalty and temporary deviations from party by collections of voters. Even though the same set of individuals does not turn out to vote in each election, we use the election returns over the years to indicate the collective partisanship of the electorate. From these data an estimate is made of the expected vote for the Democratic and Republican Parties. It is then possible to say, for example, that the electorate deviated from its normal voting pattern in favor of the Republican Party in 1904 or that the voters departed from their normal Democratic loyalty in 1952.

Our estimates of the expected vote nationwide in presidential voting for the Democratic Party from 1840 to 1968 and for the Republican Party from 1872 to 1968 are shown in Figures 3-2 and 3-3, respectively. The actual vote in these elections is also shown to indicate the amount of departure from underlying partisan patterns that occurred in each election.

FIGURE 3-2   Democratic Expected Vote in Presidential Elections, 1840–1968

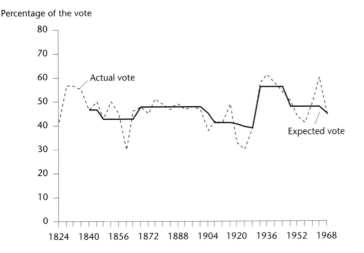

Source: Jerome M. Clubb, William H. Flanigan, and Nancy H. Zingale, *Partisan Realignment* (Beverly Hills, Calf.: Sage Publications, 1980), 92–93, Table 3.1a.

FIGURE 3-3   Republican Expected Vote in Presidential Elections,
1872–1968

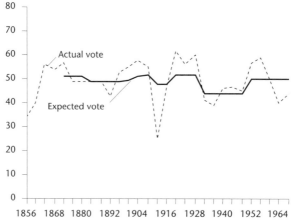

Percentage of the vote

Source: Jerome M. Clubb, William H. Flanigan, and Nancy H. Zingale, *Partisan Realignment* (Beverly Hills, Calf.: Sage Publications, 1980), 92–93, Table 3.1a.

For the more recent period, something similar to the normal vote technique developed by Philip Converse that depends on individual-level survey data can be used to create an expectation about vote choice in the absence of short-term forces. This technique uses party identification, expected defection rates, and turnout to generate an estimate of the normal vote. Using a simplified calculation method, the Democratic and Republican normal votes, along with the actual vote for president, from 1968 to 2004 are shown in Figures 3-4 and 3-5, respectively. (Note that, because normal vote calculations depend on party identifications and identifications with third parties are trivial, the Republican normal vote is a mirror image of the Democratic normal vote.) The deviation of the actual Democratic vote meanders under the Democratic normal vote line, meaning that Democratic presidential candidates since 1968 have rarely done as well as would be expected, given the distribution of party identification. In elections in which a third-party candidate won a significant number of votes—1968, 1992, and 1996—both the Democratic and Republican candidates performed below what the normal votes would predict.

Types of Electoral Change

As we have said, the utility of the concept of the expected vote in part lies in providing a base against which to measure and analyze de-

FIGURE 3-4   Democratic Normal Vote, 1968–2004

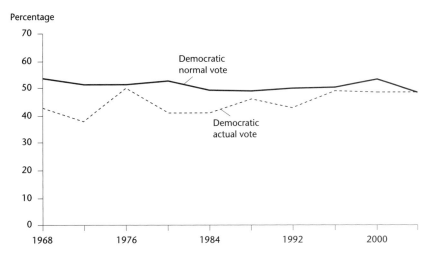

Source: U.S. House of Representatives, Office of the Clerk, clerk.house.gov; and National Election Studies, available at www.umich.edu/~nes.

Note: The normal vote calculations are a simplified version of Philip E. Converse's original analysis. See Philip E. Converse, "The Concept of a Normal Vote," in *Elections and the Political Order,* ed. Angus Campbell, Philip E. Converse, Warren E. Miller, and Donald E. Stokes (New York: Wiley, 1966), 9–39.

partures from the expected pattern. One type of departure is usually referred to as *deviating change:* the temporary deviations from normal party loyalty attributable to the short-term forces of candidate images or issues.[5] The amount of deviating change in an election tells how well a candidate or party did relative to the party's normal performance. In these terms, the Dwight D. Eisenhower victories in 1952 and 1956 and the Richard M. Nixon landslide in 1972 appear even more dramatic because they represent big Republican margins during a time when the Democratic Party held an advantage in party loyalists. These deviating elections involved substantial departures from the underlying strength of the two parties in the electorate.

Temporary deviating changes may be dramatic and reflect important electoral forces, but another type of change is of even greater interest. On rare occasions in American national politics, a permanent or *realigning change* in voting patterns occurs. In such instances the electorate departs from its expected voting pattern but does not return to the old pattern afterward. The changes sometimes are large enough to alter the competitive balance between the parties, with significant consequences for the policy directions of the government. Such a period of change is usually referred to as a *partisan realignment.*[6]

FIGURE 3-5   Republican Normal Vote, 1968–2004

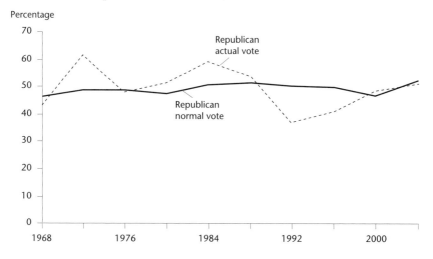

Source: U.S. House of Representatives, Office of the Clerk, clerk.house.gov; and National Election Studies, available at www.umich.edu/~nes.

Note: The normal vote calculations are a simplified version of Philip E. Converse's original analysis. See Philip E. Converse, "The Concept of a Normal Vote," in *Elections and the Political Order,* ed. Angus Campbell, Philip E. Converse, Warren E. Miller, and Donald E. Stokes (New York: Wiley, 1966), 9–39.

Electoral analysts usually discuss three major realignments in American history. One occurred during the time of the Civil War and the emergence of the Republican Party; another followed the depression of 1893 and benefited the Republicans; and the most recent followed the depression of 1929 and led to Democratic Party dominance. These abrupt changes in the expected votes of the parties can be seen in Figures 3-2 and 3-3. Each realignment of partisan loyalties coincided with a major national crisis, leading to the supposition that a social or economic crisis is necessary to shake loose customary loyalties. But major crises and national traumas have not always led to disruptions of partisanship, suggesting that other political conditions must also be present for a crisis to produce a realignment. The nature of the realignment crisis has political significance, however, because it generally determines the lines along which the rearrangement in partisan loyalties will take place, as different segments of the electorate respond differently to the crisis and to attempts to solve it.

In general, realignments appear to happen in the following way. At a time of national crisis, the electorate rejects the party in power, giving a decisive victory to the other party, a victory that includes not only the presidency but also large majorities in both houses of Congress. Armed with a political mandate, the new party in office acts to meet the crisis, often with innovative policies that are sharp departures from the past. *If the administration's policy initiatives are successful in solving the nation's problems (or at least if they are widely perceived as successful), then significant numbers of voters will become partisans of the new administration's party* and continue voting for this party in subsequent elections, thus causing a lasting change in the division of partisan strength in the electorate. If the administration in power is *not* perceived as successful in handling the crisis, then in all likelihood the voters will reject that party in the next election, and its landslide victory in the previous election will be regarded, in retrospect, as a deviating election.

In a realignment the people who become partisans of the new majority party likely are independents and previously uninvolved members of the electorate, not partisans of the other party. In other words, in a realignment few Democrats or Republicans switch parties. It appears more likely that independents drop their independent stance and become partisan. Thus, for a realignment to occur, a precondition may be a pool of people without partisan attachments who are available for realignment. This, in turn, suggests a longer sequence of events that forms a realignment cycle.

First there is the crisis that, if successfully handled, leads to a realignment. This initiates a period of electoral stability during which the parties take distinct stands on the issues that were at the heart of the crisis. Party loyalty is high during this period, both within the electorate and among the elected political leaders in government. However, as time passes, new problems arise and new issues gradually disrupt the old alignment and lead to greater electoral instability. During this period, often referred to as a *dealignment,* voters are much more susceptible to the personal appeals of candidates, to local issues, and to other elements that might lead to departures from underlying party loyalty. As the time since the last realignment lengthens, more and more new voters come into the electorate without attachments to the symbols and issues of the past that made their elders party loyalists. This group of voters without strong attachments to either party may provide the basis for a new realignment should a crisis arise and one or the other of the parties be perceived as successfully solving it.

Party Systems and Realignments

Political historians often divide American electoral history into five *party systems*—eras that are distinguished from each other by the different political parties that existed or by the different competitive relationships among the parties.[7] The transition from one party system to another has usually been marked by a realignment.

The first party system, which extended from the 1790s until about 1824, saw the relatively rapid formation of two parties, the Federalists and the Jeffersonian Republicans. The issue that divided the parties most clearly was their attitude toward the power of the central government. The commercial and financial interests supported the Federalist position of increasing the authority of the central government, whereas Jeffersonian Republicans distrusted the centralizing and, in their view, aristocratic tendencies of their rivals. The parties began as factions within Congress, but before long they had gained organizations at the state and local level and had substantially broadened the base of political participation among the voting population. After 1815, competition between the two parties all but ceased as the Jeffersonian Republicans gained supremacy, moving the country into the so-called Era of Good Feelings.

The second party system is usually dated from 1828, the year of the first presidential election with substantial popular participation, which marked the resurgence of party competition for the presidency. Emerging ultimately from this renewed competition were the Democrats and the Whigs, parties that competed almost evenly for national power until the 1850s. Mass political participation increased and party organizations were strengthened as both parties sought electoral support from the common people. Although the Democratic Party had come to prominence led by frontiersman Andrew Jackson, by the 1850s both Democrats and Whigs had adherents in all sections of the nation. Thus, when the issue of slavery broke full-force on the nation, the existing parties could not easily cope with the sectional differences they found within their ranks. As the Whigs and Democrats compromised or failed to act because of internal disagreements, a flurry of minor parties appeared to push the cause of abolition. One of these, the Republican Party, eventually replaced the floundering Whigs as one of the two major parties that would dominate party systems thereafter.

The intense conflicts that preceded the Civil War led to the basic regional alignment of Democratic dominance in the South and Republican strength in the North that emerged from the war and that characterized the third-party system. But the extreme intensity and durability of the partisan loyalties were also significantly dependent on emotional attachments associated with the war. The strength of partisan attachments after the Civil War was not lessened by the sharp competitiveness of the two parties throughout the system. Electoral forces were so evenly balanced that the Republican Party could effectively control the presidency and Congress only by excluding the southern Democrats from participation in elections. Once Reconstruction relaxed enough to permit the full expression of Democratic strength, the nation was narrowly divided, with the slightest deviation determining the outcome of elections.

The most dominant characteristic of the Civil War realignment was the regional division of party strongholds, but considerable Republican vote strength was found throughout much of the South and Democratic strength in most of the North. Especially in the North, states that regularly cast their electoral votes for Republican presidential candidates did so by slim margins. Within each region persistent loyalty to the minority party was usually related to earlier opposition to the war. The intensity of feelings surrounding the war overwhelmed other issues, and the severity of the division over the war greatly inhibited the emergence of new issues along other lines. Thus, a significant feature of the Civil War realignment is its "freezing" of the party system.[8] Although later realignments have occurred and a fourth and fifth party system can be identified, after the Civil War the same two parties have remained dominant. New parties have found it impossible to compete effectively (although they may affect electoral outcomes). The subsequent realignments changed only the competitive position of these two parties relative to each other. Thus, although the choices were frozen following the Civil War, the relative strength of the parties was not.

Toward the end of the nineteenth century, Civil War loyalties weakened enough to allow new parties, particularly the Populists in the Midwest and South, to make inroads into the votes of both major parties. Following the economic recession of 1893 for which the Democrats suffered politically, the Republican Party began to improve its basic voting strength. In 1896 the formation of a coalition of Democrats and Populists and the unsuccessful presidential candidacy of their nominee, William Jennings Bryan, resulted in increased Republican strength in the East and a further strengthening of the secure position of the Democratic Party in the South. Republican domination was solidified in the Midwest by the popularity of Theodore Roosevelt in the election of 1904. By the early twentieth century, competitive areas were confined to the border states and a few mountain states.

The realignment of 1896 and the fourth party system that followed are appropriately viewed as an adjustment of the Civil War alignment. Few areas shifted far from the previous levels of voting; most individuals probably did not change their partisanship. The issue basis of the alignment was economic. The Republicans advocated development and modernization while opposing regulation of economic activity. The Democrats supported policies intended to provide remedies for particular economic hardships. At a minimum these issues led the more prosperous, more modern areas in the North to shift toward the Republicans and the more backward, more depressed areas in the South to shift toward the Democrats. These tendencies are based on normal vote patterns and should not obscure the considerable variation in the vote for president during these years, particularly in the elections of 1912 and 1916.

Following the onset of the Great Depression in 1929 under a Republican president, Democrat Franklin D. Roosevelt rode the reaction to economic hardship to a landslide victory in 1932. In his first administration, Roosevelt launched a program of economic recovery and public assistance called the New Deal. The Democrats emerged as the majority party, signaling the start of the fifth party system. The New Deal realignment resulted in far greater shifts than the earlier realignment of 1896, because it moved many of the northern states from Republican to Democratic status. Because the policies of the Democratic administration during the New Deal appealed more to the working class than to the middle class, more to poor farmers than to more prosperous farmers, these groups responded differently to Democratic candidates. The New Deal and the electorate's response to Roosevelt's administration considerably sharpened the social class basis of party support. Especially for younger voters during these years, class politics was of greater salience than it had been before or has been since.

This realignment resulted in adjustments in previous loyalties, but it did not override them completely. The New Deal coalition was based on regional strength in the South, which was independent of social class, and further reinforced an already overwhelming dominance there. The most incompatible elements in the New Deal coalition were southern middle-class whites, mainly conservative, and northern liberals, both white and black, and this incompatibility is what led to the current unraveling of the New Deal alignment. The disintegration of the New Deal coalition occurred first in presidential voting with the departure of southern white voters from the Democratic Party. In 1964 the states of the Deep South were the only states carried by Republican candidate Barry Goldwater, a stark reversal of one hundred years of history. This pattern continued in subsequent presidential elections. Only when the Democratic candidate was a southerner (Jimmy Carter in 1976 and Bill Clinton in 1992 and 1996) did the Democrats have a chance to carry some southern states. In 2000 Gore, also a southerner, was given a chance of winning only two southern states, Florida and his home state of Tennessee. Ultimately, he won neither. (Of course, he was running against another southerner.) To a degree, working-class whites in the North also have been attracted to the Republican Party on occasion, and middle-class voters have sometimes shifted toward the Democrats.

Survey data on party identification over the past fifty years also yield evidence of the New Deal alignment, as well as its recent deterioration (see Table 3-1). In the early years of this period, the advantage that the Democrats enjoyed nationwide was largely a result of having an overwhelming Democratic majority in the South, as shown in Table 3-2.

TABLE 3-1 Party Identification of the Electorate, 1952–2004

Party identification	1952	1956	1960	1964	1968	1972	1976	1980	1984	1988	1992	1996	2000	2004
Democrats	47%	44%	46%	51%	45%	40%	39%	41%	36%	35%	35%	38%	36%	32%
Independents	22	24	23	22	29	35	36	35	34	36	38	32	42	38
Republicans	27	29	27	24	24	23	23	22	28	28	25	29	20	29
Nothing, don't know	4	3	4	2	2	2	2	2	2	2	2	1	2	2
Total	100%	100%	100%	99%	100%	100%	100%	100%	100%	101%	100%	100%	100%	101%
(N)	(1,799)	(1,762)	(1,954)	(1,571)	(1,557)	(2,705)	(2,872)	(1,614)	(1,989)	(2,040)	(2,485)	(1,714)	(977)	(1,212)

Source: National Election Studies, available at www.umich.edu/~nes.

TABLE 3-2   Party Identification of the Electorate for the Nation, the Non-South, and the South, 1952–2004

The Nation

	1952	1956	1960	1964	1968	1972	1976	1980	1984	1988	1992	1996	2000	2004
Strong Democrats	22%	21%	20%	27%	20%	15%	15%	18%	17%	17%	18%	19%	19%	16%
Weak Democrats	25	23	24	25	25	26	25	23	20	18	17	20	17	15
Independents	22	23	22	22	29	35	36	34	34	36	38	32	42	38
Weak Republicans	14	14	14	13	14	13	14	14	15	14	14	16	10	12
Strong Republicans	13	15	15	11	10	10	9	8	13	14	11	13	10	16
Apolitical, other	4	4	5	2	2	2	2	2	2	2	2	1	2	2
Total	100%	100%	100%	100%	100%	101%	101%	99%	101%	101%	100%	101%	100%	99%
(N)	(1,799)	(1,762)	(1,954)	(1,571)	(1,557)	(2,705)	(2,872)	(1,614)	(1,989)	(2,040)	(2,485)	(1,714)	(977)	(1,212)

The Non-South

	1952	1956	1960	1964	1968	1972	1976	1980	1984	1988	1992	1996	2000	2004
Strong Democrats	18%	17%	18%	23%	17%	13%	12%	15%	15%	16%	16%	17%	18%	15%
Weak Democrats	22	19	20	23	24	22	22	22	18	16	17	20	17	14
Independents	26	26	25	25	28	37	38	37	33	36	39	32	44	42
Weak Republicans	16	16	16	16	17	16	17	14	17	16	15	17	11	12
Strong Republicans	17	18	17	12	12	12	10	9	14	15	12	14	9	16
Apolitical, other	2	2	4	1	1	1	2	2	2	2	1	1	1	1
Total	101%	98%	100%	100%	99%	101%	101%	99%	99%	101%	100%	101%	100%	100%
(N)	(1,290)	(1,249)	(1,293)	(1,087)	(1,076)	(1,799)	(1,623)	(1,050)	(1,352)	(1,322)	(1,650)	(1,123)	(642)	(793)

The South

	1952	1956	1960	1964	1968	1972	1976	1980	1984	1988	1992	1996	2000	2004
Strong Democrats	31%	29%	23%	36%	26%	17%	19%	23%	19%	21%	21%	22%	21%	18%
Weak Democrats	32	32	33	30	28	32	30	25	23	21	18	19	15	19
Independents	14	15	17	15	30	29	32	29	35	35	37	32	38	32
Weak Republicans	8	9	8	8	8	10	11	13	11	10	12	14	10	13
Strong Republicans	6	8	12	8	4	9	7	7	9	11	9	13	12	17
Apolitical, other	9	9	6	3	2	2	2	3	3	2	3	0	4	2
Total	100%	102%	99%	100%	98%	99%	101%	100%	100%	100%	100%	100%	100%	101%
(N)	(509)	(513)	(661)	(484)	(481)	(906)	(780)	(564)	(596)	(718)	(835)	(591)	(335)	(419)

Source: National Election Studies, available at www.umich.edu/~nes.

Today, Democrats are about equally strong in the North and South, and the proportion of Republicans in the South has increased to about the same level as in the North. In both the South and the North, independents hold the balance of power between Democrats and Republicans.

Another important element in the breakup of the New Deal alignment, also reflected in these tables, was the increase beginning in 1966 in the proportion of independents. Supporters of George Wallace in the South represented part of this increase initially, but an even larger portion is composed of young voters who have not chosen sides in politics as quickly as their elders did. The increase leveled off in the 1970s, and although the proportions have fluctuated, the number of independents remains near its highest point since the era of survey research began. The 42 percent independent in 2000 is the largest proportion of independents in the history of the National Election Studies.

The New Deal partisan realignment established in the 1930s remained intact longer in congressional voting. However, by the 1970s additional shifts in the New Deal alignment became evident, as conservative Republicans began to show strength in races for other offices in many parts of the South. Long-standing southern Democratic incumbents in Congress were safe from competition. As they stepped down, though, their seats were won, more often than not, by Republicans. Conversely, in some areas of the North moderate Republicans were replaced by liberal Democrats. These trends are shown in Figure 3-6, plotting the Democratic vote for Congress in the North and South since 1936. Clearly, Democratic strength in the South was crucial for the Democrats' control of the House of Representatives for much of this period.

We should be clear about what is changing and what is not. White southerners have always been conservative, especially on racial matters. From the Civil War until the 1960s, the Democratic Party was at least as conservative as the Republican Party on the crucial issue of race. When the national Republican Party took the more conservative position on race in 1964, white southerners began to vote for Republican presidential candidates. They continued to vote for southern conservative Democratic candidates in state and local races. Meanwhile, for the same reasons in reverse, newly enfranchised black southern voters were moving into the Democratic Party. Over the years, the positions of the two parties have become more clearly distinguished—the Democratic Party as the more liberal party on racial as well as economic issues, the Republican Party as the more conservative party. Particularly in the South, but also in the North, some voters have changed their partisanship and their votes accordingly. The congressional elections of 1994 were perhaps the culmination of this process. As the Republicans took control of the House of Representatives and Senate, their leadership was predominantly southern.

FIGURE 3-6   Democratic Vote for Congress, North and South, 1936–2004

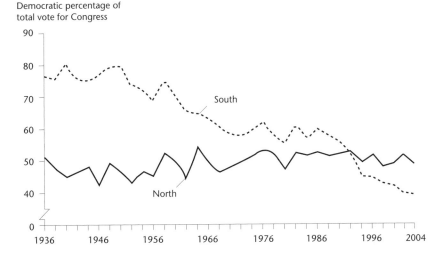

Democratic percentage of
total vote for Congress

Source: U.S. Bureau of the Census, *Statistical Abstract of the United States, 1993,* 113th ed. (Washington, D.C.: U.S. Government Printing Office, 1992); "Election '96," *Congressional Quarterly Weekly Report,* February 15, 1997, 444; and U.S. House of Representatives, Office of the Clerk, clerk.house.gov.

Are Conditions Right for a Realignment?

Some analysts have argued that the movement of white southerners into the Republican Party and the movement of blacks and some northern whites toward the Democratic Party constitutes a realignment and should be regarded as the start of a new party system. Disagreement arises about when this realignment occurred. Some date it from the 1960s, with the start of Republican dominance in presidential voting. Others view it as a Reagan realignment of the 1980s.

Voter movement and electoral volatility have been in evidence since the 1960s. Furthermore, much of this movement has been a sorting-out process whereby some voters are finding their natural home in a political party that shares their views on issues that concern them most. However, over this same time period, a sizable number of voters have found neither political party a congenial place to be and have demonstrated this by becoming independent, by not adopting a party identification in the first place, or by supporting an independent candidate such as Perot or, to a lesser extent, Nader. Through the 1990s, neither party was able to gather the political support to take firm control of government or complete initiatives that would appear to solve societal problems and win converts to their ranks. Bill Clinton perhaps had the opportunity to do so in 1993 when the House, the Senate, and the presidency were held by the Democrats. The opportunity was lost as his health care initiative went down to defeat. As a result of the 1994 elections, the Republicans gained control of the House of Representatives for the first time in forty years. For the remainder of that decade, gridlock reigned in Washington, D.C., as the parties engaged in increasingly acrimonious battle over the budget and Clinton's impeachment. With a substantial portion of the electorate standing on the sidelines as independents and professing frustration with the ideologically polarized political parties, it seemed reasonable to consider this as a continuation of a period of *dealignment.*

The situation changed in 2003. As a result of the midterm election of 2002, the Republicans gained a razor-thin majority in the Senate to add to their control of the House of Representatives and the presidency. In the election of 2004, the Republicans widened their majority in the Senate and George W. Bush claimed the mandate of a popularly elected president that he had been denied in 2000. Given the realignment perspective presented above, the Republicans now have achieved the unified control of government that gives them the opportunity to put into effect the initiatives that—if perceived as successful—could win converts to their party from the large pool of self-identified independents and produce a Republican majority for the future.

Might this scenario come about? On the one hand, the September 11, 2001, attacks provided a major crisis to which the president and Congress responded. The public rallied to support President Bush and, in the short term, his popularity soared. Bush has continued to do enough in the war on terror to maintain high job approval in this area. Indeed, this seems to have been a major key to his victory in 2004. (While it would be difficult to demonstrate that the president's efforts have contributed significantly to winning the war on terror, appearances are important. His position is similar to Franklin Roosevelt's during the Great Depression. Roosevelt's New Deal policies may not have contributed to the eventual economic recovery, but the public believed he accomplished much.)

On the other hand, the war in Iraq and, in the late summer of 2005, Hurricane Katrina brought additional challenges. Whether or not the Republicans can convert the opportunity provided by their unified control of government into a new realignment will rest on the Bush administration's ability to appear to be successful in dealing with these challenges. The responsibility for the United States being in Iraq and for establishing a viable democratic Iraqi government clearly lies with the administration. And, in the immediate aftermath of Katrina, the Bush administration was perceived as responsible for, but not adequately leading, the disaster relief efforts. If the administration fails to handle these challenges, and if President Bush and his fellow Republicans take the blame, then the electorate may "throw the rascals out" at their next opportunities in 2006 and 2008. The country would remain as it seems to be now, with closely balanced and deeply polarized partisan divisions and with a large middle group of independents holding the key to electoral success. If, however, the administration is able to get out of Iraq with the appearance of success and if it is ultimately perceived as successfully leading the rebuilding of New Orleans and the Gulf Coast communities, it might win enough converts to produce a solid Republican majority and a new partisan alignment.

Notes

1. *CQ Almanac Plus 2003* (Washington, D.C.: Congressional Quarterly Inc., 2004), 1-3, 1-4.
2. The most important work on party identification is in Angus Campbell, Philip E. Converse, Warren E. Miller, and Donald E. Stokes, *The American Voter* (New York: Wiley, 1960), 120–167. For a treatment of this subject in comparative perspective, see Ian Budge, Ivor Crewe, and Dennis Farlie, eds., *Party Identification and Beyond* (New York: Wiley, 1976), Part I.
3. For the most important statement of these ideas, see Philip E. Converse, "The Concept of a Normal Vote," in *Elections and the Political Order*, ed. Angus Campbell, Philip E. Converse, Warren E. Miller, and Donald E. Stokes (New York: Wiley, 1966), 9–39.
4. This discussion and data presentation are based on our earlier work in William H. Flanigan and Nancy H. Zingale, "The Measurement of Electoral Change," *Political Methodology* 1 (summer 1974): 49–82.
5. This and most discussions of the classification of elections are based on the work of V. O. Key and Angus Campbell. See V. O. Key, "A Theory of Critical Elections," *Journal of Politics* 17 (1955): 3–18; and Angus Campbell, "A Classification of Presidential Elections," in *Elections and the Political Order,* ed. Angus Campbell, Philip E. Converse, Warren E. Miller, and Donald E. Stokes (New York: Wiley, 1966), 63–77.
6. This and the following discussion draw heavily on Jerome M. Clubb, William H. Flanigan, and Nancy H. Zingale, *Partisan Realignment: Voters, Parties, and Government in American History* (Boulder, Colo.: Westview Press, 1990). See especially chaps. 5 and 8.
7. See, for example, William N. Chambers and W. Dean Burnham, eds., *The American Party Systems: Stages of Political Development* (New York: Oxford University Press, 1975).
8. This concept was developed by S. M. Lipset and Stein Rokkan in their discussion of the development of the European party systems in *Party Systems and Voter Alignments* (New York: Free Press, 1967), 1–64.

Suggested Readings

Beck, Paul Allen. "The Dealignment Era in America." In *Electoral Change in Advanced Industrial Democracies: Realignment or Dealignment?* edited by Russell J. Dalton,

Scott C. Flanagan, and Paul Allen Beck. Princeton: Princeton University Press, 1984. A good survey of recent politics as an example of dealignment.

Burnham, W. Dean. *Critical Elections and the Mainsprings of American Politics.* New York: W. W. Norton, 1970. An early, important statement of the electoral realignment perspective.

Campbell, Angus, Philip E. Converse, Warren E. Miller, and Donald E. Stokes. *The American Voter.* New York: Wiley, 1960. The classic study of public opinion and voting behavior in the United States.

Clubb, Jerome M., William H. Flanigan, and Nancy H. Zingale. *Partisan Realignment: Voters, Parties, and Government in American History.* Boulder, Colo.: Westview Press, 1990. A conceptualization of realignments that emphasizes both electoral behavior and political leadership.

Converse, Philip E. "The Concept of a Normal Vote." In *Elections and the Political Order,* edited by Angus Campbell, Philip E. Converse, Warren E. Miller, and Donald E. Stokes. New York: Wiley, 1966. This chapter established the role of party identification as a baseline for the analysis of vote choice.

MacKuen, Michael B., Robert S. Erikson, and James A. Stimson. "Macropartisanship." *American Political Science Review* 83 (December 1989): 1125–1142. A sophisticated analysis of trends in aggregate party identification, arguing that the sizable amount of instability undermines the realignment perspective.

Internet Resources

The Web site of the National Election Studies, www.umich.edu/~nes, has basic information on partisanship and party identification. Click on "Partisanship and Evaluation of the Political Parties." For information on partisan voting patterns, click on "Vote Choice."

During election years news organizations may have Web sites with election statistics in historical depth. A site with extensive historical data is David Leip's Atlas of U.S. Presidential Elections at www.uselectionatlas.org.

Another source of current information on elections and public opinion is the Elections U.S.A. Web site at www.geocities.com/CapitolHill/6228. Click on "Elections" for election returns for the states and nation.

Partisans and Partisan Change

PARTISANSHIP is a useful concept for tracing the dynamics of American political history. It is also crucial for understanding the political behavior of individuals. We begin this chapter by examining the impact of having—or not having—a party identification on the way people respond to politics. We then turn to the question of partisan change, looking first at change in individuals' partisanship over their lifetimes and then at changes across generations.

Voting Behavior

The standard party identification question, used in almost all political surveys, asks respondents whether they are Republicans, Democrats, or independents and whether they are "strong" or "not very strong" Republicans or Democrats. The likelihood of voting loyally in support of one party varies with the strength of individuals' partisanship. The defection rates of strong and weak (not very strong) partisans in each presidential election since 1952 are illustrated in Figure 4-1. Declining party loyalty is apparent with a decrease in the intensity of partisanship. Strong partisans consistently support the candidate of their party at higher rates than do weak partisans. (In most years Republicans have been more loyal to their party than Democrats, although this is partly accounted for by southern Democrats who regularly deserted their party in presidential elections. By the end of the twentieth century, southern Democrats were no longer distinctive in this regard. Previously defecting Democrats had become independents or Republicans.)

Differences in candidate appeal affect the propensity to defect. Few Republicans deserted Dwight D. Eisenhower in the 1950s, Richard M. Nixon in 1972, or Ronald Reagan in 1984; many more left Barry Goldwater

FIGURE 4-1   Defection Rates, by Party Identifiers in Presidential Elections, 1952–2004

Source: National Election Studies, available at www.umich.edu/~nes.

in 1964. Similarly, most Democrats were loyal to Lyndon B. Johnson in 1964 but abandoned George McGovern in large numbers in 1972.

Another potential cause of defection is attractive third-party candidates. In 1992 Ross Perot drew defectors from both parties, although more from the Republican side. Ten percent of strong Republicans and

25 percent of weak Republicans defected to Perot. Although few strong Democrats defected to Perot, 17 percent of the weak Democrats did. John B. Anderson in 1980 and George C. Wallace in 1968 similarly account for part of the upsurges in defections in those years.

Historically, third-party candidates often have been viewed as "halfway houses" for partisans moving from one party to another. Not as dramatic for a partisan as defection to the opposition party, a vote for such a candidate may be a first step away from party loyalty. In any event, support for third parties and an increase in defection rates have generally been symptomatic of the loosening of party ties in a dealignment.

A different pattern—one of high party loyalty on both sides—was exhibited in the last three presidential elections (1996, 2000, and 2004) as well as 1976 and 1988. In these elections partisans of both parties remained loyal to candidates who were relatively balanced in their appeal. This return to party loyalty, not seen so consistently since the 1950s, is perhaps an indicator of the greater partisan polarization that has occurred in recent years.[1]

Although strong partisans vary in their loyalty from year to year depending on the candidates offered by their party, this tendency is much more pronounced among weak partisans. For example, the defection rate of strong Republicans falls in a narrow range from around 2 percent in a good Republican year to 10 percent in a bad year. In contrast, weak Republicans are almost as loyal as strong Republicans when an attractive Republican candidate is on the ticket, but nearly 50 percent defected in the disastrous 1964 election. The behavior of Democrats is similar, although both strong and weak Democrats are more likely to desert their party than are Republicans. Clearly, marked departures from the expected vote of a party are accomplished by wooing away the weaker partisans of the opposite party.

The tendency of both strong and weak partisans to vote according to their party identification becomes even more pronounced as one moves down the ticket to less visible and less publicized offices. This is a product of the dominant two-party system nationwide. Even highly successful third-party or independent candidates down the ticket are merely local disruptions that have virtually no impact on national patterns. The voting behavior of partisans in congressional races since 1952 differs from the presidential data in two significant ways (see Figure 4-2). First, differences between the party loyalty of strong and weak partisans are usually smaller. Second, the defection rate does not fluctuate from year to year nearly as much as in the presidential elections, particularly among weak partisans. Both differences are attributable to the lower visibility of congressional races. In a presidential election, the flood of available information means that a particularly attractive candidate or a stirring issue may touch the consciousness of the weak partisans, causing

FIGURE 4-2   Defection Rates, by Party Identifiers in Congressional
Elections, 1952–2004

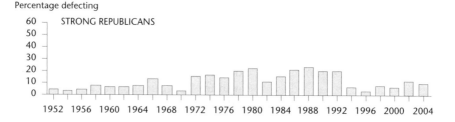

Source: National Election Studies, available at www.umich.edu/~nes.

them to defect from traditional party ties; the firmly attached, strong partisans are more likely to resist. In the less publicized congressional races, the information that might cause weak partisans to defect is less likely to even reach them. In the absence of information about the candidates and issues, weak partisans vote their party identification.

In congressional voting, unlike presidential voting, Democrats were, until 1994, regularly more party loyal than were Republicans. This was both cause and effect of the recent disjuncture of national politics, whereby Republicans were stronger in presidential politics and Democrats dominated in congressional politics. Throughout the 1970s and 1980s the Republicans were able to field more attractive presidential candidates than the Democrats, leading more Democratic partisans to defect in presidential races. In contrast, congressional races saw Republican partisans often defecting to vote for a long-term Democratic incumbent running against token Republican opposition. The situation changed dramatically in 1994, when the Republicans gained control of the House of Representatives in large part by fanning the flames of anti-incumbent, anti-Democratic sentiment. Thereafter, with more Republican incumbents to vote for, Republican partisans were noticeably more party loyal than they had been in previous congressional elections.

The intensity of partisanship affects political behavior beyond its influence on the likelihood of voting for or defecting from a party's candidate. Strong partisans are also more likely to vote in all kinds of elections than are either weak partisans or independents. In fact, one explanation sometimes offered for the decline in turnout in recent years is the declining partisanship of the American public.[2] The turnout rates of the various categories of partisans and independents for three types of elections—presidential, off-year congressional, and primary—are illustrated in Figure 4-3. Presidential primaries, despite all their accompanying publicity and frenetic campaigning, typically have a lower average turnout than off-year congressional elections. Turnout declines in all categories as the presumed importance of the race decreases, but the rate is much steeper among the less partisan. As a result, the less salient the election, the more the electorate will be dominated by the intense partisans, who are also less likely to defect from party ties in casting their ballots.

These ideas led Angus Campbell to suggest an intriguing theory of electoral change to explain the often observed phenomenon in American politics whereby the party winning the presidency almost always loses seats in the legislature in the next congressional election.[3] Because, the argument goes, presidential elections are usually accompanied by a high level of interest, large numbers of weak partisans and independents are drawn to the polls. Because weak partisans and independents are more easily shifted from one party to another, they add disproportionately to the vote for one presidential candidate, usually the winner. In congressional elections these less committed voters do not turn out, whereas relatively large numbers of intense partisans do. The strong party identifiers are not so likely to shift their vote away from their party. As a consequence, support declines in off-year congressional

FIGURE 4-3   Turnout by Partisans and Independents in Presidential,
Congressional, and Primary Elections

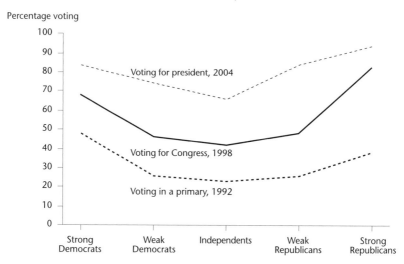

Source: National Election Studies, available at www.umich.edu/~nes.

elections for the party that won the previous presidential election with
disproportionately large numbers of less interested voters.

Persuasive as Campbell's argument may be, it rests on some assumptions that may be questionable. First, it assumes that high-stimulus
elections will be landslides—that is, it assumes that the short-term
forces bringing the less interested voter to the polls will work to the advantage of only one candidate. Even though this has often been the
case, it is not invariable. The extremely close 1960 presidential election,
with its emphasis on the religion (Catholicism) of Democratic candidate
John F. Kennedy, was a high-turnout election, but different groups of
voters were affected in different ways. Similarly, both George W. Bush
and John Kerry benefited from the high turnout in 2004.

Second, Campbell's argument suggests that the less interested voters who come to the polls to vote for the attractive presidential candidate will also vote for that party's candidate in congressional elections.
In fact, the evidence shows that in many cases weak partisans who defect
in presidential elections return to their own party in congressional elections or, in the case of Perot voters in 1992 and 1996, have no congressional candidates on the same ticket to vote for. In addition, independents often split their tickets instead of voting for the congressional
candidate of the same party as their presidential choice. To some extent,
the argument also rests on the assumption that independents are not

only less partisan but also less informed, concerned, and interested in politics, a view that is frequently called into question.

Are Independents Apolitical?

Independents, who now account for more than one-third of the national electorate, are the most obvious source of additional votes for either party. Although partisans, especially weak partisans, sometimes abandon their party, year after year independents are the largest bloc of uncommitted voters available to both parties. The independents' capacity for shifting back and forth between the major parties is shown in Table 4-1. Each party has, on occasion, successfully appealed to the independents, winning over a large majority to its side. In 1984 the independents voted almost two to one for Reagan over Walter F. Mondale, and Johnson held a similar advantage over Goldwater in 1964. The elections of 1976 (Jimmy Carter versus Gerald R. Ford) and 1960 (Kennedy versus Nixon) demonstrate the situation Republican presidential candidates faced for many years: They had to win a healthy majority of the independent vote even to stay in close contention. The election of George W. Bush in 2000 depended on, among other things, the substantial advantage he enjoyed over his opponents among independents. This represented a strong Republican recovery from the weak showings of Bush's father in 1992 and Bob Dole in 1996.

Third-party or independent candidates find unaffiliated voters a major source of votes. In 1992, 27 percent of the independents voted for Perot. His failure to hold those votes in 1996 turned his earlier, impressive showing into a minor story. In 1968 more than 20 percent of the independents gave their votes to Wallace; and in 1980, 14 percent voted for Anderson. Put another way, more than half of a third-party candidate's votes typically come from independents. Furthermore, independents may shift dramatically in voting for president and remain stable in voting for Congress.

On what basis do independents make their vote choices? Two views of independents have competed for popularity. The civics textbook view is of an intelligent, informed, dispassionate evaluator of candidates and issues, who, after careful consideration, votes for "the person, not the party." An alternate view—often attributed to campaign strategists—is of the independent as uninformed and uninterested, on whom intelligent, issue-oriented appeals and reasoned debate would be lost.

To pursue the analysis of independents, we need to make two distinctions that have not intruded on the discussion to this point. We will note these distinctions and then drop them because they complicate the analysis and are usually ignored.

TABLE 4-1   The Distribution of Votes for President by Independents, 1948–2004

	1948	1952	1956	1960	1964	1968	1972	1976	1980	1984	1988	1992	1996	2000	2004
Democratic	57%	33%	27%	46%	66%	32%	33%	45%	26%	34%	46%	42%	49%	43%	55%
Republican	43	67	73	54	34	47	65	55	56	66	53	30	37	50	40
George C. Wallace[a]						21									
John G. Schmitz[b]							2								
John B. Anderson[c]									14						
Ross Perot[d]												27	14		
Pat Buchanan[e]														1	
Ralph Nader[f]														6	1
Other									4		2				4
Total	100%	100%	100%	100%	100%	100%	100%	100%	100%	100%	101%	99%	100%	100%	100%
(N)	—	(263)	(309)	(298)	(219)	(228)	(908)	(532)	(306)	(334)	(364)	(573)	(304)	(194)	(255)

Sources: Source: National Election Studies, available at www.umich.edu/~nes.

[a]American Independent Party candidate in 1968.
[b]American Party candidate in 1972.
[c]Independent candidate in 1980.
[d]Independent candidate in 1992, 1996.
[e]Reform Party candidate in 2000.
[f]Green Party candidate in 2000.

First, important differences exist between nonpartisans who identify themselves as independents and those who lack any political identification. A sizable segment of the electorate answers the party identification question by saying that they identify themselves as nothing or that they do not know what they are. According to the coding conventions used by the National Election Studies, most nonidentifiers are included with the independents, but important conceptual distinctions may exist between them and self-identified independents.[4] The two types of nonpartisans are highlighted in the box in Table 4-2. Those in one set identify themselves as *independents;* the others do not think of themselves in terms of political labels. Since 1972, between about one-sixth and one-third of the nonpartisans failed to identify themselves as independents. Even though the electorate generally has become more nonpartisan, it is not necessarily more independent. These situations present different implications for the political parties. Self-identified independents think of themselves as having a political identity and are somewhat antiparty in orientation. The nonidentifying nonpartisans have a less clear self-image of themselves as political actors, but they are not particularly hostile to the political parties. They are less self-consciously political in many ways.

Second, within the large group of people who do not identify with either the Democratic or the Republican Party are many who say they "lean toward" one or the other. These leaners make up two-thirds of all nonpartisans, and they complicate analysis in a significant way. On crucial attitudes and in important forms of political behavior, the leaning independents appear partisan. Independents who lean toward the Demo-

TABLE 4-2   Party Identifiers, Self-Identified Independents, and People Claiming No Preference, 1968–2004

	1968	1972	1976	1980	1984	1988	1992	1996	2000	2004
Identify with a party	69%	64%	64%	64%	64%	63%	60%	66%	57%	61%
Identify as independents	27	28	30	24	25	31	32	26	29	33
Have no preference	3	8	5	12	10	6	7	8	13	5
Don't know	a	0	a	0	0	0	1	a	1	1
Not ascertained	a	a	1	a	1	a	a	a	a	a
Total	99%	100%	100%	100%	100%	100%	100%	100%	100%	100%
(N)	(1,557)	(2,702)	(1,320)	(1,614)	(1,989)	(2,040)	(2,485)	(1,714)	(981)	(1,212)

Source: National Election Studies.

[a]Less than 0.5 percent.

cratic Party behave somewhat like weak Democratic partisans, and independents who lean toward the Republican Party behave like weak Republicans.[5] As can be seen in Figure 4-4, independent leaners are more similar to weak partisans than strong and weak partisans are to each other.

How appropriate, then, is it to include all independents in one category? On some characteristics such as ideological self-identification and interest in public affairs much more variation is evident within the three independent categories than between the several partisan categories. The differences between leaners and pure independents are often greater than the differences among Republicans or Democrats. Because the concept of "independent" embraces these three dissimilar groups, there is little wonder that some disagreement exists over what the true independent is like.

As a consequence of including various types of people under the label "independent," making generalizations about the degree of political interest and information of independents is difficult. Some independents have considerable interest in politics, and others are apathetic. There are more informed, concerned voters among the leaning independents than among other nonpartisans, and the leaning independents are more likely to register and to vote. So, are independents attentive or apathetic toward politics? They are both.

To the student of contemporary American politics, these characteristics of the independent remain important because they determine

FIGURE 4-4   Percentage of Turnout, High Interest, and Democratic Vote for President by Partisanship, 2004

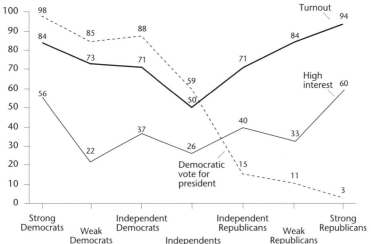

Source: 2004 National Election Study, available at www.umich.edu/~nes.

the independent's susceptibility to political appeals. We and others have argued that the American electoral system is presently at a time when a fairly large group of potential voters has weak ties to the political parties. The argument is that, when a large portion of the electorate is either independent or exhibits more independent behavior, these people form a pool of potential recruits for one of the parties or a new party. Should one or another political party be able to capture the imagination of this pool of available recruits on a lasting basis, it would lead to a significant change in the partisan division in the electorate.

Partisan Change

Partisanship can be thought of as a basic attitude that establishes a normal or expected vote, an estimate about how individuals or populations will vote, other things being equal. However, partisanship itself is not unchangeable. Individuals may change not only their vote but also their long-term party identification from one party to another. More important, over extended periods of time the partisan composition of the electorate may be altered as new voters of one political persuasion replace older voters of another. When the basic partisan division of the electorate changes, a partisan realignment occurs.

In the past the absence of survey data limited analysis of realignments, but during the current period the individual processes of partisan change that underlie aggregate shifts in the partisan division of the electorate can be studied. These processes have been a matter of some controversy. One perspective holds that individual partisans are *converted* from one party to the other during a realignment. Other analysts, noting the psychological difficulty in changing long-held and deeply felt attachments, argue that such change probably comes about through *mobilization*, not conversion. In other words, the independents or nonpolitical individuals, perhaps predominantly young voters just entering the electorate without strong partisan attachments, fuel a realignment by joining the electorate overwhelmingly on the side of one party.

Some evidence on these points comes from the New Deal era. Although survey research was then in its infancy, some scholars have creatively used data from early surveys to try to answer these questions. Research by Kristi Andersen, reported in *The Changing American Voter,* reveals high levels of nonvoting and nonpartisanship among young people and new citizens before the Great Depression.[6] Those uninvolved, uncommitted potential participants entered the electorate in the 1930s disproportionately as Democrats. Andersen's findings on the electorate of the 1920s and 1930s support the view that realignments are based on the mobilization of new, independent voters instead of on the conversion of partisans. In contrast, Robert S. Erikson and Kent L. Tedin argue on the basis of early Gallup poll data that much of the increase in the Democratic vote in the 1930s came from voters who had previously voted Republican.[7]

In the next section we will examine the processes of partisan change in the contemporary period. Although we are in a better position to do so than we were for earlier eras, efforts are still hampered by a scarcity of panel data—that is, repeated interviews with the same individuals at different times. In most cases it will be necessary to infer individual changes from the behavior of different individuals over time.

Changes in Individuals over a Lifetime

Two types of change in partisan identification can be distinguished, both of which have significant implications for political behavior. First, an individual may change from one party to another or to independent, or from independence to partisanship. Such change is important if a large proportion of the electorate shifts in the same direction at about the same time. Second, an individual's partisanship may strengthen or weaken in intensity. A long-standing hypothesis states that the longer individuals identify with a party the stronger their partisanship will become.[8] In the electorate as a whole, the two types of change are not necessarily related to one another, so the occurrence of one form of change does not dictate or prevent the other. For example, recent decades saw an increase in the number of independents in the electorate, which can be accounted for by young people not choosing a party or by partisans moving to independence or both. At the same time, the remaining partisans are becoming more firmly committed and more party loyal, and the polarization between the parties is increasing.

Analysts have attempted to explain partisan change by referring to three types of causal effects: (1) *period effects,* or the impact of a particular historical period that briefly affects partisanship across all age groups; (2) a *generation effect,* which affects the partisanship of a particular age group for the remainder of their political lives; and (3) a *life-cycle effect,* which produces changes associated with an individual's age. In current political behavior all three can be illustrated: a period effect that has resulted in an increasing independence in all age groups, a generation effect that keeps Democratic partisan loyalty high in the generation that entered the electorate during the New Deal, and a life-cycle effect that yields greater independence among the young than among their elders.

The difference between 1960, 1980, and 2004 in the proportion of independents in various age groups is shown in Figure 4-5. The solid line represents the percentage of independents in each age group in 1980, and the dotted line represents 2004. The left end of each line re-

FIGURE 4-5   Distribution of Independents by Age Cohorts, 1960, 1980, and 2004

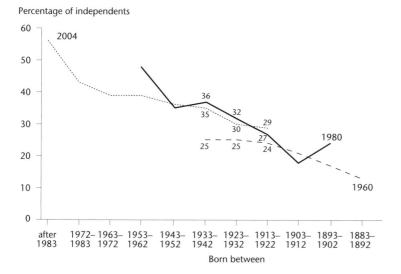

Percentage of independents

Source: National Election Studies, available at www.umich.edu/~nes.

Note: The youngest cohort in each year includes only those old enough to vote.

flects a higher rate of independence among the young in 1980 and 2004 when compared with 1960, the broken line.

Each line reveals a downward slope to the right. This indicates that older individuals in each year were less likely to be independents compared with younger people in the same year. By looking at the first point on the left of each line, the youngest respondents can be compared in each of the three years; the second point represents the second youngest group; and so on. In general, the cohorts in the 1980 and 2004 surveys have higher levels of political independence at each age than the cohorts from the 1960 survey.

The change in particular age cohorts also can be examined between 1960 and the later years using Figure 4-5.* The youngest cohort

---

*In the absence of repeated observations of the same individuals over time, studying many aspects of change is impossible. The use of age cohorts is an analytical technique that attempts to assess individual change through the use of surveys of different individuals over the years. Individuals of a certain age are isolated in an early survey—say thirty- to forty-year-olds in 1960—and they are compared with forty- to fifty-year-olds from a 1970 survey. Thus, an age cohort can be compared at two different times. This technique has been used in several studies of partisanship. See,

in 1960 was more than forty years old in 1980 and reveals a higher level of independence (36 percent) than it did when entering the electorate (25 percent). By 2004 the cohort was more than sixty years old and had stayed about the same in its level of independence (35 percent). At each point along the lines, the vertical distance between them represents the changing percentage of independents in that age cohort. Most age cohorts became more independent before 1980 and did not change much after that.

Contrary to political folklore, little evidence exists that people become Republicans as they grow older—that is, that a life-cycle effect favors Republicans. Older members of the electorate were, for some years, more likely to be Republicans than younger members. The generation of young people who came of age before the Great Depression contained large proportions of Republicans, an understandable situation given the advantage the Republicans enjoyed nationally at that time. Relatively few members of this generation changed partisanship over the years, and these individuals constituted the older, more heavily Republican segment of the electorate. By the same token, the generation that entered the electorate during the New Deal was disproportionately Democratic. Because they also have remained stable in partisanship, older voters now look increasingly Democratic as this generation ages. For the next decade or so it will appear that the older the voters are, the more likely they are to be Democratic.

The tendency of individual partisanship to strengthen with age is the subject of some controversy.[9] During periods of stable party voting, increased partisanship is likely the longer individuals identify with and vote for their party. In a multi-wave panel study by M. Kent Jennings, the proportion of respondents who called themselves "strong Democrats" or "strong Republicans" increased from 15 percent in 1973 (when the respondents were about twenty-five years old) to 26 percent in 1997 (when they were around fifty).[10]

However, when party voting is frequently disrupted, this reinforcement of partisanship may not occur. Even if the strength of partisanship does not increase with age, older partisans are less likely to abandon their party and become independents. This explains in part why older partisans are less likely to vote for independent or third-party candidates than are younger partisans. In 1992, 19 percent of the Republican and Democratic partisans aged twenty-five and younger voted for Perot, but only

---

for example, Paul R. Abramson, "Generational Change in American Electoral Behavior," *American Political Science Review* 68 (March 1974): 93–105; David Butler and Donald Stokes, *Political Change in Britain: Forces Shaping Electoral Choice* (New York: St. Martin's Press, 1969), especially chaps. 3, 11; and Philip E. Converse, *The Dynamics of Party Support: Cohort-Analyzing Party Identification* (Beverly Hills, Calif.: Sage Publications, 1976).

11 percent of partisans aged forty-five and older voted for him. In 2000, Nader's vote, although small, was greatest among the young.

Gradual changes in individual partisanship have not been assessed satisfactorily for the entire public because the few election studies based on repeated interviews of the same individuals have covered at most four years. Nevertheless, the possibility that individuals change their partisanship over longer time periods is of considerable interest. Speculation has focused on the possibility that the large number of young independents will become identified with one party or the other, thus creating a substantial shift in the overall partisan balance of the electorate, with or without a realigning crisis.

The best evidence on this point comes from a major study of political socialization conducted by M. Kent Jennings. He surveyed a national sample of high school students and their parents in 1965, with follow-up interviews in 1973, 1982, and 1997.[11] This study provides a before-and-after picture of young people during the political traumas of the late 1960s and early 1970s, as well as later snapshots after a more quiescent period.

Table 4-3 shows the amount of change in partisanship between each wave of the study. As can be seen by looking at the highlighted cells, partisanship was least stable when the respondents were youngest, between 1965 and 1973. About two-thirds of the sample reported the same partisanship when interviewed in 1982 as in 1973 and, again, between 1982 and 1997. Most of the changes that did occur were between partisanship and independence; relatively few reported switching from Democrat to Republican or vice versa.

Changes across Generations

A shift in the partisan composition of the electorate owing to generational change is ordinarily a gradual one, because political attitudes, including partisanship, tend to be transmitted from parents to their children. Normally, more than two-thirds of the electorate identify with their parents' party if both parents had the same party identification. Adoption of parents' partisanship by their children is consistent with the notion of family socialization. Children pick up the partisanship of their parents while young, but the parents' influence diminishes as the child comes into contact with other political and social influences during the teenage years. For most individuals the political influence of their surroundings will be consistent with their family's political leanings, so the similarity between parents' and offspring's partisanship remains strong. In contrast, people who remember their parents as having conflicting loyalties are more likely to be independents than either Democrats or Republicans. This is even more true of the children of parents without

TABLE 4-3   Stability and Change of Partisanship, 1965–1997

		1973					1982		
		Dem.	Ind.	Rep.			Dem.	Ind.	Rep.
	Dem.	24	14	3		Dem.	23	9	3
1965	Ind.	7	24	5	1973	Ind.	8	32	7
	Rep.	3	9	10		Rep.	2	4	13

Total = 99%   N = 952   Total = 101%   N = 924

		1997		
		Dem.	Ind.	Rep.
	Dem.	23	7	2
1982	Ind.	5	27	5
	Rep.	4	10	17

Total = 100%   N = 896

Source: Youth-Parent Socialization Study Panel, 1965–1997, Youth Wave. Data provided by Inter-university Consortium for Political and Social Research.

Note: Dem. = Democrat; Ind. = Independent; Rep. = Republican. The highlighted cells (along the diagonal) represent those individuals who remained stable in their partisanship from one time period to the next. The off-diagonal cells represent individuals who changed their partisan identification.

any partisan attachments. Thus, in each political generation a sizable number of voters lacks an inherited party loyalty.

The Jennings study also permits the examination of the process of generational change because it allows a comparison of party identification for parents and their children. As can be seen in Figure 4-6, 58 percent of the seventeen-year-olds in 1965 had adopted the party identification of their parents. Of the high school seniors, 30 percent were Democratic and came from Democratic families. Another 10 percent of the seniors were Democratic but came from independent or Republican families. Although not explicitly shown in Figure 4-6, Democrats had a somewhat higher transmission rate than either Republicans or independents. Despite the higher transmission rate, there were so many more Democratic parents that their children also contributed substantial numbers to the independent ranks.

The latest wave of the Jennings study allows an examination of generational change in a more recent time, by comparing the partisanship of the 1965 high school seniors, now parents, with the partisanship of their high school–age children (see Figure 4-7). (Not all the original

FIGURE 4-6   Party Identification of High School Seniors and Their Parents, 1965

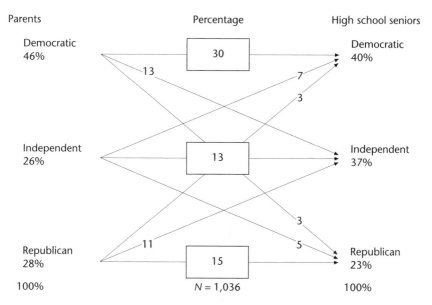

Source: Adapted from Paul A. Beck, Jere W. Bruner, and L. Douglas Dobson, *Political Socialization* (Washington, D.C.: American Political Science Association, 1974), 22.

Note: On the left of the figure is the distribution of the parents' party identification and on the right is their children's. The numbers in the three boxes highlight the percentages of the children who had the same party identification as their parents. The numbers on the remaining arrows show various amounts of change from their parents' partisanship by the children. For example, 7 percent of the total number of children had independent parents but became Democrats.

1965 students had children of that age in 1997, so the focus is on only a subset of those in the original sample reinterviewed in 1997. Therefore the distribution of partisanship of these parents will not be the same as for the whole 1997 sample covered in Table 4-3. The group of parents is somewhat less Democratic and more Republican than the full group.) Figure 4-7 suggests that parents transmitted their partisanship to their children at a lower rate in the 1990s than they had a generation earlier. Hidden in these numbers, however, are traces of a modest recovery in partisanship. Unlike 1965, the younger generation is only slightly more independent than the parents, and the number of children leaving their parents' parties for independence is about equally offset by the children of independents adopting a partisanship. In 1965, twice as many children opted for independence as moved toward partisanship.

FIGURE 4-7   Party Identification of High School Seniors and Their Parents,
               1997

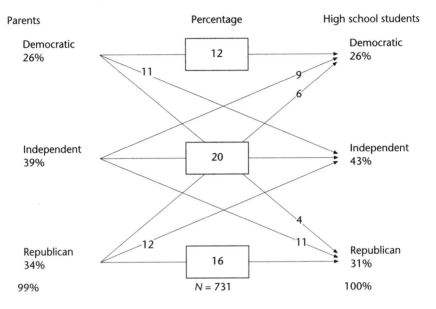

Source: Youth-Parent Socialization Panel Study, 1965–1997: 1997 Youth-Parent Wave.
Data provided by the Inter-university Consortium for Political and Social Research.

The Future of Parties and Partisanship

Since the 1970s some political observers have commented on the
weakness of political parties, citing especially the overall increase in independents and the appeal of independent candidates, such as John
Anderson in 1980 or Ross Perot in 1992 and 1996. These factors, combined with declines in trust and confidence in government, turnout,
and attention to political news, have suggested to some that the American public has lost its capacity to identify with political parties in a meaningful way. A corollary would suggest there would likely never be another realignment because political parties would not be able to attract
new partisans to their camps.

A contrary point of view argues that many of these trends slowed or
stopped in the late 1970s, that partisan stability and party loyal behavior
since then have been nearly as high as in the 1950s. Analysts cite increases in party-line voting in Congress, sharper ideological division between the parties, and an increase in uncivil political discourse in the
mass media and in Congress as evidence of the increased commitment
to, as well as the polarization of, political parties.

So, is partisanship becoming stronger or weaker? It seems to us that both these phenomena are occurring—in different parts of the electorate. On the one hand, among political elites and party activists, the polarization and hostility are becoming greater. On the other hand, a large pool of individuals remains who do not identify with either of the major parties and for whom the increased intensity of the partisan debate is off-putting.

The close competitiveness of the last two presidential elections has raised the intensity of feelings about politics. In 2004 almost half of the public reported trying to influence other people's votes. This is a substantial increase over percentages reported in any election in the past fifty years. Higher percentages than in previous elections reported having a strong preference for their presidential choice and caring who won the election. However, this does not seem to translate to stronger partisanship. The percentage of strong party identifiers has not increased in almost twenty years and is not as high today as it was in the 1950s and early 1960s. The percentage of people who call themselves "extremely liberal" or "extremely conservative" has not increased either and is generally less than 5 percent of the population.

A sizable segment of the electorate distrusts political parties, even feels hostility toward them. In the 2004 National Election Study, a majority (54 percent) of the public preferred to see divided control of government; only 22 percent said it would be better if one party controlled both Congress and the presidency. A third of the public would prefer that candidates run without party labels.

For at least some of these nonparty people, the problem with the parties is the same partisan and ideological intensity that has been increasing. They see the party elites and activists as extreme in their views while they see themselves as moderate. They view party conflict in Washington as divisive and contributing to, instead of solving, the country's problems. For such people, heightened partisan debate is unlikely to move them to embrace a political party. Becoming more engaged in political discussion, turning out to vote, and trying to influence the views of others are not unimportant aspects of the public's behavior, and they may signal changes in the partisan feelings of American citizens. However, the largest changes in partisan behavior are among leaders and political actives.

Notes

1. Larry Bartels argues that partisan loyalty has been steadily increasing since its nadir in 1972, but this trend has been overlooked by analysts focusing on the weakness of the political parties. See Larry Bartels, "Partisanship and Voting Be-

havior, 1952–1996," *American Journal of Political Science* 44 (January 2000): 35–50.

2. Paul R. Abramson and John H. Aldrich, "The Decline of Electoral Participation in America," *American Political Science Review* 76 (September 1982): 502–521.

3. Angus Campbell, "Surge and Decline: A Study of Electoral Change," in *Elections and the Political Order,* ed. Angus Campbell, Philip E. Converse, Warren E. Miller, and Donald E. Stokes (New York: Wiley, 1966), 40–62.

4. Arthur H. Miller and Martin P. Wattenberg, "Measuring Party Identification: Independent or No Partisan Preference?" *American Journal of Political Science* 27 (February 1983): 106–121.

5. John Petrocik, "An Analysis of Intransitivities in the Index of Party Identification," *Political Methodology* 1 (summer 1974): 31–47.

6. Norman H. Nie, Sidney Verba, and John R. Petrocik, *The Changing American Voter* (Cambridge, Mass.: Harvard University Press, 1976), chap. 5.

7. Robert S. Erikson and Kent L. Tedin, "The 1928–1936 Partisan Realignment: The Case for the Conversion Hypothesis," *American Political Science Review* 75 (December 1981): 951–962.

8. Philip E. Converse, *The Dynamics of Party Support: Cohort-Analyzing Party Identification* (Beverly Hills, Calif.: Sage Publications, 1976).

9. The main participants in this controversy are Philip Converse and Paul R. Abramson. See Converse, *The Dynamics of Party Support;* and Paul R. Abramson, "Developing Party Identification: A Further Examination of Life-Cycle, Generational, and Period Effects," *American Journal of Political Science* 23 (February 1979): 78–96.

10. The major findings of the first two waves of this study have been reported in M. Kent Jennings and Richard G. Niemi, *The Political Character of Adolescence: The Influence of Families and Schools* (Princeton: Princeton University Press, 1974); and M. Kent Jennings and Richard G. Niemi, *Generations and Politics* (Princeton: Princeton University Press, 1981). A report on partisanship using the first three waves of interviews is contained in M. Kent Jennings and Gregory B. Markus, "Partisan Orientations over the Long Haul: Results from the Three-Wave Political Socialization Panel Study," *American Political Science Review* 78 (December 1984): 1000–1018.

11. The parents were also reinterviewed in 1973. By 1997, many of the original high school seniors were parents of high school–age students. The study also interviewed the children of the original sample, creating a second set of parent-child interviews to compare with the original data from 1965. See Figure 4-7.

Suggested Readings

Budge, Ian, Ivor Crewe, and Dennis Farlie. *Party Identification and Beyond.* New York: Wiley, 1977. An excellent collection of articles on partisanship and other topics.

Keith, Bruce, David B. Magleby, Candice J. Nelson, Elizabeth Orr, Mark C. Westlye, and Raymond E. Wolfinger. *The Myth of the Independent Voter.* Berkeley: University of California Press, 1992. An effort to reaffirm the importance of party identification in an era of increasing numbers of independents.

Nie, Norman, Sidney Verba, and John Petrocik. *The Changing American Voter.* Cambridge, Mass.: Harvard University Press, 1976. A major revisionist analysis of public opinion and voting behavior emphasizing the decline of partisanship.

Niemi, Richard G., and Herbert F. Weisberg. *Controversies in Voting Behavior.* Washington, D.C.: CQ Press, 2001. A collection of sophisticated articles on major topics in political behavior and public opinion.

Wattenberg, Martin P. *The Decline of American Political Parties: 1952–1988.* Cambridge, Mass.: Harvard University Press, 1990. A thorough analysis of the changing patterns of partisanship in recent decades.

Internet Resources

The Web site of the National Election Studies, www.umich.edu/~nes, has extensive information on partisanship and party identification from 1952 to the present. Click on "Partisanship and Evaluation of the Political Parties." Elaborate data are available separately on Democrats, Republicans, and independents.

Most political parties have Web sites. Any search engine will find them; www.democrats.org and www.rnc.org will reach the respective national committees of the two major parties.

c h a p t e r   f i v e

Social Characteristics of Partisans and Independents

ATTEMPTS TO EXPLAIN American voting behavior have relied on social and economic factors to account for both stability and change in American politics. Research based on the National Election Studies has documented a wide range of relationships in the American electorate between social and economic characteristics and political behavior. Furthermore, many descriptions of voting patterns offered by American journalists and party strategists are based on social and economic factors. Analysis regularly attributes political trends to such categories as "soccer moms" or "born-again Christians"; frequently these explanations rely on so-called bloc voting, such as "the black vote," "the senior citizens' vote," or "the union vote," implying that some social factor causes large numbers of people to vote the same way.

The social factors that underlie partisanship reflect the partisan alignment in effect at that time. During the New Deal alignment, partisan choices tended to fall along economic and social class lines. Blue-collar workers, those with lower income, those with lower education, recently immigrated ethnic groups, racial minorities, and Catholics were all more likely to vote Democratic. Higher status people—middle-class people, white-collar workers—the college educated, those with high incomes, whites of northern European background, and Protestants were more likely to vote Republican.

The remnants of the New Deal alignment can still be seen in the partisan choices of today. Table 5-1 displays the party identification of selected social groups in 2004. For example, income is associated with party identification, with lower income people more likely to be Democratic than higher income people. Blacks, Hispanics, and Jews are still much more Democratic than Republican. But significant differences

TABLE 5-1   Party Identification by Social Characteristics, 2004

Category (percentage of sample)	Democrats		Independents			Republicans		Total percentage
	Strong	Weak	Lean Democrat	Independent	Lean Republican	Weak	Strong	
Men (47)	12	15	19	10	14	14	16	100
Women (53)	20	16	17	10	9	11	17	100
Whites (80)	14	13	17	9	13	15	20	101
Blacks (15)	31	30	20	12	5	2	a	100
Hispanics (9)	16	23	17	12	11	12	11	102
18–25 (13)	5	17	34	11	12	11	10	100
26–35 (17)	18	23	15	9	10	16	10	101
36–45 (18)	14	16	17	10	14	11	20	102
46–55 (20)	16	12	18	9	13	13	20	101
56–65 (18)	21	14	11	9	12	16	18	101
66–75 (8)	23	7	11	15	13	12	20	101
76+ (6)	30	17	14	7	6	6	20	100
High school education or less (38)	17	18	16	14	13	10	13	101
Some college (33)	14	14	20	8	12	14	18	100
College graduate (30)	18	14	19	4	9	15	21	100
Under $15,000 (17)	19	17	17	16	12	9	10	100
$15,000–35,000 (21)	20	18	17	10	12	12	10	99
$35,000–70,000 (30)	15	15	20	8	12	15	16	101
$70,000–120,000 (22)	14	16	16	7	11	14	22	100
Over $120,000 (9)	14	8	24	3	10	12	29	100

Union households (18)	24	16	20	11	7	10	13	101
Mainline Protestants (14)	19	13	10	7	15	12	24	100
Fundamentalists, evangelicals (27)	18	19	14	7	11	14	17	100
Catholics (24)	17	15	17	13	9	11	18	100
No religion (15)	15	17	23	7	15	12	11	100
White fundamentalists, evangelicals (15)	6	11	9	6	15	23	31	101
Non-South (65)	15	14	20	11	12	12	16	100
South (35)	19	19	14	8	11	13	17	101

Source: 2004 National Election Study, available at www.umich.edu/~nes.

[a]Less than 0.5 percent.

also have emerged. Catholics were heavily Democratic when they were recent immigrants, but as later generations moved into the middle class, their disproportionate presence among Democratic partisans has faded. Religion still has an impact on partisanship, but it is no longer the difference between Protestants and Catholics. Instead, Protestants are divided between fundamentalists and evangelicals who are disproportionately Republican, on the one hand, and more traditional mainline denominations that are more evenly split between Democrats and Republicans, on the other. This religious distinction is further complicated by race, given that many blacks belong to fundamentalist and evangelical churches but remain overwhelmingly Democratic. The importance of religion in one's life, referred to as religiosity, is a further factor in influencing one's partisanship.

Even in the heyday of the New Deal, social and economic status was hardly a perfect predictor of partisan choice. The most obvious example of this was in the South. White southerners were overwhelmingly Democratic, a legacy from the earlier Civil War alignment, and this traditional attachment to the Democratic Party virtually wiped out the impact of any other social or economic factor on political behavior. In the 1950s the southern middle class was about as Democratic as the working class, southern Protestants as Democratic as the relatively few Catholics in that region, and so on. Since 1956 southern whites have gone from 63 percent Democratic to 26 percent, and the social factors associated with partisanship are not distinctively different from other parts of the country.

The percentage of the overall population that a particular group composes has also changed since the 1950s. The proportion of Hispanics has increased dramatically. The proportions of fundamentalists and evangelicals and of people with no religious affiliation have both increased at the expense of mainline Protestants. The proportion of people with higher education has increased while the percentage of union households has fallen.

The Social Composition of Partisan Groups

Another way of looking at the relationship between social characteristics and partisanship is to describe the Democratic and Republican Parties and independents in terms of proportions of different kinds of individuals who make up their ranks. The social composition of Democratic, Republican, and independent identifiers is illustrated in Figure 5-1, using some of the same social categories used in Table 5-1 (race/ethnicity, religion, and education). However, this way of looking at the data gives different results and answers a different set of questions. Instead of revealing to what extent particular social groups support the

FIGURE 5-1   Social Composition of Partisans and Independents by
             Race/Ethnicity, Religion, and Education, 2004

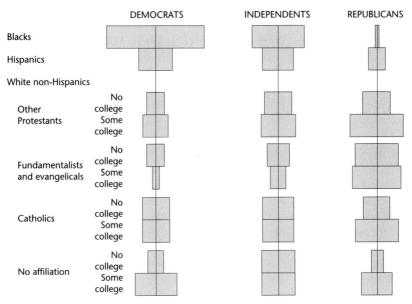

Source: 2004 National Election Study, available at www.umich.edu/~nes.

Democratic or Republican Parties, the data show the proportion of all Democrats who are black or Catholic. For example, the partisanship of various social groups presented in Table 5-1 shows blacks are heavily Democratic (61 percent in 2004 identified themselves as strong or weak Democrats). If the proportion of all Democrats who are blacks is calculated, as in Figure 5-1, however, blacks are found to make up just 32 percent of the total group of Democrats. Because blacks are a relatively small proportion of the population, their contribution to the total set of Democrats is not so large, despite their lopsided preference for the Democratic Party.

Studying the partisanship of social groups has generally been regarded as the more interesting way of looking at the relationship between social characteristics and political behavior, largely because of the causal connection between social characteristics and partisanship. Thus, one is far more inclined to say that race and ethnicity, religion, or education causes an individual to select a particular political party than to say that political affiliation causes any of the others. Familiarity with the composition of the parties is useful, however, in understanding the campaign strategies and political appeals that the parties make to hold their supporters in line and sway the independents or opposition supporters to their side. For example, the fact that blacks contribute over 30 percent of the Democratic partisans but make up just 1 percent of the Republican partisans is a significant factor that both parties take into account.

The composition of the parties affects politics in another way. In an important book on the evolution of the racial issue in the United States, Edward G. Carmines and James A. Stimson argue persuasively that the composition of the parties, particularly the composition of the party activists, influences the perceptions that less involved citizens hold about the philosophy and issue stands of the parties.[1] The fact that blacks are overwhelmingly Democratic and that vocal racial conservatives—in other words, those with a general predisposition to oppose government actions to correct racial injustices—are increasingly Republican allows the average voter to figure out which party is liberal and which is conservative on racial issues, even if race is never mentioned by candidates during the course of an election campaign.

As can be seen in Figure 5-1, the composition of the partisan identifiers is distinctively different. For example, blacks make a sizable contribution to the Democratic following and an insignificant share of the Republican following. Meanwhile, fundamentalist and evangelical Protestants and college-educated mainline Protestants make up significantly larger parts of the Republican Party than they do of the Democratic Party.

Even though the Democrats are somewhat more varied in social composition than the Republicans, the main conclusion to be drawn from an analysis of the partisan groupings is that they are basically heterogeneous. Both parties contain substantial proportions of various religious groups and people with different educational levels. They both draw substantial portions of their votes from blue-collar as well as white-collar workers, from the young, the middle-aged, the old, and so on. This diversity is also true of the independent group, as can be seen in Figure 5-1. As was pointed out in Chapter 4, independent voters hold the balance of power between the major parties and both must appeal to them to win elections.

Social Group Analysis

The impact of social groups on individual behavior is widely acknowledged. Social analysis of political behavior has examined three main units: primary groups, secondary groups, and social classes. *Primary groups* are the face-to-face groups with which one associates, such as family, friends, and coworkers. *Secondary groups* are those organizations or collections of individuals with which one identifies, or is identified, that have some common interest or goal instead of personal contact as their major basis. *Social classes* are broad groupings based on position in society according to social status.

Primary Groups

Although investigations of the political behavior of primary groups are not numerous, all available evidence indicates that families and groups of friends are likely to be politically homogeneous. Groups of coworkers appear somewhat more mixed politically. Presumably, the social forces in families and friendship groups are more intense and more likely to be based on, or to result in, political unanimity, but in most work situations people are thrown together without an opportunity to form groups based on common political values or any other shared traits. Friendship groups, even casual ones, may be formed so that individuals with much in common, including political views, naturally come together.

Table 5-2 presents findings from the 1987 General Social Survey that illustrate the homogeneity of primary groups. Respondents were asked the political party of those people with whom they regularly discussed politics. The table shows that agreement on partisanship between spouses is highest, with 75 percent of the Democrats and 70 percent of the Republicans reporting that their spouses shared their party preference. Agreement was not so high with friends and coworkers but still reflects considerable like-mindedness. Perhaps as important is the relatively low occurrence of mismatches of Democrats and Republicans in primary groups. The fact that significant percentages do not know the partisanship of friends and coworkers may reflect an avoidance of potential conflicts.

The discussion of primary groups has implications for the celebrated gender gap in the political preferences of men and women, a favorite topic of political commentators since the early 1980s. Women were less favorably inclined toward Presidents Ronald Reagan, George Bush, and George W. Bush (in 2000), and toward Republicans in general, than were men. Conversely, women were more supportive of President Bill Clinton and Vice President Al Gore than were men. Women were not more likely to vote for John Kerry in 2004, and, as evident from Table 5-1, the gender gap in partisanship is small, with women being slightly more likely to call themselves "strong Democrats" and less likely to be independents than were men. This gender gap would be reduced further if controls were introduced for race and socioeconomic variables.[2] Given what was said about the influence of primary groups, the small size of the gender gap should not be surprising. Men and women interact with each other in primary groups throughout society. They

TABLE 5-2　Reported Partisan Preferences of Primary Groups by Respondent's Party Identification

Primary group	Respondent's party identification		
	Democrat	Independent	Republican
Reported party identification of spouse			
Democrat	75%	18%	14%
Independent	9	57	10
Republican	10	18	70
Don't know	6	8	6
Total	100%	101%	100%
(N)	(176)	(120)	(142)
Reported party identification of friends			
Democrat	66%	27%	19%
Independent	8	33	7
Republican	11	16	53
Don't know	15	23	19
Total	100%	99%	98%
(N)	(542)	(379)	(410)
Reported party identification of coworkers			
Democrat	65%	26%	23%
Independent	8	34	6
Republican	11	11	50
Don't know	16	29	20
Total	100%	100%	99%
(N)	(138)	(107)	(133)

Source: General Social Survey, 1987. Data provided by the Inter-university Consortium for Political and Social Research.

Note: Respondents were asked to name three people with whom they discussed "important matters," after which their relationship with those mentioned was established. Reports only on those people with whom respondents talked about "political matters" on a regular basis.

select friends and spouses from like-minded individuals; they respond, as family units, to similar social and economic forces. In the next chapter we will consider ways in which the views of men and women differ on certain issues, but given the general influence of primary groups, differences in overall political preferences are seldom large.

Lately, another gap, the "marriage gap," has gained some notoriety. It has been suggested that married people are more likely to gravitate to the Republican Party, while unmarried people are more likely to be Democrats. The reasons alleged for this range from commitment to traditional values to the economic position of married men versus unmarried women as heads of household. In looking at a possible marriage gap, the effects of age need to be taken into account, given that younger people are both more likely to be unmarried and to identify themselves as politically independent. Figure 5-2 shows the net advantage in partisanship for white married and unmarried men and women. At every age level, the married are more likely to be Republican than their unmarried counterparts, with married men being the most decidedly so. The marriage gap is at its largest in the oldest category of men, and smallest in the oldest category of women.

We have avoided use of the term *conformity* to describe the patterns of primary group behavior because these group processes are more casual and more a matter of give-and-take than the term implies. Most people care little about politics, and it plays a small part in their per-

FIGURE 5-2   Net Partisan Advantage among White Married and Unmarried Men and Women, 2004

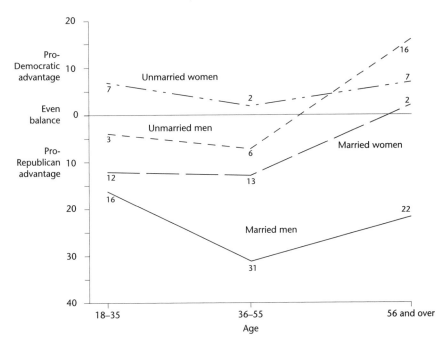

Source: 2004 National Election Study, available at www.umich.edu/~nes.

Note: Values represent the percentage difference between strong and weak Democrats and strong and weak Republicans.

sonal relationships. In few primary groups is politics of any consequence, so the things that happen in the group that lead to political homogeneity are of low salience. Individuals gradually create, evaluate, and revise their images of the world under the influence of social processes. Many of these processes are face-to-face exchanges of information or reassurances that others share views or consider them plausible, realistic, and acceptable. Most individuals are not pressured by primary groups to conform or to change politically, at least not nearly as much as they are influenced by casual, impromptu expressions of similar ideas and values. Ordinarily, primary groups do not tolerate high levels of political tension and conflict. Also, few people are subject to the social forces of only one or two primary groups, so conformity to group pressure would mean conformity to a large number of groups.

In addition to what happens within primary groups, another factor produces political similarity: the likelihood that primary group members share the same social background and experiences outside the group. Members of any primary group are apt to be socially, economically, ethnically, and racially alike, and being alike in these ways means that the same general social influences are at work on them. Much happens outside the primary group to make it politically homogeneous.

Secondary Groups

Secondary groups form around some common interest and may or may not involve personal contact among members. The term *secondary groups* covers a range of groups in society, such as labor unions, religious or fraternal organizations, and professional groups. Secondary groups are presumably composed of overlapping primary groups whose pressures toward political homogeneity spill over, tending to make the members of secondary groups alike. In addition, members of secondary groups are usually subject to the same social forces outside the group. For example, members of a labor union are likely to be in the same income group, to live in the same type of neighborhood, and to have the same social and educational background, all of which would tend to make them alike politically.

A third factor at work is the role that a secondary group may play as a reference group. A group serves as a reference group for an individual who uses the group as a guide in forming opinions. For example, if union members, identifying with their labor union, perceive that a particular policy is good for the union, perhaps because the union leadership says that it is, and favor the policy because of this, the union is a political reference group for those individuals. In the same way, if a union member believes that other union members support a policy and supports the policy in part for this reason, then the union members serve as a reference group. Also, if a businessperson perceives that unions favor a policy, and he or she opposes it in part for that reason, then unions serve as a negative reference group.

The most sophisticated analysis of social groups and political behavior applied to national survey data appeared in the classic work *The American Voter* by Angus Campbell, Philip E. Converse, Warren E. Miller, and Donald E. Stokes.[3] By controlling many outside social influences with matched groups, the authors demonstrated the degree to which an individual's political behavior was influenced by secondary group membership among union members, blacks, Catholics, and Jews. They were able to show that union members, blacks, and Jews were considerably more Democratic than one would expect from the group members' other social characteristics, such as urban–rural residence, region, and occupational status. The fact that Catholics were not more Democratic in the 1950s than would be expected from their other social characteristics is consistent with what we observed earlier: As Catholics moved into the middle class, they have ceased to be disproportionately Democratic. However, union members, blacks, and Jews have remained more Democratic than expected, based on other social characteristics. In other words, group membership appears to play a role in the Democratic partisanship of union members, blacks, and Jews, but not Catholics.

The American Voter concluded that the influence was even greater if the individual identified with the group. To establish the importance of identification with the group and belief in the legitimacy of the group's involvement in politics, the authors analyzed the 1956 presidential votes of the same four social groups. The increasing impact of identification with the group and of its perceived legitimacy was associated with an increasing Democratic vote. In other words, the stronger the belief in the legitimacy of the group's political involvement and the stronger the group identification, the greater the impact of group standards on vote choice.

Among the groups usually studied, blacks and Jews are the most distinctive politically. Jews have remained strongly Democratic in their partisanship over the years in spite of social and economic characteristics more typical of Republicans. And although Jews have at times not supported the Democratic ticket, Jewish partisanship remains close to what it was in the 1950s—54 percent Democratic, 25 percent independent, and 21 percent Republican.[4] As shown in Table 5-1, blacks also are strongly Democratic in partisanship and typically vote more than 90 percent Democratic in presidential contests. The impact of group identification is most dramatically revealed by increased turnout and overwhelming support for black candidates, such as Jesse Jackson in the 1988 presidential primaries.

The behavior of union members in recent years, in contrast, illustrates a decline in group identification. Despite one-sided Democratic partisanship, union members have been volatile in voting for president and willing to ignore the announced preferences of their union leaders. Despite an all-out effort by union leadership for Walter F. Mondale in 1984, Mondale barely outpolled Ronald Reagan among union households. Conversely, Bill Clinton did very well among union members, despite union leaders' general lack of enthusiasm. In 2004, 43 percent of union members identified with the Democratic Party versus 18 percent Republican, and John Kerry out-polled George W. Bush 67 percent to 34 percent among union members.

Over the years, the partisanship of American religious groups, other than Jews, has not been seen as particularly distinctive, or at least other factors have been considered more important in determining political behavior. In recent years analysts have focused increased attention on religious groups in American society, especially within the highly varied Protestant category. Over recent decades the composition of the Protestant category has changed dramatically. Mainline Protestant denominations such as Methodists and Presbyterians have declined from roughly 40 percent to 15 percent of the adult population. Evangelicals and fundamentalists have grown to one quarter of the electorate, about the same proportion as Catholics.

In a probing analysis of religious groups spanning 1960 to 1992, David C. Leege has demonstrated the political distinctiveness of Catholics and evangelical Protestants in comparison with mainline Protestants.[5] Leege shows that for both Catholics and evangelical Protestants significant differences in political behavior are associated with regularity of church attendance. In general, those who rarely attend church are similar to those unaffiliated with any religion.

Figure 5-3 looks at some political characteristics of white fundamentalists and evangelicals in 2004. Those who attend church most regularly are considerably more Republican and conservative than those who attend less regularly. Political strategist Karl Rove's plan to utilize the evangelical churches as a way of mobilizing conservative votes for George W. Bush in 2004 was based on an understanding of the importance of group interaction in reinforcing opinions and motivating political activity.

It should be emphasized that Figure 5-3 looks only at whites who are fundamentalists and evangelicals. If black fundamentalists and evangelicals were considered, even greater uniformity in political behavior would be found—but in a Democratic direction, and it would not depend so much upon regularity of church attendance. A similar point can be made, however. Group identification, reinforced by social interaction, leads to distinctive political behavior. It is the interaction with like-minded individuals, represented by church attendance, that likely creates and reinforces political distinctiveness.

FIGURE 5-3   Voting and Political Identification for White Fundamentalists and Evangelicals according to Church Attendance, 2004

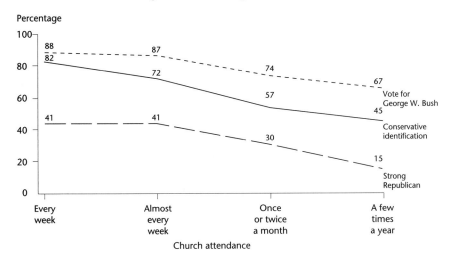

Source: 2004 National Election Study, available at www.umich.edu/~nes.

Social factors, such as religion or union membership, vary in their relative importance from election to election. After years of dormancy a social factor may temporarily become significant during a political campaign and subsequently recede in importance. The 1960 presidential election provides a good example of how secondary groups become relevant in a particular election and temporarily have great influence on voting behavior. John F. Kennedy's Catholicism was a major issue throughout the campaign and of great importance to both Catholics and non-Catholics. Researchers at the University of Michigan showed that Protestant Democrats who were more regular in church attendance were more likely to defect from the Democratic candidate. Among the nominal Protestants who never attended church, Kennedy's Catholicism exerted no such negative effect.[6]

Social Classes

The third major focus of analysis is social class. Some of the leading hypotheses of social and political theory link social classes and political behavior. In general, analysis of social class assumes that differences exist in the economic and social interests of social classes and that these conflicting interests will be translated into political forces. The critical variable in this view appears to be the importance of social class interests. In American society the importance of social class fluctuates but never becomes extremely high. The major political and sociological theories of social class have taken for granted the supreme importance of class interests, an assumption that seems unrealistic in American society. About one-third of all American adults say that they never think of themselves as members of a social class.

Given a choice between "middle class" and "working class," a majority of Americans are able to place themselves in a general social position, even to the point of including themselves in the "upper" or "lower" level of a class. Even though individual self-ratings are not perfectly congruent with the positions that social analysts would assign those individuals on the basis of characteristics such as occupation, income, and education, a general social class structure is apparent. The political significance of social class varies from election to election in much the same way as that of secondary groups. In Figure 5-4 the relationship between self-identification as a member of the working or middle class and party identification is charted from 1952 through 2004 in the nation as a whole and in the South and non-South. The values shown in the graph represent the strength of the relationship between social class and party, indicated by Somer's d. If all working-class people identified with the Democratic Party and all middle-class people with the Republican Party (with independents split evenly between the two parties), the Somer's d would be +1.0; if the reverse were true, it would be −1.0. If there were

FIGURE 5-4   The Relationship between Social Class Identification and Party Identification, 1952–2004

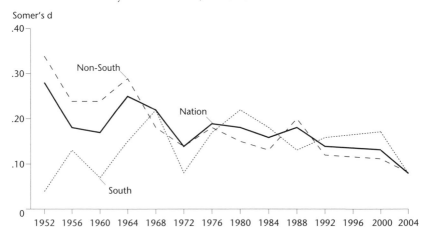

Source: National Election Studies, available at www.umich.edu/~nes.

Note: The coefficients represented by points on the graph are Somer's d. The social class identification question was not asked in 1996.

no differences in the partisan preferences of middle- and working-class people, the coefficient would be 0.0. Because working-class people have been more likely to be Democratic than have middle-class people in each year since 1952, all the values in Figure 5-4 are positive.

A number of points can be made about the data presented. Although the strength of the relationship between social class and party has varied over the years, the national trend in the relationship is downward. In other words, since 1952 the differences in partisan preference between working- and middle-class people are getting smaller. In this context, 1964, 1976, and 1988 stand out as temporary reversals of the trend. Figure 5-4 also shows that the relationship between class and party has followed different patterns in and outside the South. Whereas the relationship has been declining elsewhere, the trend was upward in the South. During the early 1950s middle- and working-class southerners were overwhelmingly Democratic; there were virtually no differences between them. Later, a modest, class-based partisan alignment emerged. The middle class became increasingly Republican, whereas the working class, particularly the black working class, remained solidly Democratic. This class-based alignment in the South, as well as the difference between North and South, disappeared—at least temporarily—in 2004.

Another common expectation about the relationship between social class and partisanship has to do with upward and downward social mobility. To put it simply, the argument has been that upwardly mobile individuals abandon a Democratic identification and become Republicans, whereas the downwardly mobile abandon their Republican identification and become Democrats. Presumably the individual becomes an independent during the period of maximum social and political stress associated with this mobility. It has not been easy to assess mobility at a national level in the United States, so the surprisingly weak relationship usually found may result from inadequate measurement. In broad terms, most members of society are neither upwardly nor downwardly mobile, and the socially mobile seem no more apt to abandon their parents' party loyalty than the socially stable. Little political difference exists between the upwardly and downwardly mobile, and this appears to hold for several measures of mobility.

Along with Canada, the United States is usually regarded as an extreme case among developed democracies for the insignificance of social class in political behavior; in most European democracies social class is of greater consequence.[7] This remains true even as the disparity between rich and poor in the United States has reached, since the 1980s, historically high levels. Two factors may depress the apparent relationship between social class and voting behavior in the United States. Aggregating data for the entire population can hide stronger relationships in subgroups and in particular communities. Probably more important are the cultural values of freedom and individualism that exalt the ability and responsibility of the individual to get ahead by talent and hard work. As a result, American political leaders tend not to emphasize or exploit highly divisive social class lines and are often criticized if they do. Social class may serve as a political guide for some citizens on certain issues, but it does not appear to be extremely important in American politics.

Red and Blue States

Political commentary in recent years has often focused on the division of the country into "red" and "blue" states—red for Republican, blue for Democratic.[8] The implication is that dramatic differences in social characteristics and political culture exist between the two sets of states that lead them to vote in distinctively different ways for president. The fact that the country is so evenly divided in presidential voting and only three states—Iowa, New Mexico, and New Hampshire—shifted between 2000 and 2004 has increased the fascination.

Are there two Americas, one red and one blue? To try to answer this question, we divided the respondents in the 2004 National Election Study according to their residence in "safe red," "safe blue," or "battleground" states and compared their characteristics on a number of demographic and attitudinal dimensions.* The results are in Table 5-3. (Because the battleground states are presumably the most competitive, separating them in the analysis should make the remaining states appear more distinctive.)

Whether we conclude the red and blue states are distinctly different or rather similar depends on which characteristics are considered. The top half of Table 5-3 shows characteristics in which the differences are small or nonexistent. Red and blue states appear virtually the same in some characteristics, such as the percentage of Hispanics or whether one attends church regularly, as well as on attitudes toward several issues. Even the frequency of Democratic and Republican party identifiers is similar.

Some other differences are dramatic, as can be seen in the bottom half of Table 5-3. The red states are overwhelmingly southern—the only

---

*Dividing states into "red" (Republican) and "blue" (Democratic) on the basis of the 2004 (or 2000) presidential vote winner is a more common way to classify the states. We thought that assigning the states with a narrow margin of victory—the battleground states—to one category or the other might obscure the distinctive qualities of the more purely red and blue states. Putting the battleground states in a separate category would thus be a better test of the idea.

TABLE 5-3   Political and Social Characteristics of Safe Red States, Safe Blue
States, and Battleground States, 2004

	Blue states (Democratic)	Battleground states	Red states (Republican)
Number of states	13	12	25
Percentage of total U.S. population	38	24	38
Total electoral college votes	183	142	213
Characteristics with little or no differences between states (in percent)			
Hispanic	9	7	8
Attend church every week	20	23	25
Democratic party identifiers	32	29	34
Republican party identifiers	26	31	30
Favor death penalty	67	68	69
Iraq war decreased risk of terrorism	21	26	25
United States must be ready to use military force	30	31	29
Very important to combat international terrorism	82	81	81
Favor tax cuts George W. Bush initiated	36	37	38
Government should try to improve the social and economic position of blacks	23	17	22
Characteristics with noticeable differences between states (in percent)			
Turnout	77	83	72
Live in the South	9	14	79
Blacks	12	9	23
College graduates	34	28	27
Catholics	30	29	15
White fundamentalists, evangelicals	6	16	25
Family income under $15,000	12	13	21
Conservatives	38	41	46
Favor governmental medical insurance	46	42	39
Approve of job Bush doing as president	44	53	53
Voted for Bush	48	50	54
Opposed to gay marriage	56	65	69
Pro-life on abortion	7	15	21

Source: 2004 National Election Study, available at www.umich.edu/~nes.

Note: The blue states are California, Connecticut, Delaware, District of Columbia, Hawaii, Illinois, Maine, Maryland, Massachusetts, New Jersey, New York, Rhode Island, Vermont, and Washington. The battleground states are Colorado, Florida, Iowa, Michigan, Minnesota, Nevada, New Hampshire, New Mexico, Ohio, Oregon, Pennsylvania, and Wisconsin. The red states are Alabama, Alaska, Arizona, Arkansas, Georgia, Idaho, Indiana, Kansas, Kentucky, Louisiana, Mississippi, Missouri, Montana, Nebraska, North Carolina, North Dakota, Oklahoma, South Carolina, South Dakota, Tennessee, Texas, Utah, Virginia, West Virginia, and Wyoming.

southern blue state is Maryland. People in blue states are twice as likely to be Catholic as red state residents. Those in red states are more likely to be white fundamentalists or evangelicals. Issue differences are in the expected direction—red states are more conservative—but the differences are not large. Even the vote for president is not dramatically different for red and blue states, which means there are many Democratic sympathizers in red states and many Republican sympathizers in blue states.[9]

We should conclude from this analysis that the red states and the blue states are hardly pure political types. The red states are distinctive in that they are primarily southern, but southern states have large percentages of black citizens whose social and political characteristics differ from the white majority. (The non-southern red states tend to be small in population and, therefore, do not loom large in a national sample, such as we are using here.) The blue states are primarily large, non-southern states with diverse populations. In sum, it is the aggregate stability of the red and blue states—and their current even balance nationwide—that is impressive, not the purity of the political culture within their borders.

Social Cross-Pressures

One of the major ideas developed in the early voting studies by Paul Lazarsfeld, Bernard Berelson, and other researchers at the Bureau of Applied Social Research of Columbia University was the "cross-pressure hypothesis."[10] The cross-pressure hypothesis is simple in outline, but it can be confusing because it takes so many different forms. The hypothesis concerns the situation in which two (or more) forces or tendencies act on the individual, one in a Republican direction and the other in a Democratic direction. In the diagram below, we use the dimensions of occupation and religion, although these particular dimensions are not as politically relevant today as they were in the 1940s when Lazarsfeld and his colleagues introduced the concept.

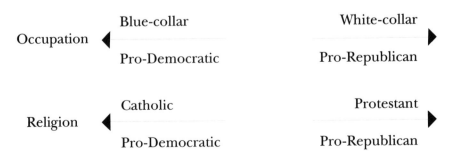

Some individuals are predisposed or pushed in a consistent way, such as white-collar Protestants, whose occupation and religion both predispose them in a Republican direction, or blue-collar Catholics, who are predisposed in a Democratic direction.

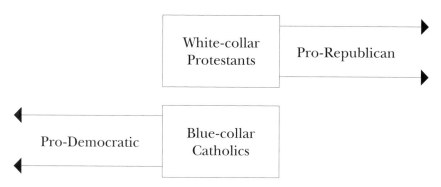

Some individuals are predisposed in both directions, or cross-pressured.

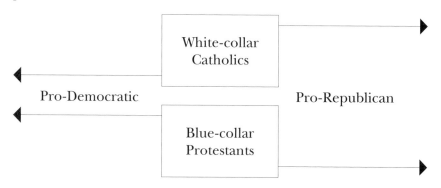

The cross-pressure hypothesis asserts that individuals under consistent pressure behave differently than individuals under cross-pressure. The predictions under the hypothesis are listed below.

Consistent pressure	Cross-pressure
Straight-ticket voting	Split-ticket voting
Early decision on vote	Late decision on vote
High interest in politics	Low interest in politics
High level of information	Low level of information
Consistent attitudes	Conflicting attitudes

These expectations about voting behavior under cross-pressure are specific applications of more general patterns investigated by sociologists and psychologists in a variety of ways. The responses to cross-pressure predicted by the hypothesis are avoidance reactions—efforts to avoid or to minimize the anxiety produced by conflict.

The cross-pressure hypothesis also has some implications for empirical political theory. According to the cross-pressure hypothesis, many large social groups are expected to be stable politically—that is, they are consistently predisposed to be Republican or Democratic by the social forces working on them. Therefore, these social pressures lead to political stability among both Republicans and Democrats because they have politically consistent social backgrounds.

Between these politically consistent social groups are cross-pressured groups predisposed toward both parties. According to the cross-pressure hypothesis, these groups are politically unstable, contributing to the voters who switch from one party to another. Thus, the available voters—the voters to whom the parties must appeal to win because they hold the balance of power in elections—are in a middle position between Democrats and Republicans. These arguments lead to a reassuring view of the American electorate. A relatively stable social system produces widespread political stability. Political flexibility and sensitivity are provided by groups between the partisans who are therefore politically moderate. As long as the stable partisan groups are roughly the same size, stable competitive conditions are guaranteed. As long as social groups overlap somewhat, the necessary cross-pressures will exist to produce the switching political moderates. It appears to be an electoral system that guarantees both competition and stability.

Nevertheless, some difficulties arise with this picture of the electoral system. For one thing, the social cross-pressure hypothesis is merely a tendency and not a perfect description of the impact of social forces on political behavior. The politically stable are more heterogeneous than the previous account implies, and the politically flexible are not under dramatic social cross-pressure, according to the best data available.

Discussion supporting the cross-pressure hypothesis is most extensive in the Elmira study, *Voting,* by Bernard Berelson, Paul Lazarsfeld, and William McPhee, which surveyed residents of Elmira, New York, from June through November 1948. They found that cross-pressures affected the time when individuals decided how to vote. A slight tendency existed for cross-pressures caused by religion and socioeconomic status to be associated with late decisions on voting. Stronger relationships were associated with conflicts in primary groups.

Social cross-pressure can be conceptualized as leading to cross-pressure on political attitudes, which in turn leads to the predicted patterns of behavior. Attitudinal cross-pressure is the only form of cross-pressure that is strongly confirmed by national survey data. When attitudes toward the candidates and parties were measured by the National Election Studies in 1952 and 1956, conflicting attitudes—those of an individual holding pro-Democratic and pro-Republican opinions—were associated with nonvoting, indecision, and indifference toward the election. These findings linking conflicting political attitudes with patterns of behavior have not always been confirmed in subsequent election studies, depending on which attitudes are examined. Nevertheless, it remains reasonable to expect conflicting political attitudes to be associated with indecisiveness in voting behavior.

The American electoral system appears to operate in a way predicted by the cross-pressure hypothesis. Partisan stability exists among both Republicans and Democrats, and the shifting of political fortunes is accomplished without intensity or extreme political appeals. One should, however, be skeptical of explaining these political patterns as a result of the social forces postulated by the cross-pressure hypothesis. Neither short-run partisan stability nor independent flexibility appears strongly associated with social group predispositions.

Notes

1. Edward G. Carmines and James A. Stimson, *Issue Evolution: Race and the Transformation of American Politics* (Princeton: Princeton University Press, 1989).
2. Richard A. Seltzer, Jody Newman, and Melissa Voorhees Leighton, *Sex as a Political Variable: Women as Candidates and Voters in U.S. Elections* (Boulder, Colo.: Lynne Rienner, 1997).
3. Angus Campbell, Philip E. Converse, Warren E. Miller, and Donald E. Stokes, *The American Voter* (New York: Wiley, 1960), 295–332.
4. The number of respondents identifying themselves as Jewish in the 2004 National Election Study is too small for analysis. However, the Pew Research Center for the People and the Press analyzed combined surveys from September 2001 to October 2003. The combined sample had 934 Jews out of a total of some 56,000 cases. Of the Jewish respondents, 49 percent were Democrats, 19 percent were Republicans, and presumably the rest were independents.
5. David C. Leege, "The Decomposition of the Religious Vote: A Comparison of White, Non-Hispanic Catholics with Other Ethnoreligious Groups, 1960–1992," paper presented at the annual meeting of the American Political Science Association, Washington, D.C., 1993.
6. Philip E. Converse, Angus Campbell, Warren E. Miller, and Donald E. Stokes, "Stability and Change in 1960: A Reinstating Election," in *Elections and the Political Order,* ed. Angus Campbell, Philip E. Converse, Warren E. Miller, and Donald E. Stokes (New York: Wiley, 1966), chap. 5.
7. There are several important works on social class and political behavior. See Campbell, Converse, Miller, and Stokes, *The American Voter,* chap. 13. Students interested in this area of analysis should also see Robert Alford, *Party and Society* (Chicago: Rand McNally, 1963); and Richard Rose, ed., *Electoral Behavior* (New York: Free Press, 1974). Perhaps the most significant work is David Butler and

124 *Political Behavior of the American Electorate*

Donald E. Stokes, *Political Change in Britain: Forces Shaping Electoral Choice* (New York: St. Martin's Press, 1969).

8. A recent, extensive analysis of divisions within the country can be found in a Pew Research Center for the People and the Press survey report, "The 2004 Political Landscape: Evenly Divided and Increasingly Polarized," November 5, 2003, available at www.people-press.org. Most of the analysis depends on differences between Democrats, Republicans, and independents, but the report also looks at partisanship within red, blue, and battleground states. Morris P. Fiorina disputes this view of polarization in *Culture War: The Myth of a Polarized America* (New York: Pearson Longman, 2005). A direct challenge to Fiorina can be found in Alan Abramowitz and Kyle Saunders, "Why Can't We All Just Get Along? The Reality of a Polarized America," *Forum* 3 (2), Article 1, available at www.bepress.com/forum/vol3/iss2/art1.

9. The results are not much different if only voters are examined as opposed to the entire sample. The data in each of the three types of states are dominated by the more numerous respondents from the larger states, but that seems unavoidable.

10. Paul Lazarsfeld, Bernard Berelson, and Hazel Gaudet, *The People's Choice* (New York: Columbia University Press, 1944); and Bernard Berelson, Paul Lazarsfeld, and William McPhee, *Voting* (Chicago: University of Chicago Press, 1954).

Suggested Readings

Campbell, Angus, Philip E. Converse, Warren E. Miller, and Donald E. Stokes. *The American Voter.* New York: Wiley, 1960. A classic study of the social psychological factors influencing political behavior.

Fiorina, Morris P., with Samuel J. Abrams and Jeremy C. Pope. *Culture War? The Myth of a Polarized America.* New York: Pearson Longman, 2005.

Huckfeldt, Robert, and Carol Weitzel Kohfeld. *Race and the Decline of Class in American Politics.* Urbana: University of Illinois Press, 1989. A study arguing that racial cleavages have become more important than social class divisions in influencing electoral decisions, with serious consequences for the Democratic Party's coalition.

Huckfeldt, Robert, and John Sprague. *Citizens, Politics, and Social Communication.* Cambridge, England: Cambridge University Press, 1995. An important study examining political attitudes and behavior within their social context.

Lazarsfeld, Paul, Bernard Berelson, and Hazel Gaudet. *The People's Choice.* New York: Columbia University Press, 1944. A classic study of Erie County, Ohio, and the first study of voting to make extensive use of survey research.

Leege, David C., and Lyman A. Kellstedt. *Rediscovering the Religious Factor in American Politics.* New York: M. E. Sharpe, 1993. A collection of articles exploring the impact of religious beliefs on political behavior.

Lipset, Seymour M., and Stein Rokkan. "Cleavage Structures, Party Systems, and Voter Alignments: An Introduction." In *Party Systems and Voter Alignments,* edited by Seymour M. Lipset and Stein Rokkan. New York: Free Press, 1967. An important conceptual statement about the role of party and social cleavages in historical perspective.

Petrocik, John. *Party Coalitions: Realignments and the Decline of the New Deal Party System.* Chicago: University of Chicago Press, 1981. An analysis of American politics that emphasizes social and economic characteristics.

Internet Resources

The Web site of the National Election Studies, www.umich.edu/~nes, has extensive data on social characteristics and party identification from 1952 to the present. Click on "Partisanship and Evaluation of the Political Parties." For every political item there is a breakdown for each social characteristic in every election year.

For current data on partisans and independents you can find analysis on Web sites such as the Pew Research Center for the People and the Press at www.people-press.org and the Gallup Poll at www.gallup.com.

Public Opinion and Ideology

PUBLIC OPINION—the collective attitudes of the public, or segments of the public, toward the issues of the day—is a significant aspect of American political behavior. Public opinion polls are an ever-present feature of American journalism. The public is constantly informed about what samples of Americans think on all manner of topics. The questions then arise: Are Americans informed, issue-oriented participants in the political process? Do they view problems and issues within a coherent ideological framework? Which issues divide Democrats and Republicans? These questions address the nature and quality of American public opinion.

A *political ideology* is a set of fundamental beliefs or principles about politics and government: what the scope of government should be; how decisions should be made; what values should be pursued. In the United States the most prominent current ideological patterns are those captured by the terms *liberalism* and *conservatism*. Although these words are used in a variety of ways, generally liberalism endorses the idea of social change and advocates the involvement of government in effecting such change, whereas conservatism seeks to defend the status quo and prescribes a more limited role for governmental activity. Another common conception of the terms portrays liberalism as advocating equality and individual freedom and conservatism as endorsing a more structured, ordered society. However, these dimensions are not always joined in the political thinking of Americans. Also, some evidence indicates that since the election campaign of 1964 the terms have become increasingly associated with attitudes on racial integration. To complicate the matter further, public opinion data suggest that a segment of the American electorate uses these terms to signify a set of social attitudes or lifestyles, not any particular political beliefs.

Despite these ambiguities, most commentators on the American political scene, as well as its active participants, describe much of what happens in terms of liberalism or conservatism. Political history (and current news analysis) portrays situations in terms such as a "trend toward conservatism," "middle-of-the-road policies," and "rejection of liberalism." Furthermore, most political commentary treats the Democratic Party as the liberal party and the Republican Party as the conservative one. Although considerable ideological variation remains in both parties, the trend in recent years is toward greater ideological distinctiveness between the two parties. Candidates of both parties attempt to pin ideological labels on opposing candidates (usually candidates of the other party, but sometimes within their own). In recent years *liberal* has been portrayed more negatively than *conservative,* and some candidates for office portray themselves as "progressive" or use other such terms to avoid the liberal label.

Consideration of the ideological positions of the parties is complicated by the many dimensions of public policy: economic affairs; race relations; international affairs; and a variety of moral, social, and cultural concerns. These issue areas have many facets, and only a few themes dominate public attention at any one time. Not only does public attention to particular issues rise and fall, but the pattern of interrelationships among different sets of issues also changes over time.

Analysts of American political history pay special attention to those rare periods when a single-issue dimension dominates the public's views of governmental policy. Periods such as the Civil War or the New Deal revealed deep divisions in the public, paralleled by a distinctiveness in the issue stands of the political parties. Electoral realignments of voters are forged by unusually strong issue alignments, and during such times a close correspondence can be expected between attitudes on the relevant issues and partisanship.

At other times, highly salient issues may capture the attention of the public, but they are likely to cut across, rather than reinforce, other issue positions and party loyalties. If the parties do not take clearly differentiated stands on such issues and if party supporters are divided in their feelings toward the issues, party loyalty and the existing partisan alignment are undermined. In a complex political system such as that of the United States, new, dissimilar issue divisions accumulate until a crisis causes one dimension to dominate and obscure other issues.

The most consistent and the most distinctive ideological difference between the parties emerged during the New Deal realignment. It focused on domestic economic issues, specifically on the question of what role the government should take in regulating the economy and providing social welfare benefits. These issues still underlie the division between the parties. Since the 1930s, the Democratic Party has advocated more government activity, and the Republicans have preferred less. Historically, American political parties have not been viewed as particularly ideological, in part because other issues, such as racial or social issues, have cut across the economic dimension and blurred distinctions between the parties. For example, in the 1940s and 1950s, the Republican Party was at least as liberal on race (i.e., supportive of civil rights legislation) as was the Democratic Party with its strong southern base. Similarly, in the 1970s the two parties were both divided internally on the issue of abortion. Today, however, the two parties have become more ideologically polarized over a broader range of issues. The parties' supporters seem to have sorted themselves out, and now the Democratic Party takes liberal positions and the Republican Party conservative positions on racial and social issues as well as economic ones.

In this chapter we will consider public opinion on several important issues and explore the relationship of social characteristics and partisanship to these opinions. We will look at the extent to which Americans have a political ideology representing a coherent set of fundamental beliefs or principles about politics that serves as a guide to current political issues, much as partisanship does. Finally, we will briefly consider the impact of public opinion on political leaders.

The Measurement of Public Opinion

The commercial opinion-polling organizations have spent more than sixty years asking Americans about their views on matters of public policy. Most of this investigation has taken one of two forms: (1) asking individuals whether they "approve or disapprove of" or "agree or disagree with" a statement of policy or (2) asking individuals to pick their preference among two or more alternative statements of policy. This form of questioning seriously exaggerates the number of people who hold views on political issues. People can easily say "agree" or "disapprove" in response to a question, even if they know nothing at all about the topic. If given the opportunity, many people will volunteer the information that they hold no views on specific items of public policy. In 1964, for example, more than one-third of the American electorate had no opinion on U.S. involvement in Vietnam. In contrast, on issues such as abortion or the death penalty in the past several decades, less than 5 percent of all adults were without an opinion. More typically, in recent years approximately 10 percent of the electorate has had no opinion on major issues of public policy. Philip Converse has shown, in addition, that a number of those individuals who appear to have an opinion may be regarded as responding to policy questions at random.[1]

The lack of opinion and information on topics of public policy can be explained in several ways. In general, the same factors that explain nonvoting also account for the absence of opinions. Individuals with little interest in or concern with politics are least likely to have opinions on matters of public policy. Beyond this basic relationship, low socioeconomic status is associated with no opinion on issues. Low income and little education create social circumstances in which individuals are less likely to have views and information on public policies.

Some issues of public policy, such as abortion or the death penalty, are relatively easy to understand; other issues may be much more difficult, requiring individuals to face complex considerations. Edward G. Carmines and James A. Stimson have argued that different segments of the public respond to "hard" issues that involve calculation of policy benefits and "easy" issues that call for symbolic, "gut responses." Relatively unsophisticated, uninterested members of the electorate respond to "easy" issues; the more sophisticated, most interested citizens take positions on "hard" issues.[2]

It is no simple matter to describe the distribution of opinions in the American electorate because no obvious, widely accepted method has been established to measure these opinions. Asking different questions in public opinion polls will elicit different answers. Even on the issue of abortion, on which most people have views, the distribution of opinions can be substantially altered by asking respondents whether they approve of "killing unborn children" as opposed to "letting women have control over their own bodies." Furthermore, no direct means exists to validate measures of opinions as there is with reports of voting behavior. As a consequence, descriptions of public opinion must be taken as more uncertain, more tentative than conclusions drawn from the discussion of partisanship because independent indicators of opinions on public issues are rare.

Domestic Economic Issues

The Republican victory in the 1994 congressional elections was widely heralded as a "conservative revolution." Speaker Newt Gingrich called it an endorsement of the Contract with America, which was a blueprint for, among other things, reducing government involvement in the economy and cutting support for various social programs. Similarly, Ronald Reagan's victory in 1980 and his administration's subsequent slashing of taxes and social programs had been portrayed as a reversal of fifty years of economic liberalism. In policy terms, these have certainly been consequences of the Republican victories of the 1980s and 1994. In terms of public opinion, however, broad public support remains for many governmental initiatives. As George W. Bush has discovered from his efforts to privatize Social Security, long-standing programs that appear to benefit "deserving" segments of the population are difficult to "reform" because they enjoy widespread support.

The responses to public opinion questions, and public opinion itself, can be affected by political rhetoric and election slogans. For example, the General Social Survey asks a long series of questions on whether spending on various programs is "too much, not enough, or about right." Over the years, sizable proportions of the public have said that too much is being spent on "welfare." At the same time, similarly large proportions have said not enough is being spent on "assistance to the poor."[3] Clearly, years of anecdotes about "welfare queens" and promises to "end welfare as we know it" have had their effect on the way particular programs are perceived, if not on the public's general willingness to use government as an instrument for social purposes.

The distribution of attitudes toward spending for different governmental purposes is shown in Figure 6-1. These data were collected by the General Social Survey from 1973 to 2004. The form of these questions— whether too much or too little is being spent on a problem—elicits answers that reflect the attitude of the respondents, the wording of the question as noted previously, and the current state of public policy. Thus, a period of cutbacks in public spending, such as in the 1980s, would be expected to produce more responses of "too little" even if public attitudes about the ideal level of such spending had not changed. Figure 6-1 shows a drop in negative attitudes toward welfare spending after the Reagan administration slashed these programs, as well as a rise

FIGURE 6-1   Attitudes toward Domestic Spending, 1973–2004

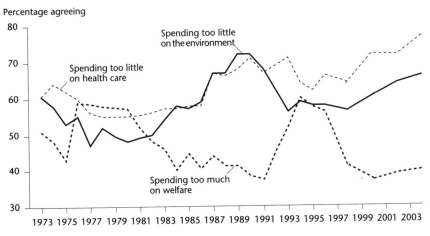

Source: National Opinion Research Center, *General Social Surveys, 1972–2004, Cumulative File.* Data provided by the Roper Center at the University of Connecticut.

in proportions saying "too much" is spent in the 1990s as both political parties promised welfare reform. The implementation of those reforms, in turn, led to a sharp drop since 1996 in the proportion believing too much is being spent. Attitudes favorable toward spending on the environment show a steady increase during the 1980s. Support for more spending on health care has been high for several decades. Overall, Figure 6-1 shows fairly widespread willingness to support government spending on domestic social programs.

When one examines the relationship between social characteristics and issue stands on traditional economic issues, one can expect to find dramatic differences among social groups. Figure 6-2 is based on a question in the 2004 National Election Study that offers respondents a choice between "cutting spending and decreasing services" and "increasing services and increasing spending." We look at responses to this question for several social categories, using race and ethnicity, education, and religion as variables. The pattern in the figure is not difficult to describe. The least economically secure—blacks, Hispanics, and less well educated whites—support government services most strongly. The only group distinctively in favor of cutting spending and services is the better-educated evangelicals. The other religious groups are either

FIGURE 6-2   Attitudes toward Cutting Spending versus Increasing Government Services by Race/Ethnicity, Religion, and Education, 2004

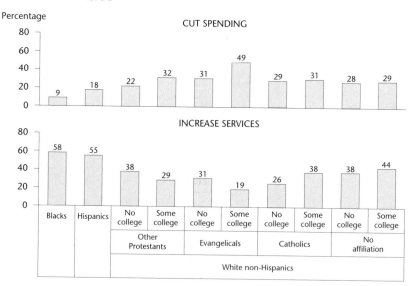

Source: 2004 National Election Study, available at www.umich.edu/~nes.

evenly balanced between cutting spending and cutting services, or they favor increasing spending and services. The lack of relationship between attitudes and social status—different from previous years—may result from the lowered spending on services during the George W. Bush administration.

Men and women do not respond to domestic economic issues in exactly the same way. In general the distribution of men's attitudes runs in a conservative direction and women's attitudes in a liberal direction. In the 2004 National Election Study, 29 percent of the men surveyed supported decreasing government services and reducing spending, whereas only 18 percent of the women polled agreed with that position. Controls for socioeconomic circumstances do not significantly alter these results, so we can conclude that men and women from the same social backgrounds have somewhat different views on certain domestic economic policies.

Favoring services over spending cuts represents the type of choice in governmental policy that characterized the New Deal. Thus, it would be reasonable to expect a dramatic difference between Democrats and Republicans on such an issue. Economic issues have divided Democrats and Republicans since the 1930s. During the past sixty years, partisans have supported or opposed economic policies consistently, whereas other issues have been of only temporary significance for the parties. As a consequence, the relationship in Table 6-1 showing that Democrats disproportionately favor increased government services and Republicans favor cuts is no surprise. Strong Democrats favor increased services over a reduction in spending by a margin of 75 percent to 7 percent; strong Republicans are just the opposite, favoring a reduction in spending over increased services by a margin of 47 percent to 31 percent. This

TABLE 6-1   Attitudes toward Cutting Spending versus Increasing Government Services by Party Identification, 2004

	Strong Demo- crats	Weak Demo- crats	Indepen- dents	Weak Repub- licans	Strong Repub- licans
Favor cutting spending	7%	11%	20%	35%	47%
Neutral	18	27	31	30	22
Favor increasing government services	75	62	50	35	31
Total	100%	100%	101%	100%	100%
(*N*)	(168)	(153)	(401)	(133)	(175)

Source: 2004 National Election Study, available at www.umich.edu/~nes.

TABLE 6-2   Attitudes on Health Care by Party Identification, 2004

	Strong Demo- crats	Weak Demo- crats	Indepen- dents	Weak Repub- licans	Strong Repub- licans
Favor governmental health insurance	66%	53%	53%	36%	18%
Neutral	19	23	19	22	13
Favor private health insurance	16	24	28	42	69
Total	101%	100%	100%	100%	100%
(*N*)	(186)	(161)	(415)	(143)	(186)

Source: 2004 National Election Study, available at www.umich.edu/~nes.

basic pattern has existed for decades, but it is also important to observe that noticeable proportions of Democrats and Republicans hold opinions opposed by a majority of their fellow partisans.

Rising health care costs have been a concern for years. In his first presidential campaign in 1992, Bill Clinton raised the issue of a national health care program and, early in his administration, appointed first lady Hillary Rodham Clinton to head a group to develop a proposal. The managed competition program eventually proposed was not the national health care program favored by the most liberal advocates, but the ensuing debate was cast in terms of governmentally mandated and regulated programs versus private insurance companies with individual choice in health care providers. Ultimately, the Clinton administration lost the battle in Congress and in the arena of public opinion. By 1996, 40 percent of the National Election Study sample said they thought medical expenses should be paid by private insurance plans whereas 34 percent opted for a governmental plan. This was a rather sharp change from 1992 when a governmental insurance plan was preferred 44 to 24 percent over private plans. In 2004 the public remained divided on the health care issue, with 39 percent favoring a government program and 27 percent favoring private health insurance. Like most other issues of government involvement in social programs and regulation of the economy, clear differences between Democratic and Republican partisans appear on the issue of health care, as can be seen in Table 6-2.

Racial Issues

Race and attitudes associated with race hold a prominent place in American political history. For many years after Reconstruction, little overt public attention was paid to racial issues. The South was allowed to impose its system of segregation on its black population by law, while informal, de facto methods created much the same system of separate neighborhoods leading to segregated schools in the North. After integration became a major national and international focal point of attention in the 1940s and 1950s, a number of significant developments in the political attitudes of the public occurred. First, during the past fifty years southern blacks have become increasingly concerned with public policies affecting them and have changed from a largely apathetic, uninterested group to a concerned, involved, politically motivated group. As chronicled in Chapter 2, removing the legal barriers to voting in the South has enabled the black population in southern states to command the attention of politicians at the ballot box and in state legislatures and governors' mansions.

Second, large numbers of southern whites have adjusted their opinions to accept the realities of the new legal and political position of blacks. The public, as a whole, has come to support the general principle of racial equality. Figure 6-3 shows the evolution of public opinion on support for school integration from the 1940s to 2000. The recent near unanimity on this point means that Americans no longer support policies and practices that discriminate against racial groups, and mak-

FIGURE 6-3   Public Attitudes toward School Integration and Fair Employment Practices, 1942–2000

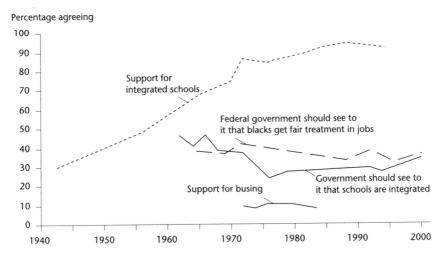

Source: Hadley Cantril, *Public Opinion, 1935–1946* (Princeton: Princeton University Press, 1951), 508; National Opinion Research Center, 1956–1985, NBC News, 1989, and Princeton Survey Research Associates, 1995, all available at the Roper Center at the University of Connecticut; and National Election Studies, available at www.umich.edu/~nes.

ing political appeals based on blatant racism is no longer consistent with the dominant political culture.

At the same time the public has not moved significantly closer to supporting government programs designed to improve the economic and social position of racial groups. Northern, as well as southern, whites have consistently opposed busing for the purposes of integration. More than 80 percent of whites oppose affirmative action on behalf of racial minorities, and less than half support the federal government enforcing fair employment practices. The proportion of the public supporting various forms of governmental action to aid blacks is shown in Table 6-3. In contrast to the near unanimity of support for "letting black and white children go to school together," less than half the public supports positive actions on the part of government to improve the social and economic position of blacks.

The lack of connection between broad principle and policy implementation has been the focus of both political debate and scholarly disagreement. One side argues that opposition to programs to aid blacks is based on opposition to government activities in general and, in particular, programs that benefit a subgroup of society.[4] This position, often referred to as "racial conservatism," is seen as stemming from a general philosophical commitment to limited government and a belief in individualism. The attitudes, it is argued, are based on principles, not racism.

The other view argues that opposition to policy proposals to use governmental programs to aid the social and economic circumstances of blacks and other minorities stems from racial hostility, even though racial conservatives may have learned to cloak their racism in acceptable philosophical language. To complicate the matter further, scholars take different views of how racial hostility expresses itself in political attitudes. Scholars have used three dimensions of racial hostility to explain white support for or opposition to government policies regarding race.

1. Racial resentment (the feeling that blacks are getting more than they deserve) or racial disapproval (the feeling that blacks do not live up to certain value expectations like working hard, etc.).[5] These contentions are often referred to as "symbolic racism."
2. Group conflict (zero-sum conflicts over scarce resources).[6]
3. Social dominance (protection of the status quo by a dominant group).[7]

Dimensions of this type can be interrelated and may reinforce one another. It is difficult to separate them or to be confident in measuring them or evaluating which dimension contributes the most to racial attitudes.*

To connect these dimensions with attitudes about policies designed to provide governmental aid to minorities, it seems reasonable to assume that people must view potential beneficiaries of government aid as deserving. How deserving blacks and other minorities are viewed by

TABLE 6-3   Public Attitudes on School Integration and Employment Practices

		Whites	
	Blacks	South	Non-South
Do you think the government in Washington should see to it that white and black children go to the same schools or stay out of this area as it is not the government's business? (2000)			
Government should see to it	78%	39%	50%
Not government's business	17	54	45
Other, don't know	5	7	5
Total	100%	100%	100%
(*N*)	(137)	(255)	(604)
There is much discussion about the best way to deal with racial problems. Some people think achieving racial integration of schools is so important that it justifies busing children to schools out of their own neighborhoods. Others think letting children go to their neighborhood schools is so important that they oppose busing. Where would you place yourself on this scale, or haven't you thought much about this? (1984)			
Bus to achieve integration	29%	4%	7%
Neutral	15	4	8
Keep children in neighborhood schools	56	92	85
Total	100%	100%	100%
(*N*)	(84)	(197)	(585)
Should the government in Washington see to it that black people get fair treatment in jobs or is this not the federal government's business? (2004)			
Government should see to it	86%	49%	44%
Not government's business	9	47	52
Other, don't know	4	5	4
Total	99%	101%	100%
(*N*)	(114)	(149)	(365)
Some people say that because of past discrimination, blacks should be given preference in hiring and promotion. Others say that such preference in hiring and promotion of blacks is wrong because it gives blacks advantages they haven't earned. What about your opinion—are you for or against preferential hiring and promotion of blacks? (2004)			
For preferential treatment of blacks	47%	13%	12%
Against preferential treatment	41	83	83
Other, don't know, refused to say	12	4	5
Total	100%	100%	100%
(*N*)	(167)	(254)	(587)

Source: National Election Studies, available at www.umich.edu/~nes.

white Americans may depend on whether blacks are seen as individually responsible for their position or whether they are seen as victims of social and economic forces beyond their control. Presumably whites who believe that blacks can improve their situation through their own efforts will not view them as deserving of special government programs on their behalf. This basis of opposition would fit the symbolic racism perspective. Whites who see social structures and conditions imposing special hardships on blacks regardless of their individual efforts will view blacks as deserving of special assistance.

Even if blacks are viewed as deserving, special programs may be opposed if whites see these programs as coming at the expense of whites. Another, similar basis for opposition to programs for blacks would be the expectation that the status quo, which favors whites, would be disrupted, which would be undesirable from the point of view of whites. These objections are examples of the group conflict and social dominance perspectives.

A racial conservative might make the argument that there once was a time when all the relevant democratic principles were on the side of helping blacks but that more recently such principles work both ways. Blacks should have an equal chance to get an education, find a job, and so forth, but they should not be given advantages over other deserving people. However, great differences are found in the perceptions of blacks and whites about whether or not blacks have an equal chance in American society.

Racial attitudes have had a profound effect on the American political landscape. In their book *Issue Evolution*, Carmines and Stimson argue that an evolution of the racial issue since the early 1960s has led increasingly to the Democratic Party being perceived as the liberal party on civil rights issues and the Republican Party being perceived as the conservative party.[8] They see this distinction as the dominant perception of the parties in the eyes of the public. If this is so, it represents a fundamental redefinition of the issue alignment that has characterized the parties since the New Deal.

Before the 1960s, the Republican Party was seen as more progressive on civil rights than the Democrats, particularly in light of the strongly segregationist cast to the southern wing of the Democratic Party. Carmines and Stimson show that a change occurred during the 1960s and 1970s, when the elites of the two parties—members of Con-

---

*Although these dimensions are often labeled as if they were positive or negative in content, they have both pro-black and anti-black extremes. In other words, if a black person believes strongly that black people are not getting what they deserve, racial resentment may be involved just as much as when a white person believes that blacks are getting more than they deserve.

gress, presidential candidates—as well as party activists became distinctive in their racial views. The Democratic Party became dominated by northern liberals advocating stronger governmental action to ensure equal rights. At the same time the leadership of the Republican Party became racially conservative, that is, opposed to government intervention to ensure equal rights for minorities. As the elites and activists sorted themselves into distinct groups on the basis of their attitudes toward racial issues, the perceptions that the mass public held of the parties followed suit. Increasingly through the late 1960s and 1970s, Carmines and Stimson argue, the partisan choices of individual citizens fell in line with their attitudes on racial questions.

The role of race and racial issues in American politics is not always easy to trace, however. Because certain issues that are not explicitly stated in terms of race are nevertheless symbols of race in the minds of some people, candidates can make appeals based on racist attitudes without using racial language. For example, "law and order" may mean "keeping blacks in their place" to some, "welfare" may carry racial overtones, and so on.

Furthermore, the lack of support among whites for policies that target assistance to blacks gives both parties an incentive to avoid embracing such policies, according to Donald R. Kinder and Lynn M. Sanders. Republican leaders can oppose these policies and win support from their overwhelmingly white constituency, particularly southern whites. But Democratic leaders also have an incentive to avoid endorsing policies that would help blacks so as not to alienate white support. Leaders of both parties thus have incentives to avoid advocating policies favorable to blacks.

If race is not an issue to be openly discussed in political campaigns, then uncovering the political significance of race in people's attitudes and perceptions of the political parties becomes difficult. On the whole, straightforward efforts to capture distinctive party images along racial lines do not succeed. Although more than half of the public in 2004 believed there were differences in what the parties stand for, only a small percentage characterized the differences in racial terms. Overwhelmingly, when people articulate differences between the parties it is in terms of symbols and issues associated with the New Deal realignment. This in all likelihood reflects the lack of overt discussion of racial issues by the political leadership of either party.

Social Issues

When presidential candidate Pat Buchanan issued a call for a "cultural war" at the Republican national convention in 1992, he reflected an emphasis on so-called traditional values that increasingly divide the two political parties. Issues such as abortion, pornography, gay rights, and sex education and prayer in the public schools have become prominent in recent years. Although common wisdom positions Democrats on the liberal side and Republicans on the conservative side of such issues, significant numbers of political activists and leaders in both parties are not so easily placed. E. J. Dionne has argued that a major reason that Americans are disenchanted with politics is that the parties insist on defining *liberal* and *conservative* in terms of the New Deal policy dimension, whereas the public is more interested in the traditional value dimension.[9] Certainly one of the most potent of these social issues is abortion. The 1973 Supreme Court decision in *Roe v. Wade* immediately generated a polarized response, turning election races in some areas into one-issue campaigns. Thirty years later, so-called partial birth abortion is a hot-button issue and both sides in the abortion debate gird for battle over any anticipated retirement on the U.S. Supreme Court.

One of the difficulties in examining public opinion on the issue of abortion lies in the responses that different question wording elicits. Although responses to the same question are similar over time, different phrasing of questions produces differing proportions of "pro-choice" or "pro-life" answers. In the following analysis, we use data from the National Election Studies (NES), which has used the same question in each biennial survey since 1980.

The public's views on abortion are associated with several personal characteristics, most notably age, education, and religion. No matter what combination of characteristics is examined in the general public, invariably more than half of the people in the NES surveys support the right to abortion under at least some circumstances.** In simple terms, young people generally favor the right to abortion, the elderly are much more likely to oppose it, and the less educated are less supportive of legal abortion than are the better educated. Given the frequent labeling of abortion as a "women's issue," it is worth noting that virtually no difference turns up in the views of women and men.

Perhaps surprisingly, given the Roman Catholic Church's clear position in opposition to abortion, little difference is found between

---

**These figures undoubtedly underestimate the proportion taking the pro-life position. The two response choices at the pro-life end of the continuum are that abortion should never be permitted and that abortion should be permitted only in cases of rape or incest or to save the life of the mother. The first is a more extreme position than many pro-life advocates would take; the second includes circumstances that have been explicitly rejected by pro-life advocates in and out of Congress. Thus, neither category is an entirely satisfactory indicator of pro-life sentiment. The most extreme pro-choice alternative offered is that by law a woman should always be able to obtain an abortion as a matter of personal choice. We have used the most extreme category at either end of the continuum to indicate pro-life and pro-choice positions.

Catholics and Protestants in their positions on abortion. This is true even when the frequency of church attendance is taken into account. Figure 6-4 shows the percentages taking the most extreme pro-life position and the most extreme pro-choice position for Catholics and Protestants with different frequencies of church attendance. Among both Catholics and Protestants, opposition to abortion increases with frequency of church attendance, but the percentages expressing pro-choice and pro-life sentiments are remarkably similar for the Catholic and Protestant groups. If anything, Protestants are slightly more pro-life and less pro-choice than Catholics at similar levels of church attendance.

The data in Figure 6-4 mask the different attitudes on abortion among Protestant groups, especially among whites. Table 6-4 divides white mainline Protestants from evangelicals and compares them with white Catholics and those with no religious affiliation, again controlling for frequency of church attendance. The evangelical Protestants who regularly attend church are more pro-life than the Catholics who regularly attend. However, the mainline Protestants who regularly attend church are considerably more pro-choice than the frequent attenders of other faiths. Because most mainline Protestant churches take a position of individual moral responsibility on the question of

FIGURE 6-4   Attitudes toward Abortion among Catholics and Protestants by Frequency of Church Attendance, 2004

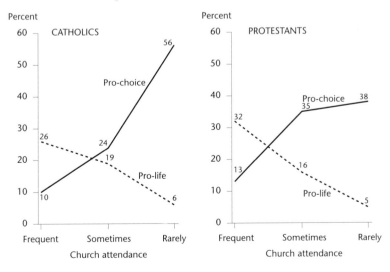

Source: 2004 National Election Study. Available at www.umich.edu/~nes.

TABLE 6-4   Whites' Views on Abortion by Religion and Frequency of Church Attendance, 2004

	Evangelical Protestants			Other Protestants			Catholics			No affiliation
	Frequent	Sometimes	Rarely	Frequent	Sometimes	Rarely	Frequent	Sometimes	Rarely	
Pro-life	36%	37%	0%	15%	10%	0%	27%	13%	6%	5%
Pro-life, with exceptions	46	30	42	37	12	38	41	37	21	23
Pro-choice, with limitations	10	17	29	21	22	17	17	16	18	18
Pro-choice	5	16	29	25	54	45	13	32	55	53
Other, don't know	2	0	0	2	2	0	1	2	0	1
Total	99%	100%	100%	100%	100%	100%	99%	100%	100%	100%
(N)	(72)	(38)	(24)	(99)	(32)	(31)	(97)	(31)	(46)	(206)

Source: 2004 National Election Study, available at www.umich.edu/~nes.

TABLE 6-5   Attitudes on Abortion by Party Identification, 2004

	Strong Demo- crats	Weak Demo- crats	Indepen- dents	Weak Repub- licans	Strong Repub- licans
Never permit abortion	13%	16%	10%	15%	23%
Permit only in special cases	22	33	33	31	39
Permit for other reasons	12	19	18	27	17
Always permit as woman's right	53	33	40	28	21
Total	100%	101%	101%	101%	100%
(N)	(165)	(155)	(396)	(133)	(180)

Source: 2004 National Election Study, available at www.umich.edu/~nes.

Note: The full text of choices is:
1. By law, abortion should never be permitted.
2. The law should permit abortion only in case of rape, incest, or when the woman's life is in danger.
3. The law should permit abortion for reasons other than rape, incest, or danger to the woman's life, but only after the need for the abortion has been clearly established.
4. By law, a woman should always be able to obtain an abortion as a matter of personal choice.

abortion, the pro-choice stance of many of their adherents is not un-expected.

Position on abortion has become a litmus test for presidential candidates in both parties ever since the 1970s. Not surprisingly, then, a fairly strong relationship exists between partisanship and views on abortion, as can be seen in Table 6-5. Perhaps more unexpected is that the relationship is not stronger. Sizable minorities of both Republicans and Democrats take positions contrary to the stand of their party. This is one

TABLE 6-6   Attitudes toward Gay Marriage by Party Identification, 2004

	Strong Demo- crats	Weak Demo- crats	Indepen- dents	Weak Repub- licans	Strong Repub- licans
Allow gay marriage	47%	37%	41%	20%	14%
Not allow but permit civil union (volunteered answer)	3	4	3	4	3
Should not allow gay marriage	50	59	57	76	83
Total	100%	100%	101%	100%	100%
(N)	(183)	(178)	(439)	(139)	(191)

Source: 2004 National Election Study, available at www.umich.edu/~nes.

of several ways in which the polarization of the political activists and elites of the parties is not reflected in the rank and file.

In the summer of 2004, the Supreme Court of Massachusetts ruled that denying gays and lesbians the right to marry was unconstitutional in that state. At about the same time, the mayor of San Francisco began issuing marriage licenses to gay couples. Without any help from the Democratic Party leadership, who doubtless would have liked to avoid the issue, gay marriage was suddenly injected into the presidential campaign. This was a no-win situation for the Democrats and their presidential candidate, given that the American public opposes gay marriage by a two-to-one margin. At the same time, as can be seen in Table 6-6, Democratic partisans are more accepting of the idea than Republicans. Nevertheless, even strong Democrats are split 50–50 over the issue.

Homeland Security and the War on Terrorism

Since September 11, 2001, the eight-hundred-pound gorilla of American public opinion has been terrorism. Not only have the events of that day been seared into people's memories, but the fear of future terrorist attacks also remains strong. Even without another attack, many years will pass before substantial numbers of the public have no personal memory of September 11, so the feelings and issues surrounding terrorism will be around for a long time.

In the fall of 2004 a CBS News poll found that 71 percent of the public believes that the threat of terrorism will always exist.[10] An even larger percentage believes that a terrorist attack against the United States likely will take place fairly soon.[11] Americans' concerns about a terrorist attack focus on chemical and biological weapons as the most worrisome.[12] Terrorism is seen as multifaceted, taking many possible forms with a wide array of possible targets.

Terrorism is a "valence issue," that is, one in which virtually every citizen of the United States agrees that it is bad, as opposed to a "position issue" in which some are for and others are against. At one level, terrorism is also an "easy" issue in the sense that Carmines and Stimson use the term. It is easy, on a gut level, to understand what happened on September 11 and to find it abhorrent. Beyond this, however, the terrorist threat becomes more complicated—a "hard" issue—as one tries to imagine who might be terrorists, what motivates them, and what array of possible weapons they might use. Even more difficult is the assessment of steps proposed and taken to thwart terrorists. Do they work? Are they cost-effective? How would one know?

Although almost everyone believes that the terrorist threat is important, not everyone believes it is the most important issue. In 2004 the

NES asked a battery of questions about the goals of American foreign policy. Among other things, respondents were asked how important it is to combat international terrorism. Over 80 percent said it was "very important." The relatively small number who saw combating terrorism as less important overwhelmingly rated nuclear proliferation (67 percent) and protecting American jobs (78 percent) as very important.

More than most other wars, the war on terrorism involves domestic policies aimed at thwarting terrorist attacks, such as security searches at airports and on mass transit systems. Most survey research in this area has focused on the public's reaction to the Patriot Act. Apparently not everyone is paying much attention, because several years after the adoption of the Patriot Act, one-third of the public said they had heard or read nothing about it. Among the two-thirds of the public who knew something about it, opinion was fairly evenly divided between those who saw it as a necessary tool for finding terrorists and those who thought it goes too far and threatens civil liberties. These responses were strongly influenced by partisanship. Only 10 percent of Republicans thought the Patriot Act goes too far, while 68 percent of Democrats held that view.[13]

Up to some unknown point, Americans are willing to see their civil liberties compromised if they believe doing so will help prevent terrorism, even though three-fourths of the public has little confidence that the government will use personal information, gained through anti-terror measures, appropriately.[14] Respondents are more willing to sacrifice the civil liberties of others than their own. For example, a CBS News poll in the spring of 2005 found that 56 percent of the public was willing to have government agencies monitor the telephone calls and e-mails of Americans the government finds suspicious; only 29 percent favored allowing this monitoring of "ordinary Americans."[15]

Typically, important valence issues such as terrorism have components that can be treated as position issues when segments of the public and their leaders hold differing views. So while everyone is opposed to terrorism, dissimilar views can be held about how well President George W. Bush is handling the war on terrorism or whether the Iraq war made the United States more or less safe from terrorism. As might be expected, the positions people take on these matters may be influenced by partisanship.

Using data from the 2004 National Election Study, Figure 6-5 shows the relationship between party identification and three attitudes toward the war on terrorism. In 2004 Democrats were likely to believe that the war in Iraq increased the terrorist threat; Republicans did not. Republicans were likely to approve of President's Bush's handling of the war on terrorism; Democrats did not. Even views on spending money on the war on terrorism were related to partisanship, with Democrats and independents more likely to support increased spending than Republi-

FIGURE 6-5   Attitudes toward the War on Terrorism according to Party
                Identification, 2004

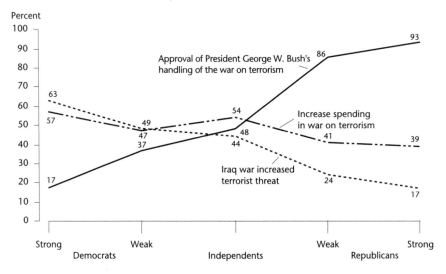

Source: 2004 National Election Study, available at www.umich.edu/~nes.

cans. As discussed in Chapter 8, the war on terrorism was a significant
factor in Bush's appeal in the 2004 election.

International Affairs

During the cold war years, foreign policy—and the study of public
opinion about foreign policy—focused on relations between the United
States and the Union of Soviet Socialist Republics. Questions centered
on the relative strength of the two countries, the likelihood of nuclear
conflict between them, and the preference for negotiation or military
strength as a strategy for keeping the peace. With the breakup of the Soviet Union, the focus of foreign policy has shifted away from superpower
military relations toward involvement, or noninvolvement, in trouble
spots around the world, such as the Persian Gulf in 1991 and Afghanistan and Iraq since 2001 and 2003, respectively.

Issues of foreign affairs vary greatly in salience, particularly in response to involvement of the nation in a military conflict. In analyzing
the public's attitudes toward international events, a distinction needs to
be made between brief conflicts and longer-lasting wars. A truism now
in American politics says the American public will support—usually

enthusiastically—brief military involvement in a foreign conflict that seems to be successful (and they will quickly forget if it is not successful). If, however, combat drags on, support will diminish, especially if there are significant U.S. casualties. In the case of Vietnam, opposition to the war developed at a sluggish pace over a considerable period of time, as did recognition of the seriousness of U.S. involvement. In the early years, opposition to the war (as measured by support for a prompt withdrawal) was low—less than 10 percent. By 1968, it had grown to 20 percent; by 1970, it was more than 30 percent; and by 1972, more than 40 percent. Clearly, as the war dragged on, support for military involvement declined dramatically. The Korean War more than fifty years ago offers similar evidence of the failure of public support for prolonged conflicts.

In contrast, military episodes that develop rapidly command great public attention and almost always garner public support. In the Persian Gulf War, deployment of American military forces to Saudi Arabia began in the late summer of 1990, in response to Iraq's invasion of Kuwait. In the late fall, as deployment of U.S. troops continued, the public was somewhat divided in its support of this policy. Fifty-nine percent of the public polled said they believed it was the correct policy to pursue, and 39 percent said they believed it was not. These views shifted fairly dramatically after the brief and well-televised war with Iraq in early 1991. When the same people were interviewed again in June 1991 following the war, 81 percent felt the war had been the right thing to do and only 18 percent thought the United States should have stayed out.

In the beginning, support for the second war in Iraq was high among the American public. In March 2003, immediately after the invasion, 69 percent of the public thought the United State had done the right thing in taking military action against Iraq. Only a quarter of the public thought the United States should have stayed out.[16] A little over a year later, on the anniversary of the declared end of formal hostilities, the public was evenly divided on whether or not the United States had done the right thing—47 percent thought so, 46 percent did not.[17] Small bursts of support appeared after the patriotic displays at both parties' national nominating conventions in the summer of 2004 and right before the presidential election in November 2004, but, generally, the trend of support has been downward.

Political analysts have long noted a "rally 'round the flag" phenomenon that occurs at times of international crisis.[18] Presidents invariably get a boost in popularity ratings in the polls in the midst of an international incident, even when the actions of the administration are not particularly successful. John F. Kennedy got such a boost after the disastrous Bay of Pigs invasion of Cuba in 1961, as did Jimmy Carter—temporarily—when hostages were taken at the American Embassy in Iran in 1979. And public approval of President George Bush's handling of the Gulf War was extremely high during and immediately following the conflict, representing a substantial increase over his earlier ratings. Similarly, George W. Bush saw an immediate gain in presidential job approval after the attacks on the World Trade Center and Pentagon on September 11, 2001. ABC News and the *Washington Post* completed a national survey the weekend before the attacks in which Bush's job approval was at 55 percent, about average for modern presidents in the first year of their first term. Immediately after the disaster, his job approval climbed to 86 percent. The change in "strong" approval was from 26 to 63 percent.[19] Not all of this enthusiasm survives the passage of time.

As with domestic issues, partisan differences are apparent, with partisans of the president in office more supportive of whatever actions are taken than are partisans of the party out of power. This was seen most clearly during the war in Vietnam. Republicans were more likely to think getting involved in Vietnam was a mistake before 1969, when Democratic president Lyndon B. Johnson was in charge; thereafter, with Republican Richard M. Nixon in the White House, Democrats were more likely to view the war as a mistake.

Similarly, in 2004, 61 percent of Republicans said that Iraq was an immediate threat that required military action, whereas only 14 percent of Democrats and 26 percent of independents held that view. The partisan differences extend to many attitudes toward the Iraq war. Republicans, for example, are much more likely than Democrats or independents to believe that the war in Iraq is a major part of the war on terrorism. Republican support for the war in Iraq has remained strong, whereas the support of Democrats and independents has fallen faster. In March 2003, 87 percent of Republicans said that attacking Iraq was the right thing to do. A year later, their support was still at 80 percent. Democratic support, meanwhile, dropped from 50 percent to 24 percent over the same time period, and independent support declined a comparable amount from 70 percent to 45 percent.[20] As can be seen in Table 6-7, what question was asked about Iraq did not matter much. Democrats, independents, and Republicans responded consistently. Republicans were still supportive of the Republican president and Democrats were not. Independents were somewhere in between but not, on balance, positive about the war.

The public makes a distinction between the war in Iraq and the war in Afghanistan, although they both have the common characteristic of dragging on inconclusively. By the fall of 2004 a little over two-thirds of the public thought the war in Afghanistan was worth it, while only 39 percent held that view of the Iraq war. Republicans overwhelmingly thought both wars had been worth it, but Democrats were less sure. Fifty-two percent of all Democrats thought Afghanistan had been worth

TABLE 6-7   Attitudes toward the War in Iraq according to Party
             Identification, 2004 (in percentages)

	Democrat	Independent	Republican
Think the United States did the right thing in taking military action against Iraq	24	45	80
Think the result of the war with Iraq was worth the loss of American life and other costs of attacking Iraq	12	33	62
Think Iraq was a threat to the United States that required immediate military action	14	26	61
Think the Bush administration tried hard enough to reach a diplomatic solution in Iraq	12	31	64
Think most Iraqi people are feeling grateful to the United States for getting rid of Saddam Hussein	23	34	61
Think of the war with Iraq as a major part of the war on terrorism	22	32	64
(*N*)	(363)	(304)	(299)

Source: CBS News Poll, April 6–8, 2004. Data provided by the Inter-university Consortium for Political and Social Research.

it, but only 12 percent felt that way about Iraq.[21] Because the war in Afghanistan has lasted longer, simple duration of a conflict does not determine the level of support. The cost in American lives and dollars has been much less in Afghanistan than Iraq. News coverage of successes and failures has been much more extensive in Iraq. Perhaps most important, the connection between terrorism and the war in Afghanistan has not been questioned.

Issues and Partisanship

As noted in previous sections, fairly strong and consistent relationships exist between partisanship and domestic and foreign policy issues. A leading assumption is that partisan identification provides guidance for the public on policy matters—that is, most Americans adopt opinions consistent with their partisanship. It also is likely that policy positions developed independently of one's partisanship but consistent with it will reinforce feelings of party loyalty or that attitudes on issues will lead to a preference for the party most in agreement with them. Furthermore, issue preferences inconsistent with party loyalty can erode or change it. For any particular individual it would be extremely difficult to untangle the effects of partisanship and policy preferences over a long period of time.

Even though on many issues most partisans of one party will hold a position different from that held by the majority of the other party, considerable numbers of people with issue positions "inconsistent" with their party identification remain loyal to that party. To account for this, it is variously suggested that (1) issues are unimportant to many voters; (2) only the issues most important to individuals need be congruent with their partisanship; (3) individuals regularly misperceive the positions of the parties to remain comfortable with both their party loyalty and their policy preferences; or (4) the positions of each party are ambiguous or dissimilar enough in different areas of the country that no clear distinction exists between the parties. Undoubtedly, all these explanations have some degree of truth, and no one should expect to find extremely strong relationships between partisanship and positions on particular issues. Nevertheless, as an indication of the recent increased polarization of the parties, racial issues and so-called moral issues have joined traditional domestic economic issues to clearly differentiate Democrats from Republicans.

Political Ideology

A political ideology is a set of interrelated attitudes that fit together into some coherent and consistent view of or orientation toward the political world. Americans have opinions on a wide range of issues, and political analysts and commentators characterize these positions as "liberal" or "conservative." Does this mean, then, that the typical American voter has an ideology that serves as a guide to political thought and action, much the same way partisanship does?

When Americans are asked to identify themselves as liberal or conservative, most are able to do so. The categories have some meaning for most Americans, although the identifications are not of overriding importance. Table 6-8 presents the ideological identification of Americans over the past three decades. A consistently larger proportion of respondents call themselves conservative as opposed to liberal. At the same time, about a quarter of the population regards itself as middle-of-the-road ideologically. The question wording provides respondents with the opportunity to say they "haven't thought much about this," and fully a

TABLE 6-8   Distribution of Ideological Identification, 1972–2004

	1972	1974	1976	1978	1980	1982	1984	1986	1988	1990	1992	1994	1996	2000	2004
Liberal	9%	13%	8%	10%	8%	7%	9%	7%	7%	9%	10%	8%	9%	11%	11%
Somewhat liberal	10	8	8	10	9	8	9	11	9	8	10	8	11	9	8
Middle-of-the-road	27	26	25	27	20	22	23	28	22	25	23	27	24	25	25
Somewhat conservative	15	12	12	14	14	13	14	15	15	14	15	14	16	13	12
Conservative	12	14	13	14	15	14	15	15	17	12	15	21	19	16	19
Haven't thought about it	28	27	33	27	36	36	30	25	30	33	27	22	21	27	25
Total	101%	100%	99%	102%	102%	100%	100%	101%	100%	101%	100%	100%	100%	101%	100%
(N)	(2,155)	(2,478)	(2,839)	(2,284)	(1,565)	(1,400)	(2,229)	(2,170)	(2,035)	(1,987)	(2,481)	(1,795)	(1,714)	(838)	(1,212)

Source: National Election Studies, available at www.umich.edu/~nes.

quarter to a third typically respond in this way. The series of liberal and conservative responses has been remarkably stable over the years. Ideological identification, in the aggregate, is even more stable than party identification. The slight drop in the percentages saying they "haven't thought about" themselves in these terms, and the corresponding increase in the proportion of those calling themselves conservatives in 1994 and beyond, may be a response to the heightened ideological rhetoric of the 1994 campaign and the increased polarization of the political parties. The overall stability of these numbers, however, should make one cautious of commentary that finds big shifts in liberalism or conservatism in the American electorate.

Table 6-9 shows the relationship between ideological self-identification and party self-identification. Democrats are more liberal than conservative, Republicans are disproportionately conservative, and independents are fairly evenly balanced. But conservatives are four times as likely to be Republicans as Democrats, and liberals are far more likely to be Democrats. The relationship between ideology and partisanship is shown in the low coincidence of liberal Republicans and conservative Democrats. Also, the electorate tends to perceive the Democratic Party as liberal and the Republican Party as conservative. Those who see an ideological difference between the parties believe the Republicans are more conservative than Democrats by a ratio of more than four to one.

Figure 6-6 presents the relationship between social characteristics and ideological self-identification. Self-identified liberals are most frequent among college-educated whites who claim no religious affiliation. Self-identified conservatives are most common among white evangelicals, but they are also found in substantial numbers among other Protestants and college-educated Catholics. The major impact of education is to reduce the proportion of respondents who opt for the middle category. The college-educated are more likely to call themselves either liberal or conservative than the high school–educated. This tendency

TABLE 6-9   Relationship between Ideological Self-Identification and Party Identification, 2004

	Democrats	Independents	Republicans	Total
Liberal	14%	10	2	26%
Middle-of-the-road	11	16	6	33
Conservative	5	11	25	41
Total[a]	30%	37	33	100%

Source: 2004 National Election Study, available at www.umich.edu/~nes.

[a]$N = 901$. "No opinion" and "haven't thought about it" responses are omitted.

FIGURE 6-6   Ideological Identification by Race/Ethnicity, Religion, and
             Education, 2004

Source: 2004 National Election Study, available at www.umich.edu/~nes.

would be even greater if those who offered no self-identification were included.

Approximately half the public identifies itself as liberal or conservative. Do these individuals use ideological orientation to organize political information and attitudes? Does political ideology play a role for Americans similar to the role of partisanship as a basic determinant of specific political views? Analysis has usually centered on two kinds of evidence to assess the extent of ideological thinking in the American electorate: the use of ideological concepts in discussing politics and the consistency of attitudes on related issues, suggesting an underlying perspective in the individual's approach to politics.

Data reported in *The American Voter*, by Angus Campbell, Philip E. Converse, Warren E. Miller, and Donald E. Stokes, showed that few members of the electorate discussed their evaluations of the parties and

TABLE 6-10   Distribution of the Levels of Conceptualization, 1956–1988

Levels of conceptualization	1956	1960	1964	1968	1972	1976	1980	1984	1988
Ideologues	12%	19%	27%	26%	22%	21%	21%	19%	18%
Group benefit	42	31	27	24	27	26	31	26	36
Nature of the times	24	26	20	29	34	30	30	35	25
No issue content	22	23	26	21	17	24	19	19	21
Total	100%	99%	100%	100%	100%	101%	101%	99%	100%
(N)	(1,740)	(1,741)	(1,431)	(1,319)	(1,372)	(2,870)	(1,612)	(2,257)	(2,040)

Source: Richard G. Niemi and Herbert F. Weisberg, eds., *Controversies in Voting Behavior,* 3d ed. (Washington, D.C.: CQ Press, 1993), 89.

the candidates in ideological language; only 12 percent did so in 1956.[22] The work of John C. Pierce and others has contributed to similar analysis of subsequent years.[23] As shown in Table 6-10, a change occurred in 1964. The proportions of ideologues doubled in 1964 over 1956 but still constituted only about one quarter of the electorate. This does not mean that most voters have no notions about what the parties stand for or what they are likely to do when in office. Large proportions of the electorate evaluate the parties with group symbols: "The Democrats help the working man" and "Republicans are good for business." Still, the public lacks a commitment to some set of abstract principles about the role of government in society on the basis of which the parties are evaluated.

It is possible that individuals may simply be unsophisticated in the verbal descriptions of their feelings about politics and political parties. Their ideology may guide their political decisions, but they may be unable to articulate it. In that case, the individuals' attitudes toward public issues might be expected to show a degree of coherence and consistency, because those positions would be arrived at through the application of a common underlying set of political ideals. If individuals are liberal on one issue, one would expect them to be liberal on other related issues; if they are conservative on one, they would be conservative on others. The most sophisticated analysis of ideological perspectives and consistency in issue positions, usually called *issue constraint,* was carried out by Philip Converse using data from 1956, 1958, and 1960.[24] He found that the strength of the relationship among domestic issues and among foreign policy issues was about twice as strong as the relationship between domestic and foreign issues. By normal standards even the strongest relationship among domestic issues did not suggest particularly impressive issue consistency. In 1974 Norman H. Nie and Kristi Andersen augmented this analysis with an additional decade of coverage.[25]

As with several other patterns, a change occurred during the campaign of 1964. The degree of issue constraint on various policy matters increased in 1964 and remains relatively high to the present.

As might be expected, the degree of consistency among attitudes on different issues varies with the level of education of the individual; the more educated are substantially more consistent in their views than the less educated. However, increasing levels of education do not appear to account for the increase in issue constraint. The work of Nie and Andersen shows convincingly that interest in politics is more critical. In other words, as the public becomes more concerned with issues and more attentive to political leaders, the public perceives a higher degree of issue coherence. Almost certainly the electorate generally has the capacity for greater issue constraint than it has shown. However, the exercise of the capacity depends much more on political leaders and events than on the characteristics of the electorate. When political leaders use ideological terms to describe themselves and the clusters of issues that they support, the electorate is capable of following suit.

The degree of issue constraint will depend on the range of issues considered. *The American Voter* documented a coherent set of attitudes on welfare policies and governmental activity, even in the 1950s. When the analysis moves to more disparate issues, such as support for welfare policies and civil liberties, the relationship weakens substantially. It can be argued that little relationship should be expected between positions in these different issue areas because they tap different ideological dimensions with no logical or necessary connections among them. For example, there is nothing logically inconsistent in a person's opposing government regulation of business and believing in racial equality. In the past, internationalist views in foreign policy were considered the liberal position and isolationist attitudes conservative. However, the cold war and Vietnam did much to rearrange these notions as liberals argued against American involvement and conservatives became more aggressive internationalists. In considering the question of issue constraint, two points should be kept in mind: (1) the meaning of the terms *liberal* and *conservative* change with time, as do the connections between these ideologies and specific historical events; and (2) analysts, in studying issue constraint, invariably impose on the analysis their own version of ideological consistency, which, in light of the ambiguities surrounding the terms, is likely to be somewhat artificial.

A less strenuous criterion than issue constraint for assessing the impact of ideology on political attitudes is simply to look at the relationship between individuals' ideological identification and their positions on various issues taken one at a time. Here, substantial relationships are found. The relationship between ideological identification and liberal

TABLE 6-11   Relationship between Ideological Identification and Liberal Positions on Issues, 1972–2004

	Liberal	Somewhat liberal	Middle-of-the-road	Somewhat conservative	Conservative
Increase government services (2004)	67	55	46	33	22
Favor government health insurance (2004)	70	57	50	30	17
Pro-choice on abortion (2004)	71	46	39	32	26
Should allow gay marriage (2004)	70	47	39	19	10
Iraq war increased terrorist threat (2004)	73	57	38	29	23
Government help for blacks (2004)	48	26	20	14	11
Protect the environment (2004)	63	55	40	37	27
Oppose school vouchers (2000)	44	48	52	46	28
Protect homosexuals from job discrimination (1996)	87	79	68	63	39
Not worth it to fight in Persian Gulf (1992)	66	45	41	30	24
Support for the Equal Rights Amendment (1980)	91	78	64	48	38
Legalize marijuana (1976)	60	49	24	24	10
Oppose the Vietnam War (1972)	76	61	39	33	27

Source: National Election Studies, available at www.umich.edu/~nes.

Note: The numbers in the table are the percentages taking the liberal position on each issue.

views on various policy matters over the past thirty-two years is shown in Table 6-11. Between one-fourth and one-third of the people sampled did not have an ideological position or did not profess attitudes on these issues and are, therefore, missing in the analysis. Nevertheless, the data in Table 6-11 document strong, consistent relationships between ideological identification and many issue positions. The data do not, however, demonstrate that ideology determines issue positions.

If everyone had a strong ideology, attitudes would be determined by that ideology. To a considerable extent, this appears to happen to the most politically alert and concerned in the society, but this group is only a small minority of the total adult population. To the extent that the major American political parties are ideologically oriented, then, by following the parties or political leaders in these parties, Americans have their opinions determined indirectly by ideology. American political parties are often characterized as nonideological, and the country has passed through substantial historical periods when the parties have seemed bent on obscuring the differences between them. At other times, such as 1964 and since the early 1990s, political leaders were more intent on drawing distinctions between themselves and the opposing party in ideological terms. At these times, the public responds by appearing more ideological, too.

Public Opinion and Political Leadership

The study of public opinion is of obvious relevance to public officials and political journalists who wish to assess the mood of the people on various topics, but the extent to which decision makers are influenced by public opinion on any particular policy is almost impossible to determine. Although policy makers must have some sense of the public mood, no one supposes that they measure precisely the attitudes of the public or are influenced by public opinion alone.

Political analysts and public officials both have difficulty assessing the likely impact of public opinion as measured by public opinion polls because the intensity of feelings will influence the willingness of the public to act on their views. Public officials who value their careers must be conscious of the issues that raise feelings intense enough to cause people to contribute money, to campaign, and to cast their ballots solely on the basis of that issue. As a result, public officials may be more responsive to the desires of small, intense groups than to larger, but basically indifferent, segments of the public.

In American society public attitudes toward policies usually can be described in one of two ways: as permissive opinion, whereby a wide range of possible government activities are acceptable to the public, or, in contrast, as directive opinion, either supportive or negative, whereby specific alternatives are definitely demanded or opposed. Ordinarily, policy alternatives advocated by both political parties are within the range of permissive opinion, a situation that does not create highly salient issues or sharp cleavages in the public even though political leaders may present their positions dramatically. Only when many people hold directive opinions will the level of issue salience rise or issue clashes appear among the public. For example, widespread directive support exists for public education in the United States. Most individuals demand a system of public education or would demand it were it threatened. At the same time permissive support is evident for a wide range of policies and programs in public education. Governments at several levels may engage in a variety of programs without arousing the public to opposition or support. Within this permissive range the public is indifferent.

On occasion, out-and-out opposition to programs develops, and directive opinion is formed that imposes a limit on how far government can go. For example, the widespread opposition to busing children out of their neighborhoods for purposes of integration has perhaps become a directive, negative opinion. Political analysts or politicians cannot easily discover the boundaries between permissive and directive opinions. Political leaders are likely to argue that there are supportive, directive opinions for their own positions and negative, directive opinions for their opponents' views. One should be skeptical of these claims because it is much more likely that there are permissive opinions and casual indifference toward the alternative views. Indifference is widespread and, of course, does not create political pressure. It frees political leaders of restrictions on issue positions but, on balance, is probably more frustrating than welcome.

Notes

1 Philip Converse, "The Nature of Belief Systems in Mass Publics," in *Ideology and Discontent,* ed. David Apter (New York: Free Press, 1964), 206–261.
2. Edward G. Carmines and James A. Stimson, "The Two Faces of Issue Voting," *American Political Science Review* 74 (1980): 78–91.
3. In the 1993 General Social Survey, for example, 57 percent said "too much" was being spent on "welfare"; however, 65 percent said "too little" was being spent on "assistance to the poor."
4. This view is most prominently associated with Paul M. Sniderman and Edward G. Carmines, *Reaching Beyond Race* (Cambridge, Mass.: Harvard University Press, 1997). See also Paul M. Sniderman, Philip E. Tetlock, and Edward G. Carmines, *Prejudice, Politics, and the American Dilemma* (Stanford: Stanford University Press, 1993).

5. A strong, recent statement of the symbolic racism position is in Donald R. Kinder and Lynn M. Sanders, *Divided by Color* (Chicago: University of Chicago Press, 1996).

6. This position is most commonly associated with Lawrence Bobo. See his "Race and Beliefs about Affirmative Action," in *Racialized Politics,* ed. David Sears, Jim Sidanius, and Lawrence Bobo (Chicago: University of Chicago Press, 2000), chap. 5.

7. This position is represented by Jim Sidanius in *Social Dominance: An Intergroup Theory of Social Dominance and Oppression* (Cambridge, England: Cambridge University Press, 1999).

8. Edward G. Carmines and James A. Stimson, *Issue Evolution: Race and the Transformation of American Politics* (Princeton: Princeton University Press, 1989).

9. E. J. Dionne, *Why Americans Hate Politics* (New York: Simon and Schuster, 1991).

10. CBS News Poll, September 6–8, 2004, Roper Center at the University of Connecticut, accession number 1605388.

11. In the "America Speaks Out about Homeland Security Survey" by Hart and Teeter for the Council for Excellence in Government, February 5–8, 2004, 77 percent of all adults said it was "very likely" or "somewhat likely" that a terrorist attack against the United States at home or overseas would take place in the "next few months." Roper Center at the University of Connecticut, accession number 0451077. The full report is available at www.excelgov.org.

12. "America Speaks Out about Homeland Security Survey," Roper Center at the University of Connecticut, accession number 0451122.

13. CBS News Poll, April 2005, Roper Center at the University of Connecticut, accession numbers 1622862 and 1622863, available at www.pollingreport.com/terror.htm.

14. "America Speaks Out about Homeland Security Survey," Roper Center at the University of Connecticut, accession number 0451133.

15. CBS News Poll, April 2005, Roper Center at the University of Connecticut, accession numbers 1622865 and 1622864.

16. CBS News Monthly Poll 5, March 26–27, 2003.

17. CBS News/*New York Times* Poll, April 23–27, 2004.

18. John E. Mueller, *War, Presidents, and Public Opinion* (New York: Wiley, 1973), 208–213.

19. These data were available at www.pollingreport.com, accessed on September 14, 2001.

20. CBS News Monthly Poll 5; and CBS News/*New York Times* Poll, April 23–27, 2004. Data provided by the Inter-university Consortium for Political and Social Research.

21. 2004 National Election Study, available at www.umich.edu/~nes.

22. Angus Campbell, Philip E. Converse, Warren E. Miller, and Donald E. Stokes, *The American Voter* (New York: Wiley, 1960), 249.

23. John C. Pierce, "Ideology, Attitudes, and Voting Behavior of the American Electorate: 1956, 1960, 1964," Ph.D. dissertation, University of Minnesota, 1969, Table 3.1, 63; and Paul R. Hagner and John C. Pierce, "Conceptualization and Consistency in Political Beliefs: 1956–1976," paper presented at the annual meeting of the Midwest Political Science Association, Chicago, 1981. See also Norman H. Nie, Sidney Verba, and John R. Petrocik, *The Changing American Voter* (Cambridge, Mass.: Harvard University Press, 1976), chap. 7.

24. Converse, "The Nature of Belief Systems in Mass Publics," 206–261.

25. Norman H. Nie and Kristi Andersen, "Mass Belief Systems Revisited: Political Change and Attitude Structure," *Journal of Politics* 36 (September 1974): 541–591.

Suggested Readings

Carmines, Edward G., and James A. Stimson. *Issue Evolution: Race and the Transformation of American Politics.* Princeton: Princeton University Press, 1989. A fascinating account of the role of racial issues and policies in American politics in recent decades.

Converse, Philip E. "The Nature of Belief Systems in Mass Publics." In *Ideology and Discontent,* edited by David Apter. New York: Free Press, 1964. A classic analysis of the levels of sophistication in the American public.

Hochschild, Jennifer L. *What's Fair.* Cambridge, Mass.: Harvard University Press, 1981. An intensive, in-depth study of the beliefs and attitudes of a few people that deals with traditional topics from a different perspective.

Mayer, William G. *The Changing American Mind.* Ann Arbor: University of Michigan Press, 1992. Analysis of changes in issue positions between 1960 and 1988.

Page, Benjamin J., and Robert Y. Shapiro. *The Rational Public.* Chicago: University of Chicago Press, 1992. Analysis of the American public's views on policy issues over the past fifty years.

Sniderman, Paul M., Richard A. Brody, and Philip E. Tetlock. *Reasoning and Choice.* Cambridge, England: Cambridge University Press, 1991. A political, psychological approach to the study of issues and ideology.

Internet Resources

The Web site of the National Election Studies, www.umich.edu/~nes, has extensive data on the topics covered in this chapter. Click on "Ideological Self-Identification" for ideological items in a number of election years. Click on "Public Opinion on Public Policy Issues" for a wide range of attitudes from 1952 to the present. Each political item is broken down by an extensive set of social characteristics.

The Roper Center at the University of Connecticut has an enormous collection of survey data on American public opinion from the 1930s to the present. Limited access to the data is available through LexisNexis. For complete access to the data a membership is required.

Political Communication
and the Mass Media

MUCH ATTENTION has been focused on the process of change in political opinions, both in terms of the conditions for such change and the possibilities of instigating widespread shifts in political beliefs through the mass media. At the extremes, the process of influencing political opinions is labeled *brainwashing* or *propaganda*. In reality, only a matter of degree separates these forms of influence from political persuasion, campaigning, or even education. All the efforts covered by these terms are directed toward changing individuals' political ideas, values, and opinions or toward fostering some political action. Enormous amounts of time and money are expended in American society to change political views. The diversity of the efforts to influence the public mind, along with the diversity and complexity of the society itself, makes highly unlikely a quick or uniform public response to any one of these attempts. Only dramatic events or crises can quickly change the public's views. Although news of such events comes through the media, the impact results from the events themselves, not simply the media imagery.

Political persuasion probably is most effective in casual personal relationships. The impact of the mass media likely is important in shaping the contours of political discourse but only gradually and over fairly long periods of time. At the same time, the role that the media have in making information widely available is significant in creating the conditions under which attitude change occurs. In this chapter we will consider the basic processes of opinion change and the impact of the mass media and election campaigns on individual political behavior.

Functions of Opinions for Individuals

Social psychology suggests that an individual's opinions can serve various purposes: cognitive, social, and psychological. Cognitive functions of opinions cover the efforts to give meaning to the social environment and to relate elements of belief and knowledge to one another. Opinions generally relate directly or indirectly to an individual's most significant goals or values. Somehow the policy supported by a political opinion is expected to be consistent with one's most important political values.

Opinions serve a social function if they aid the individual in adjusting to others or in becoming part of a group. In some cases individuals may use opinions to set themselves apart from others. Political and social issues may be too unimportant in general to serve social purposes for most people, and little evidence suggests that strong social conformity pressures affect their views on most political issues. Nevertheless, for highly salient issues an individual is apt to find that holding a socially unacceptable view is both uncomfortable and costly.

An opinion also may serve purposes for an individual that are not dependent on its social, economic, or political meaning but on its special psychological significance for the individual. For example, an individual might hold strongly prejudicial opinions against some group because it enhances self-esteem to feel superior to others, or an individual might project undesirable qualities onto a certain group and thereby disassociate him- or herself from those qualities. The problem with psychological attachments of this kind is that the opinions so based are not responsive to ordinary influence because of their psychological importance to the individual. Most Americans do not appear to attach strong psychological meaning to their political opinions. Furthermore, in a modern pluralistic society with its open political processes, opinions on significant political subjects are unlikely to remain privatized and solely of psychological relevance to the individual. Opinions also take on social and cognitive functions.

Most discussions of political opinions imply a more or less reasoned handling of opinions by individuals. They imply that individuals intelligently relate their opinions to one another and that a logical relationship exists between a goal and a preference for policies leading to that goal. The implication of this perspective is that opinions can be changed if the cognitive content of the attitude is changed—that is, if new information is brought to the attention of the individual. However, if individuals hold their opinions for the social or psychological purposes they serve, instead of for the cognitive, providing these individuals with more information or altering the policy implications of the opinion will not necessarily lead to opinion change.

Opinion Consistency and Dissonance

The analysis of inconsistency in opinions has much in common with the cross-pressure hypothesis (considered in Chapter 5). In psychology this analysis of opinions has taken the form of identifying elements of several opinions as consistent with one another or as being in conflict (dissonant). Because dissonance is assumed to be disturbing, an individual presumably will try to avoid or reduce it. An example of dissonance should clarify these concepts.[1]

Suppose a Republican believes that all Democratic administrations are corrupt and that Republicans stand for honest government, and the individual's party loyalty is justified on this basis. If the individual hears that a Republican governor is taking bribes, the information conflicts with the person's earlier views and may create dissonance among them. The dissonance could be reduced by justifying his or her loyalty on a new basis or by denying or discrediting the new information. A denial might take the form of deciding that the governor is being framed by opponents.

Individuals have many psychological defenses against the potential dissonance represented by new information that conflicts with their existing attitudes: *selective exposure,* not paying attention to conflicting information; *selective perception,* misinterpreting such information or rejecting the sources of the information as lacking credibility; *compartmentalization,* not making the connections between dissonant attitudes; and *rationalization,* developing an unwarranted interpretation of a situation to avoid confronting the real one. Should the meaning of the information be unavoidable, attitude change to restore harmony may result. Typically, individuals will change dissonant patterns in the easiest way. The opinions or beliefs that are least important to the individual will be changed, not important ideas or values.

Political opinions are probably most often changed simply by providing individuals with more information. The additional information may be no more than some new facts about the environment or indications that many political leaders whom an individual respects hold a particular view. The low salience of most political issues, plus the widespread emphasis on debate and discussion, leads to circumstances that improve the opportunities for changing opinions with information.

Political Communication and Attitude Change

Individuals in the public receive ideas and information intended to alter their political opinions from a variety of sources. Some sources are political leaders and commentators whose views arrive impersonally through the mass media; others are friends, coworkers, and family members who influence opinions through personal contact. Much remains to be learned about political persuasion and communication, but at least occasionally many Americans engage in attempts to influence others, and almost everyone is regularly the recipient of large quantities of political communication.

A somewhat oversimplified view of the transmission of political information would have the media beaming a uniform message to a mass audience made up of isolated individuals. The audience would receive all or most of its information from the media. Thus, public opinion would be a direct product of the information and perspective provided through the media. A more complex view suggests that information is transmitted in a "two-step flow of communication."[2] Information is transmitted from "opinion elites" (leaders in the society, such as politicians, organizational leaders, news commentators) to a minority of the public—the "opinion leaders"—and from them to the remainder of the public:

Opinion Elites

Opinion Leaders

Public

The information from opinion elites usually is sent through the mass media, but this view implies that only a portion of the audience, the opinion leaders, is attentive to any particular type of information such as political news. The opinion leaders, as intermediaries, then interpret, modify, and explain facts and events to those friends and neighbors who are less interested in or concerned with these happenings. In the process, the original message conveyed through the media becomes many somewhat different messages as it reaches the public.

The two-step flow model may not be strictly true in most cases, and public opinion research has generally failed to turn up many people who recognize themselves as opinion leaders. Even so, most members of the public probably do receive information from the mass media in the context of their social groups. Thus, they filter the information and interpretations of the media through not only their own perceptions, experiences, and existing attitudes but also those of people around them. Only when the media have the attention of most members of the audience and a virtual monopoly over the kinds of information received by a public that has few existing attitudes about the subject can the media produce anything like a uniform change in public attitudes.

A somewhat different argument, also based on the role of social influences on the development of public opinion, has been made by Elisabeth Noelle-Neumann in *The Spiral of Silence.*[3] She argues that members of society sense that some views are increasing in popularity, even if these ascending viewpoints are held only by a minority. Under such circumstances people become reluctant to express opinions contrary to the presumed ascending view, whereas individuals holding that view are emboldened and express themselves more freely. This furthers the illusion that one viewpoint is widely shared. People then adopt the viewpoint because of this largely imaginary public pressure. Although intriguing, the attractiveness of this argument is diminished somewhat by the almost total lack of evidence in support of it.

In the remainder of this chapter we will consider the impact of the mass media on political attitudes in the context of political campaigns. Because the media can be influential only if people are paying attention, we will look at the question of the overall attentiveness of the public to political news. Because the impact of the media varies depending on the existing attitudes and information of the audience, we will examine the impact of the media on different kinds of people and in different campaign contexts.

To begin, however, we need to draw some distinctions among the various types of media. First, the impact of information may be different depending on the type of media through which it is received. Precisely the same information received through television, radio, or a newspaper may impress the recipient differently. For example, viewing a speech on television may be more dramatic than hearing it on radio or reading the text in a newspaper. Something like this occurred in 1960 when television viewers of the first of three presidential debates between John F. Kennedy and Richard M. Nixon had a less favorable impression of Nixon than did radio listeners.[4] A difficult topic, however, may be more easily absorbed by reading and rereading a newspaper article rather than having a story flash by once on television.

Second, the media differ in what they offer. Simple elements of information are more quickly and dramatically presented to a large audience on television than they can be through the print media. Television, however, may systematically under-inform its audience by rarely offering more than a "headline service" of a minute or two on any one story. The more the public wants information and is motivated to seek it, the more important newspapers, magazines, and the Internet become. It is easy to search for items of information on the Internet, more difficult but possible in the print media, and much more difficult with radio and television. The characteristics of the media give them different roles in the formation of public opinion. In general, television alerts the public to a variety of topics; newspapers inform a smaller segment of the public in greater depth.

Third, an increasing diversity of news sources is available through television, especially over the past fifteen years. CNN, MSNBC, and Fox News are genuine alternatives to the broadcast networks, especially when it comes to fast-breaking news. Surveys done by the Pew Research Center for the People and the Press in 2004 estimated that more than half the public watched CNN "sometimes" and 22 percent did so "regularly."[5] The Fox News cable audience was just as large. The C-SPAN channels provide extensive coverage of both the U.S. House of Representatives and the Senate, as well as other political events, without the intermediary of network editing and commentary. Somewhat under 20 percent of the public reports watching C-SPAN at least occasionally.[6] Call-in television and radio provide lengthy discussions of public issues and, since 1992, offer a mechanism whereby candidates can bypass the normal news channels and receive unmediated coverage.

The Internet as a news source is a recent development with intriguing characteristics. Providing almost unlimited access to information, it requires the consumer actively to seek out that information. It also offers opportunities to "talk back" or comment on the news and to be put in touch with other like-minded people. Few "gatekeepers" operate on the Internet, and the issues of the reliability and credibility of information are largely left to the user to determine. Opportunities abound for whispering campaigns of rumor and misinformation.

Fourth, the impact of editorial endorsements by newspapers (television and radio stations rarely make endorsements) should be assessed independently of news coverage, although editorial preferences may bias news stories. Newspaper endorsements seemingly have a minimal impact in presidential elections, given that many other sources of influence exist.[7] In less visible, local races, a newspaper editorial may influence many voters.[8] Some concern exists that major newspaper chains could wield significant power nationally by lining up their papers behind one candidate. However, in recent years the large chains have generally left their papers free to make decisions locally.

Fifth, throughout our discussion we need to make the distinction between the impact of news coverage by the media and political advertising carried by the media. This is not easy to do, especially because the news media often cover political advertising as if it were news and consciously or unconsciously pick up themes from political ads and weave them into their own coverage.[9] The placing of political advertising in news programs increases the difficulty in separating news from ads. Even the "ad watches" that news organizations use to critique the advertising of candidates may contribute to confusion over what is news and what is paid advertising.

Attention to the Media

For the media to have an impact on an individual's political attitudes and behavior, the individual must give some degree of attention to the media when political information is being conveyed. Almost all Americans have access to television and watch political news at least some of the time. In 2004 a majority of Americans (54 percent) reported reading a daily newspaper regularly; somewhat fewer read a newspaper for political news. This represents a decline in daily newspaper readership from more than 70 percent early in the 1990s.[10] Occasional newspaper reading is higher.

Much discussion has ensued in the scholarly literature on mass media about the capacity to bring matters to the attention of the public or to conceal them.[11] This is usually referred to as *agenda setting.* The literature suggests that the media have great influence over what the public is aware of and concerned with. Television news and front-page stories in newspapers focus the public's attention on a few major stories each day. This function, sometimes called headline service, tells the public: Here are important developments you should be aware of. Major events, such as the September 11, 2001, terrorist attacks, or scandalous happenings, such as the Monica Lewinsky affair, push other stories off the agenda. The media made it almost impossible for an ordinary American to be unaware of these events. That is agenda setting.

Television often plays a critical role in bringing events and issues to the attention of the American public. Television presents certain types of information in an exceptionally dramatic or impressive way. The Persian Gulf War and the Iraq War were televised to an unprecedented extent. The American public watched a real-life video arcade of modern warfare. In January of 1991, 67 percent of a national sample reported following the Persian Gulf War "very closely."[12] Attention was not as high in 2003, but over half the public followed the Iraq War very closely.[13] In the short run, the coverage created the impression of an overwhelming military victory and great satisfaction with the performance of each president. In each instance, the president's job approval ratings soared and support for the war increased dramatically.[14] With the passage of time, evaluations became more mixed.

Perhaps nothing in television history compares with the coverage of the attacks on the World Trade Center and the Pentagon on September 11. The major news channels abandoned regular programming and focused on the attacks and their aftermath for days. Virtually everyone in the country was attentive to this coverage, and most people had a strong emotional reaction to what they saw.

The news media, particularly television, can rivet public attention on certain issues and, in doing so, limit the policy-making options of political leaders. The range of subjects on which this can be done is narrow, however. Death, destruction, intrigue, or pathos is generally an essential ingredient. More abstract or mundane political issues are easily ignored by most of the public.

However, many potential news items are never reported, either in the print media or on television. This is the result of a process often referred to as *gatekeeping*.[15] The media are more selective than a phrase such as "all the news that's fit to print" suggests. Bias in gatekeeping and agenda setting can occur when items are kept from the public that would have been of considerable interest or when items the public otherwise would have ignored are made to seem important. Neither of these effects is easily demonstrated with political information and opinions. It is fairly easy to show that a particular newspaper or a given television station may ignore certain topics or exaggerate others, but it is difficult to find evidence of any impact of selective coverage on the public.

Although the media may focus on certain news items, the public has an enormous capacity for ignoring the coverage and being highly selective about what to take an interest in. First the *Los Angeles Times Mirror* and later the Pew Research Center for the People and the Press engaged in an extensive project to explore the public's awareness of and interest in news stories.[16] Some news stories, such as the explosion of the space shuttle *Challenger* and the 1989 San Francisco earthquake, were followed with great interest by most of the public. As shown in Table 7-1, almost all the news stories from January 1986 to September 2005 that were followed "very closely" by large percentages of the public were military operations or disasters of one sort or another. In contrast, less than 25 percent of the public paid close attention to news stories about the mapping of the human genetic code, charges that Speaker Newt Gingrich violated House ethics rules, or the U.S. Supreme Court decision on campaign finance.

As would be expected, a large percentage of the public followed news about the terrorist attacks on September 11 very closely. Some of the people who did not follow the story said they were so distraught they avoided the news. Public attention to the military activities in Afghanistan, shown in Table 7-1 at 51 percent, is noticeably below the level of attention to the Persian Gulf War in 1991 at 67 percent. Public attention to the debate about going to war in Iraq during several months in the spring of 2003 (around 63 percent) was greater than the attention to the onset of the war itself in March of that year (57 percent).

TABLE 7-1   Most Closely Followed News Stories and Other Selected News
Items, 1986–2005

News stories	Percentage following very closely
Ten most closely followed news stories	
Explosion of the space shuttle *Challenger* (January 1986)	80
Terrorism attacks on the United States (September, October 2001)	74
San Francisco earthquake (November 1989)	73
High price of gasoline (September 2005)	71
Hurricane Katrina (September 2005)	70
Verdict in Rodney King case and subsequent violence (May 1992)	70
TWA 800 crash (July 1996)	69
Rescue of little girl in Texas who fell into a well (October 1987)	69
Columbine High School shooting (April 1999)	68
End of Persian Gulf War (January 1991)	67
Other news stories	
Hurricane Andrew (September 1992)	66
Sniper shootings near Washington, D.C. (October 2002)	65
News about situation in Iraq (May 2003)	63
Debate about war in Iraq (February 2003)	62
Increases in the price of gasoline (October 1990)	62
Increases in the price of gasoline (June 2000)	61
Increases in the price of gasoline (June 2004)	58
War with Iraq (March 2003)	57
News about situation in Iraq (May 2004)	54
Death of Princess Diana (September 1997)	54
News about presidential election (October 2004)	53
U.S. military effort in Afghanistan (January 2002)	51
Federal Bureau of Investigation incident at Waco, Texas (May 1993)	50
Terrorist bombings in London (July 2005)	48
Breakup of the Soviet Union (October 1991)	47
Bill Clinton health care reform proposals (December 1993)	45
News about the situation in Iraq (July 2005)	43
Debate over Elian Gonzalez (January 2000)	39
Outcome of the presidential election (November 2000)	38
George W. Bush's proposal to deal with Social Security (March 2005)	38
Debate in Congress over George W. Bush's budget and tax cut plan (February 2001)	31
Charges that Newt Gingrich violated House ethics rules (January 1997)	23
Mapping the human genetic code (July 2000)	16
U.S. Supreme Court decision on campaign finance (December 2003)	8

Source: Pew Research Center for the People and the Press, www.people-press.org.

Large numbers of Americans (70 percent) followed the news of Hurricane Katrina in the late summer of 2005.[17] Most (89 percent) relied on television coverage, especially that of cable news channels, for their news about Katrina and its aftermath. Interestingly, equally large numbers (71 percent) paid close attention to the news about high gasoline prices in the wake of the storm; Table 7-1 reflects concern about gas prices at other times as well. As events were unfolding in the Gulf Coast, only 18 percent of the public was paying close attention to the nomination of John Roberts as Chief Justice of the Supreme Court.

The combination of television, newspapers, radio, and magazines represents an extraordinary capacity to inform the public rapidly and in considerable depth about major political news items. Add to this the informal communication about the news of the day that most people engage in, and it is easy to see that the American public is in a position to be well informed. That as many people persist in *not* informing themselves about most political news is not a failure of the mass media to make the news available in a variety of forms.

A number of scholars have pointed out that it may be rational for voters to ignore much of the political information around them. Rational choice theorists, following the lead of economist Anthony Downs, argue that the benefits derived from reaching a "correct" decision on a candidate or policy may not be worth the costs the voter incurs in finding out the information.[18] It is rational, therefore, for the voter to take a number of information shortcuts, such as relying on someone else's judgment or voting according to one's established party identification. Samuel Popkin uses the analogy of "fire alarms" versus "police patrols" to explain how most people view political information.[19] Instead of patrolling the political "neighborhood" constantly to make sure nothing there requires their attention, most citizens rely on others to raise the alarm when something important happens. Television news and newspaper headlines may be enough to tell average citizens whether they need to delve deeper into a particular story.

A minority of people are motivated to follow political news and inform themselves broadly about public affairs. Some people need to be informed about government and politics—or some aspects of it—to do their jobs. Others are simply interested in politics, so searching out information is less burdensome to them. Not surprisingly, scholars studying media behavior have consistently found a strong relationship between interest in politics and attention to political news. In his study of the media behavior of voters in Erie, Pennsylvania, and Los Angeles, California, during the 1976 presidential election, Thomas E. Patterson found that the most interested voters not only paid the most attention to the media, but they also were able to recall political news heard on television or read in the newspaper better than the less interested.[20] Interested individuals are better equipped than the uninterested and inattentive to retain and use new elements of information that come their way.

Because the most interested voters are also the most partisan, a relationship also exists between attention to the media and partisanship. The fact that strong partisans and politically interested people are most attentive to the media accounts for the somewhat paradoxical finding that those with the most exposure to the media are among the least affected by it. The impact of mass media exposure on voting behavior in elections in the 1950s was studied by Philip Converse, who drew several conclusions based on findings similar to those represented in Figure 7-1.[21] The voters most stable in their preferences (whether stability is measured during a campaign or between elections) would be those who are highly attentive to mass media but firmly committed. Those who pay no attention to media communication remain stable in their vote choices because no new information is introduced to change their votes. The shifting, unstable voters are more likely to be those with moderate exposure to mass media. Unfortunately, efforts at replicating Converse's findings for other election years have failed to uncover similar patterns. One difficulty may be the virtual disappearance of voters with no exposure to the mass media in recent years. Nevertheless, the reasoning behind this expected relationship is compelling: The impact of the media is likely to be greatest when the recipients of the message have little information and few existing attitudes.

FIGURE 7-1   Hypothetical Relationship between Mass Media Attention and Stability of Voting Behavior

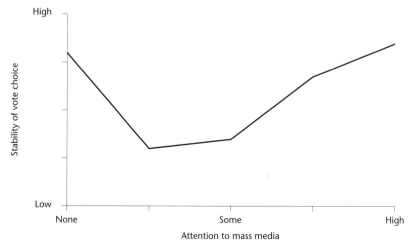

Does Iraq Have Weapons of Mass Destruction?

Attitudes may be surprisingly resistant to new information. Since President George W. Bush declared the end of "formal hostilities" in Iraq in May 2003, a large number of surveys have documented a pattern of beliefs among partisans about the factual evidence for weapons of mass destruction, nuclear arms development, and Iraqi president Saddam Hussein's involvement in the attacks on September 11. A year later, Bush supporters disproportionately believed that Iraq had weapons of mass destruction and, to a lesser degree, that weapons of mass destruction had been found in Iraq. People not sympathetic to the president believed the opposite. As can be seen in Figure 7-2, views on the existence of weapons of mass destruction in 2004 were strongly associated with vote intention, partisanship, and ideological self-identification. The belief that Saddam Hussein was involved in September 11 showed a similar, if weaker, pattern.

Misinformation or ignorance usually is considered a result of apathy or inattention, but that is not always the case. Given what has been said so far, the expectation is that the better-educated and those more interested in politics would be less likely to believe that Iraq had weapons of mass destruction. For the whole sample this is true to a moderate degree, but it is solely a function of the supporters of Democratic presidential nominee John Kerry. Among Bush supporters, those who were highly attentive and least attentive to the election campaign were equally likely to believe there are weapons of mass destruction in Iraq. In Figure 7-3, the

FIGURE 7-2   Iraq Probably Does or Probably Does Not Have Weapons of Mass Destruction by Vote Intention, Party Identification, and Ideology, 2004

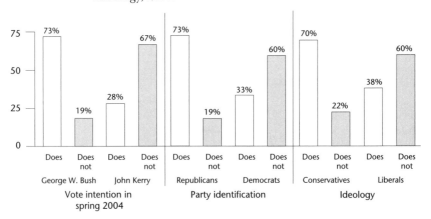

Source: CBS News/*New York Times* Monthly Poll, April 2004.

FIGURE 7-3   Percentages Believing Iraq Has Weapons of Mass Destruction
by Attention to the Campaign and Vote Intention, 2004

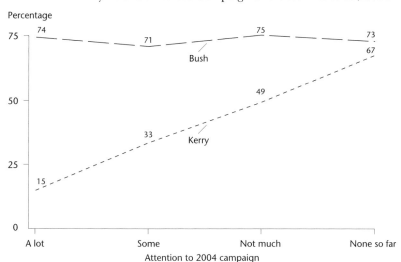

Source: CBS News/*New York Times* Monthly Poll, April 2004.

flat line at the top of the graph represents this lack of relationship. The Kerry supporters, represented by the sloping line, had different views depending on their level of interest in the campaign. The least attentive Kerry supporters had about the same views as the Bush supporters.

A study by PIPA (Program on International Policy Attitudes) shows some evidence of a relationship between viewing Fox News and believing that weapons of mass destruction have been found in Iraq.[22] A simple argument would be that Fox News' content led their audience to this belief. But that argument is too simple. Almost all of the Fox News audience also pays attention to media sources that offer a different perspective than Fox.[23] Why do these people appear to believe Fox News and not their other news sources? Even Fox News stories are not consistent in their bias.[24] Why do their viewers believe some stories but not others?

A more plausible explanation is that people who believe that weapons of mass destruction have been found in Iraq have characteristics that make them more likely to view Fox News. They may watch Fox News because they hope to view stories that will support their beliefs about weapons of mass destruction, but probably more general orientations, such as support for President Bush and the Republican Party, lead them to seek out Fox News as a conservative voice.

This pattern of behavior can be referred to as dissonance reduction. Because these individuals support Bush, who used the presence of weapons of mass destruction as a reason for going to war, accepting the idea that these weapons do not exist might create negative feelings toward Bush. To avoid the cognitive dissonance that would result, the individuals persist in believing that Iraq had such weapons.

Over time, it doubtless becomes more difficult to believe that Iraq had weapons of mass destruction and another dissonance reduction step might appear. One possibility would be changing the belief that the existence of weapons of mass destruction was a significant reason for going to war. Eventually President Bush and others offered the view that the reason for going to war was not weapons of mass destruction, but the removal of Saddam Hussein and the establishment of a democracy in Iraq. This might be considered an example of reducing dissonance through rationalization.

The Media and Presidential Approval Ratings

Presidential approval ratings, regularly measured by public opinion polling organizations, reflect both the effect media coverage can have on political attitudes and its limitations. Media polls regularly ask about and report on the public's views on how the president is handling his job.

The various polling organizations ask the question in different ways, but basically what they report, and what we report here, is the percentage of the public that approves of the way the president is doing his job—not the degree of enthusiasm people feel. The approval measure sometimes behaves oddly. For example, President Ronald Reagan's approval rating jumped 10 percent after he was shot, presumably an expression of sympathy and not an assessment of the job he was doing.

In one sense, the ratings are a function of media content, because media coverage is the only source of information about the president for most people. The most precipitous changes in approval ratings, though, result from dramatic and important events. Although the media coverage colors the recipient's perception of events, the media are usually not free to ignore them. The events themselves, not just the coverage, make them compelling.

Most presidents begin a term with high ratings, a phenomenon referred to as a "honeymoon effect." Presidents usually suffer a decline in approval ratings the longer they are in office. Not only are the ratings expected to decline over time, but, as the public becomes more knowledgeable about a president, the approval ratings also should become more stable and more retrospective. In other words, the more people know about the president, the less impact some new element of information has and the more their approval or disapproval represents a summary judgment. As this happens, the day-to-day events covered by the media, and the coverage itself, have less impact in shaping the attitudes of the public.

Extraordinary events can boost a president's popularity while in office. International crises usually produce an increase in approval ratings as the public rallies 'round the flag and its representative, the president. Winning a second term (or even campaigning for one), with the accompanying election fanfare, also lifts presidential approval scores. These boosts usually prove to be temporary, and popularity ratings usually drift downward again as time in office passes.

The approval ratings of both George Bush and George W. Bush illustrate the transitory nature of the increase in popularity associated with international crises. Both presidents' approval ratings improved dramatically during their respective wars in Iraq, both of which started far into their first term as president. Poll results varied, but generally the senior Bush received approval ratings as high as any president had ever received, approaching 90 percent. His son did not do as well, but his ratings went over 70 percent in early April of 2003.

In both cases their approval ratings began to fall immediately after the declared end of hostilities, for much the same reason initially. The public shifted its attention and concern away from war and to the economy. For the senior Bush the sagging economy drove his approval ratings down for the remainder of his presidency as the Persian Gulf War became irrelevant. By the fall of 1992, he was receiving ratings about as low as any past president.[25]

President George W. Bush found his approval ratings dropping because of the economy and because of the continuing insurgency in Iraq. His ratings dropped even further (to new lows) after Hurricane Katrina in the late summer of 2005. The approval ratings of both presidents follow a remarkably similar path over the course of their respective crises, as can be seen in Figure 7-4.

What happened to the two presidents' ratings illustrates the public's shifting focus on what matters in the assessment of the president. Throughout 1990, 1991, and 1992, President George Bush received low ratings for his handling of the economy, so when the economy mattered most to people, his overall approval ratings were low. During the Persian Gulf War, attention shifted to foreign affairs, an area in which Bush had always enjoyed high ratings, and this translated, for a while, into high overall approval ratings.

President George W. Bush had enjoyed very high approval ratings after September 11—almost as high as his father's after the Persian Gulf War. But by early 2003, the president's approval ratings had dropped 30 percent, back to their level before the terrorist attacks. Public attention on the military action in Iraq raised his job approval ratings about 20 percent. During the next year his ratings dropped to the point that

FIGURE 7-4   Approval Ratings of Presidents George Bush and George W.
                Bush before and after Middle Eastern Wars, August 1990 to
                January 1992 and October 2002 to March 2004

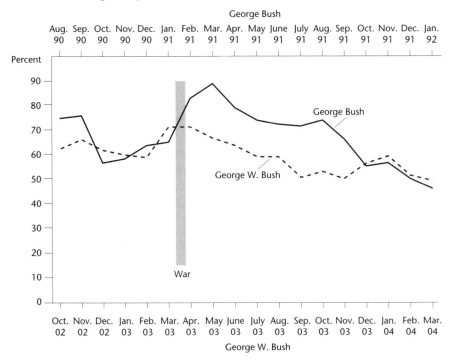

Source: CNN/ *USA Today*/Gallup Polls, available at www.pollingreport.com; and the Roper
Center at the University of Connecticut, available at web.lexis-nexis.com.

more people disapproved of the job he was doing than approved. As discussed in Chapter 6, when George W. Bush was able to refocus attention
on terrorism during the presidential campaign, his approval ratings recovered somewhat.

Figure 7-5 shows George W. Bush's approval ratings from the start
of his term until mid-2005. His ratings differ considerably depending
upon whether the question focused on his overall job performance or
his handling of the situation in Iraq or on the war on terrorism.

The trend of President Bill Clinton's approval is somewhat unusual
in that he managed to reverse a precipitous decline in popularity on the
basis of a confrontation in domestic politics, instead of an international
one. Clinton ended his term in office in January 2001 with approval ratings of 61 percent, unprecedented for a modern president at the end of
his second term. Commentators and politicians have asked repeatedly
how Clinton could maintain such high approval ratings when the pub-

FIGURE 7-5   Approval Ratings of President George W. Bush in Handling the Job as President, the War in Iraq, and Terrorism, 2001–2005

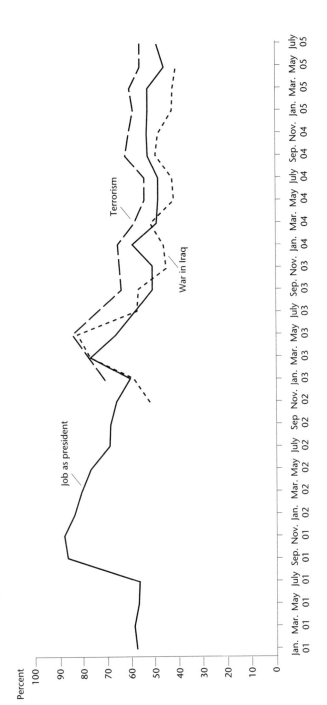

Percent

Source: CNN/ *USA Today*/Gallup Poll, available at www.pollingreport.com. The one exception is the May 2003 data on "terrorism," which came from a CBS News Poll, Roper Center for Public Opinion Research, accession number 0430556.

Note: The September 2001 poll was conducted immediately after September 11 terrorist attacks. The spike in all three lines in the spring of 2003 correspond with the "military phase" of the war in Iraq. The spike in January 2004 follows the capture of Iraqi president Saddam Hussein.

lic was thoroughly aware of his personal misbehavior and disapproved of it. An overwhelming majority of Americans thought Clinton lacked the ability to provide moral leadership for the country and that providing moral leadership was important for a president to do. The explanation, to the extent that one exists, appears to be another dissonance reduction device—compartmentalization. Republicans made the connection between personal misbehavior and the job Clinton was doing as president and reported their disapproval. Democrats and, to a lesser extent, independents did not link the two views. In July of 1998 a CBS News poll asked people whether they thought of "this whole situation (with Monica Lewinsky) more as a private matter having to do with Bill Clinton's personal life, or more as a public matter having to do with Bill Clinton's job as president."[26] Eighty percent of the Democrats and 68 percent of the independents—but only 37 percent of the Republicans—said they regarded this as a "personal matter."

Campaigns

Political campaigns are efforts to present candidates or issues to voters with information, rationales, characterizations, and images to convince them that one candidate or position is better than the alternatives and to get them to act on that preference. Massive amounts of money are spent in modern campaigns to saturate the airwaves in an effort to influence voters. A perennial question for politicians, political commentators, and scholars is, "How much difference does a campaign make?"

Although most professional politicians take for granted the efficacy of political campaigns, scholarly analysis has often questioned their impact. In most elections the majority of voters decide how they will vote before the campaign begins. Beyond this, the general low level of political information in the American electorate throws doubt on the ability of undecided voters to absorb ideas during a campaign. Andrew Gelman and Gary King have offered an especially interesting form of this argument.[27] They contend that a voter's eventual choice can be predicted satisfactorily at the start of a campaign, well before the candidates are even known. Furthermore, because a voter may move away from this ultimate choice during the course of a campaign, intermediate predictions, so popular in media coverage and campaign organizations, are misleading.

Other analysts, using economic forecasting models, argue that the outcome of the election—and the margin of victory—can be predicted well before the election campaign from such variables as the rate of economic growth, the inflation rate, and the unemployment rate.[28] That an individual voter's choice is determined at the start of a campaign may be difficult to believe. Yet evidence indicates that in most years the vote choices of most voters are not affected by the general election campaigns. The National Election Studies regularly asks voters when, during the presidential campaign, they made their voting decisions. Table 7-2 shows the time of decision for voters in the presidential elections of 1948 to 2004. In most years about two-thirds of the electorate decided before or during the conventions, with the final one-third deciding during the campaign. Over the years, fewer people report deciding during the conventions, presumably because, in recent decades, the candidates have essentially been chosen by the end of the presidential primaries in late spring.

The decision times of partisans and independents vary because the loyal party votes line up early behind the party's candidate. In all recent presidential elections, the independents and weak partisans were more likely to make up their minds during the campaign, whereas strong partisans made their decisions by the end of the conventions. Uncharacteristically, in 2004 well over half of the strong partisans made their decision before the conventions. More remarkably, barely half of the independents and weak partisans waited until the conventions or the general election campaign to make up their minds. Even so, many of the less committed partisans and independents are typically still undecided at the start of the general election campaign. In fairly close elections, this relatively uncommitted group can swing the election either way with 10 to 15 percent of the voters making a decision in the last days of the election campaign.

The possibility clearly exists that campaigning can influence a small but crucial proportion of the electorate, and many elections are close enough that the winning margin could be a result of campaigning. Professional politicians drive themselves and their organizations toward influencing undecided voters in the expectation that they are the key to providing, or maintaining, the winning margin. One can easily think of examples of elections in which the only explanation for the outcome was the aggressive campaign of one of the candidates. Multimillionaire publisher Steve Forbes could never have won the 1996 Republican presidential primaries in Arizona and Delaware without the expensive media advertising campaign he waged in those states. One can, however, just as easily think of examples of well-financed campaigns that failed. In early 1996 Sen. Phil Gramm of Texas raised more money and won fewer delegates than any other Republican presidential candidate. The simple, if unsatisfying, answer to the question "Do campaigns work?" seems to be "sometimes."

In this section we will explore the conditions under which campaigns, and the information they seek to convey, are likely to have the most impact. In general, the effect of information provided in a cam-

TABLE 7-2   Distribution of Time of Decision on Vote Choice for President, 1948–2004

Time of Decision	1948	1952	1956	1960	1964	1968	1972	1976	1980	1984	1988	1992	1996	2000	2004
Before conventions	37%	34%	57%	30%	40%	33%	43%	33%	42%	49%	32%	39%	49%	51%	56%
During conventions	28	31	18	30	25	22	17	20	17	16	28	14	13	10	14
During campaign	25	31	21	36	33	38	35	45	40	29	37	45	34	39	30
Don't remember, not ascertained	10	4	4	4	3	7	4	2	1	5	3	2	3	0	a
Total	100%	100%	100%	100%	101%	100%	99%	100%	100%	99%	100%	100%	99%	100%	100%
(N)	(424)	(1,251)	(1,285)	(1,445)	(1,126)	(1,039)	(1,119)	(1,667)	(958)	(1,376)	(1,209)	(1,684)	(1,171)	(566)	(799)

Source: National Election Studies, available at www.umich.edu/~nes.

[a]Less than 0.5 percent.

paign will depend on (1) the amount already known about the candidate (or issue), (2) the extent to which the information is countered by competing claims, and (3) the extent to which the information is in a form that resonates with the concerns and life experiences of the voter.

New information has the greatest impact in situations in which little is known about the candidate or issue and in which the voters have few existing attitudes. The application of this generalization can be seen in many areas. For example, the candidate who is less well known has the most to gain (or lose) from joint appearances, such as debates. The 1960 debates between Kennedy and Nixon, the first-ever series of televised presidential debates, appear to have had substantial impact on the election outcome, in large part because Kennedy was, at the time, not well known to the public. According to several different public opinion polls in 1960, about half of the voters reported that they were influenced by the debates in their evaluation of the candidates, with Kennedy holding an advantage of three to one over Nixon.[29] Although Nixon's poor showing is often blamed on his five o'clock shadow, it is unlikely that his appearance caused many to turn against him, because he had been in the public eye as vice president for eight years. Instead, Kennedy's advantage came from undecided Democrats who had little information about Kennedy (but were favorably disposed toward him because he was the Democratic candidate) and who were given a reason to vote for him by his attractive appearance and good performance. The immediate effect of the 1960 experience was the abandonment of presidential debates until 1976. Incumbent presidents or campaign front-runners were unwilling to offer such an opportunity to their lesser-known challengers.

Because new information has the greatest impact when little is known, voter preferences or opinions will be more volatile when candidates or public figures are not well known. Public opinion "trial heats" that are intended to gauge the preferences of the electorate during the course of the election campaign can be highly unstable when one or all of the candidates are not well known. In the spring and summer of 1992, Clinton was a virtual unknown to most voters, although he had already clinched the Democratic nomination for president. Perceptions of independent candidate Ross Perot were similarly vague, although he was recognizable as an eccentric billionaire. George Bush was, in contrast, well known to the public as the incumbent president and former vice president. Figure 7-6 shows the trial heat preferences of voters in Gallup polls during this period. The preferences for Clinton and Perot were extremely volatile and made additionally so by Perot's sudden exit from the race in July and equally sudden reentry in September. Although preferences for Bush were more stable, the changing set of alternatives with which he was compared made his support fluctuate as well. In contrast, the trial heat preferences for George W. Bush and John Kerry in the presidential race in 2004 from January to November were remark-

FIGURE 7-6   Trial Heat Results for the Presidential Elections of 1992 and 2004

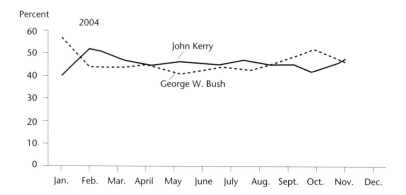

Source: CNN/ *USA Today* Gallup Polls, Roper Center for Public Opinion Research, available at web.lexis-nexis.com.

ably stable. Almost from the beginning the contest was too close to call. Although Senator Kerry was not particularly well known, it was well-developed reactions to Bush, both positive and negative, that created this stability. Polarization of opinion reduces the opportunity for campaigns to influence vote choice.

The second condition under which campaigns and the information they provide is most effective in influencing attitudes is when counter-information is not available. The obvious example is when one candidate has substantial resources for campaigning and the opponents do not. The well-financed candidate can present a favorable image of him- or herself—or an unflattering image of the opponent—without having those images contradicted. This situation is more likely to occur in primaries, when candidates must rely on their own funds and whatever they can raise from others, than in general elections, when both candidates can tap party resources. However, strategic decisions may also lead to a failure to counter information. In 2004, John Kerry delayed responding to the Swift Boat Veterans for Truth ads attacking his war record. The swift boat veterans had been following him with similar allegations for years. He may have underestimated their potential harm to him when these allegations were played on a national stage with higher stakes and with an audience less knowledgeable about him than his constituents as senator from Massachusetts.

In presidential elections, the national nominating conventions offer each party the opportunity, at least temporarily, to get its message to the public without the annoyance of sharing the stage with the other party. The televised acceptance speech of the nominee, the ability to showcase rising stars and celebrate past heroes, all before a prime-time audience, offer unique opportunities for the political parties to present themselves and their campaign themes as they wish the public to see them. Although the news media interject commentary and analysis, the media's view of what is interesting generally leads them to emphasize strategy and motives instead of outright contradiction of a party's claims. The result of this nationwide opportunity for favorable publicity is the convention "bounce" that presidential nominees typically receive in their approval ratings and trial heat results immediately after their party's convention.[30] In Figure 7-6, one can see George W. Bush's convention bounce at the beginning of September. Atypically, Kerry's campaign got virtually no bounce from the Democratic convention a few weeks earlier. If the Kerry vote was primarily an anti–Bush vote, Kerry supporters did not need the Democratic convention to tell them they were opposed to Bush.

The political parties have not always been able to use the nominating convention to their advantage. The battle-marred Democratic convention in 1968 and George McGovern's acceptance speech long after midnight in 1972 represent dramatic failures to use this opportunity to benefit the party's nominee. Opponents within one's party may present the case against a nominee as effectively as the opposing party could. In recent years, when the nomination has been a foregone conclusion months before the nominating convention, both parties have tried to control their conventions as tightly as possible, keeping controversial issues and personalities under wraps. However, as the conventions become more staged in an effort to promote the most favorable image of the candidate, the audience and the news coverage for them have shrunk, making it less likely that those images will be conveyed to the public. The shrinking number of voters who report making their decision during the conventions, shown in Table 7-2, reflects this new reality.

Another, less obvious, situation in which unchallenged information has an impact is when the characterizations of a candidate or issue are agreed on by all parties. If, for example, both candidates agree on which of them is liberal and which is conservative (although not on which position is "good" and which is "bad"), this information will be effectively conveyed to voters during the course of a campaign. An intriguing finding from a study by Thomas E. Patterson and Robert D. McClure in the Syracuse, New York, area in 1972 suggests that a major impact of television advertising may be on increasing voters' awareness of the issue stands of the candidates.[31] They concluded that television advertising contained more explicit information about the candidates' stands on issues than did news stories and had a correspondingly greater impact on voters' awareness of the issue positions of candidates. Television news stories were too brief and focused too much on campaign action to convey much issue information to the viewer.

In studying the 1976 election, Patterson found that the association between voters' issue positions and their candidate choices increased over the course of the campaign.[32] Voters in his sample did not appear to be persuaded to change their attitudes on issues by candidate appeals or to switch their vote choices. Instead, as they learned which positions the candidates took, voters discovered (in many instances) that they were closer to their preferred candidate. This finding might be used to argue that the campaign is a process of clarification, an articulation of issue linkages that were there all along.

A third factor affecting whether information in a campaign will have an impact on voter attitudes is the extent to which the voters accept the information as having relevance to their own concerns. In *The Reasoning Voter*, Samuel Popkin offers "Gresham's law of information," which states that small amounts of personal information drive out large amounts of impersonal information.[33] In other words, because personal information has more meaning to average voters—they use similar kinds of data every day in assessing friends and colleagues—they use such information about a candidate to make inferences about the kind of person that candidate is and how he or she will perform in office.

Information will also be more or less effective depending on the context in which the recipient receives or understands it. Cognitive psychologists use the concept of "framing" to study how people's preferences or decisions depend on the context or frame in which the alternatives are presented. For example, in the summer of 1979, in public opinion polls, Democrats preferred Sen. Edward M. Kennedy over President Jimmy Carter by a margin of three to one as their party's nominee for president.[34] By March 1980 Carter was ahead of Kennedy by two to one among Democrats.[35] Although a number of things had intervened between these times, an important element seems to have been reminding the voters of Senator Kennedy's involvement in the accidental death of Mary Jo Kopechne a decade earlier. When the voters' frame of reference was an unpopular president viewed as responsible for high inflation, Kennedy was an attractive alternative. Later, when Kennedy was framed as a fatally irresponsible playboy, Carter was preferred.

The fact that voters respond differently to information depending on its presentation offers opportunities for campaign managers to use sophisticated techniques to create favorable images of their candidates. Highly paid political consultants use an arsenal of social science knowledge and techniques in an attempt to do just that. Although some of these attempts have been notably successful, serious limitations also exist.

To successfully "sell" a candidate with advertising techniques, image makers must be able to control the information available about their candidate, thereby controlling the perceptions the voters hold about him or her. Reagan was more successfully handled in this way than most other presidential candidates. Perhaps his training as an actor made him more susceptible to management by his advisers. However, to a considerable degree, maintaining his public image depended on protecting him from the press and public exposure, not manipulating the content of publicity about him. This approach was especially effective in the campaign of 1980 when the focus of attention and public dissatisfaction rested on President Carter and not the challenger Reagan.

For most candidates, however, manipulating a public image by controlling information is either impossible or self-defeating. For a relatively unknown challenger, such as Michael S. Dukakis in 1988 or Clinton in 1992, this type of strategy would appear self-defeating because few candidates have had the resources to become well known nationwide through advertising and staged appearances alone. (Perot in 1992 was an exception.) Instead, unknowns must scramble for exposure in any forum they can find, and this prevents the careful manipulation of an image. Conversely, well-known candidates or incumbents, who can afford to sit back and let the public relations people campaign for them, probably already have images that are impossible to improve in any significant way over the relatively short period of time available in an election campaign. The most famous alleged attempt to repackage a candidate was the effort of the Nixon campaign staff in the 1968 presidential election.[36] However, the evidence suggests that more voters decided to vote for other candidates during the course of the campaign than decided to vote for Nixon. After about twenty years of nationwide public exposure, a "new Nixon" reinforced existing images, both negative and positive. He simply could not create a new, more favorable image.

Campaign organizations also attempt to affect the public image of their candidate by supplying the news media with information favorable to their candidates. If successful, this strategy can be particularly effective, because the information arrives through the more credible medium of news coverage, instead of paid advertising. Media events can be staged that provide the media, particularly television, with an attention-grabbing headline, sound bite, or photo opportunity. The campaigns of Nixon in 1968 and Bush in 1988 were particularly successful in manipulating news coverage favorable to their candidates by staging media events and otherwise limiting access to the candidates. In 2004 the campaign of George W. Bush went to great lengths to handpick the audiences at appearances of the president or vice president, thereby assuring the crowd would be enthusiastically supportive. In recent years campaign organizations have had difficulty in getting news stories aired or printed about their issue positions and policy stands, but they have had more success with negative stories and attacks on other candidates.

Another tactic is to seduce the media into covering paid political advertising as if it were news. In her book *Dirty Politics,* Kathleen Hall Jamieson details how, in 1988, the news media continually reinforced the premise behind the infamous Willie Horton ads that attacked Democratic candidate Dukakis's position on crime.[37] In 1992 and 1996, television and newspapers regularly featured ad watches that attempted to dissect the claims made in candidates' paid advertising, but in the course of doing so provided the ads with a wider audience.

Although selling a candidate by manipulating an image in a positive way may be difficult, a far greater opportunity exists to hurt an opponent's image through negative campaigning and advertising. In recent years candidates' campaigns and independent organizations have attacked the images of candidates in personal and political terms. The volume of this particular form of negative advertising, sometimes called attack ads, has increased greatly. Many of these ads are paid for by committees, interest groups, and organizations not connected directly to a candidate or a campaign. The swift boat ads that ran against Kerry in 2004 are an example. The Supreme Court has ruled that such attack ads are issue advocacy and therefore cannot be limited because of the First Amendment.[38] As a result, a candidate can be hit with a massive campaign that the opposing candidate need take no responsibility for and that is basically outside the regulations and agreements governing the candidates and their campaign organizations. Two generalizations about negative campaigning can be made: (1) The public disapproves of negative campaigning; and (2) even so, it sometimes works. Because the public disapproves of negative advertising, some candidates have managed to be positive in their own ads while allowing independent organizations to trash their opponents for them.

If negative campaigning illustrates the capacity to use the mass media to accomplish political purposes, the difficulty candidates have in using the media to respond to these attacks reveals its limitations. Victims of negative campaigning have tried to ignore the attacks, attempted to answer the charges, or counterattacked with their own negative campaign. None of these responses appears to be notably successful—a fact that encourages the continued use of negative campaigning. Attacks in the form of ridicule or humor may be particularly difficult to answer. Some strategists have urged the victims of negative campaigning to respond immediately and defend themselves aggressively. This may be good advice, but following it requires much from the victim. To respond promptly with advertising requires a great deal of money (perhaps near the end of a campaign when resources are limited) and a skilled staff. Moreover, victims of negative campaigning need to have a strong, effective answer to such attacks.

In their study of the 1992 presidential campaign, Marion R. Just, Ann N. Crigler, Dean E. Alger, Timothy E. Cook, Montague Kern, and Darrell M. West offer a useful way to look at the "construction" of a candidate's persona over the course of an election campaign.[39] Instead of the candidate's image being the creation of a campaign staff or the product of straight news coverage, it will evolve through the three-way interaction of the candidate's campaign, the news media, and the public. The candidates' initial attempts at establishing themselves face a range of reaction from press and public—encouragement, incredulity, boredom—and the candidates adjust accordingly. Likewise, the news reporters assess and react to the response of colleagues and the public to their coverage of candidates. Finally, the public's judgments in public opinion polls, radio call-in programs, live interviews, and e-mail indicate displeasure or support about the behavior of both candidates and news media. The final picture that emerges may not be a faithful reflection of the candidate's inner being, but neither is it an artificial creation of campaign technicians nor the distortion of an overbearing press.

Presidential Primary Campaigns

Because the impact of new information is greatest when there are few existing attitudes, the impact of campaigns should be greatest in primary elections, especially with little-known candidates. In primaries, when all the candidates are of the same party, the voter does not even have partisanship to help in the evaluation of candidates. In such situations, whenever new information is provided it can have a substantial impact.

After 1968 reforms in the presidential nominating process led to an increased use of presidential primaries as a means of selecting delegates to the Democratic and Republican nominating conventions. The purpose of the reforms was to make the choice of the presidential candidates more reflective of the preferences of the party's supporters in the electorate. In fact, the increased use of presidential primaries opened the door, at least initially, to the nomination of candidates little known to the general public. Political newcomers, such as Carter in 1976, Gary Hart in 1984, Steve Forbes in 1996, and Howard Dean in 2004, have an opportunity to focus their energy and campaign resources on a few early primaries or caucuses, gain national media attention by winning or doing surprisingly well in those early contests, and generate momentum to allow them to challenge more established and well-known potential nominees. Such candidates often do not have long-term viability. Their early appeal, based on little information, dissipates as more, often less flattering, information becomes available. Nevertheless, by the time this happens, the candidate may already have secured the nomination (Carter in 1976) or severely damaged the front-runner, as Hart damaged Walter F. Mondale in 1984. Primaries can do considerable damage to candidates' images under some circumstances. Well-known front-runners such as Bush in 1992 and Bob Dole in 1996 suffered a loss of popularity that they never recovered under the campaign attacks of fellow Republicans. Intraparty fighting is typically destructive for established candidates. Ever since 1972, segments of the Democratic Party expressed concern that the new reliance on presidential primaries was preventing the party from nominating its best or most electable candidates.

Before the 1988 election season, southern Democratic leaders decided that concentrating their states' primaries early in the election year would focus media and candidates' attention on the southern states as well as give a head start to more conservative candidates who could pick up a large bloc of delegate votes from these states. Although this strategy did not work in the short run—the Democrats nominated the liberal northeastern governor Dukakis in 1988—the creation of Super Tuesday considerably shortened the primary season by allowing candidates to amass enough delegates to secure the nomination months before the summer convention.

Every four years since 1988, additional states have moved their primaries forward, hoping to capture some media attention or, at least, to have a say before the nominations had been decided. This "front-loading" of primaries seems to have had the effect of favoring the front-runner and decreasing the opportunity for less well known candidates to ride favorable media coverage to the nomination. Because the primaries are so close together in time, candidates cannot concentrate their resources in a few states and use victories there to generate favorable coverage in other states. Instead, beginning in early March, candidates must campaign all across the country in many states. The unknown candidate has almost no time to capitalize on early success by raising money and creating state campaign organizations. Suddenly all the advantages are back with the established, well-known candidates.

In the presidential primaries of 2000, Republican John McCain challenged his party's front-runner with some success in a few early primaries. But quickly, the front-loading of the primaries took its toll. On March 7 alone, George W. Bush won 433 delegates to McCain's 113. With the next week's primaries mainly in the South where Texas governor Bush was expected to do well, McCain abandoned his challenge.

In 2004 Howard Dean broke new ground in his campaign for the Democratic nomination by using the Internet to raise a great deal of money and to create grassroots organizations across the country. Had he not self-destructed in Iowa, he might have set a new pattern for contesting multiple primaries at once. Instead, Kerry became the instant front-runner—with all the attendant news coverage and visibility—by virtue of his victory in the Iowa caucuses. With eight primaries coming up within two weeks, none of the other Democratic candidates could effectively challenge him. Kerry won all but one of those primaries and caucuses and was well ahead with 179 committed convention delegates. During the next month twenty states had primaries or caucuses with Kerry winning all but one. (Howard Dean won his home state of Vermont two weeks after his withdrawal from the race.) By early March all the meaningful challengers had withdrawn. In 2004 about three-fourths of the elected convention delegates had been chosen by the end of March. Not too many years ago, only one-third of the delegates were selected by then. Without intending to, state party leaders have moved the country close to a version of a national primary, in which candidates must campaign nationwide from the beginning.

The role of the news media in influencing presidential primaries with their coverage has changed as the format of the primaries has changed. In the 1970s and 1980s, the media had considerable potential to enhance one candidate's campaign momentum and to consign others to obscurity. Thomas E. Patterson's study of the role of the media in 1976 shows that, during the primaries, Carter benefited from the tendency of the press to cover only the winner of a primary, regardless of the narrowness of the victory or the number of convention delegates won.[40] Even the accident of winning primaries in the eastern time zone gave Carter disproportionately large, prime-time coverage on evenings when other candidates enjoyed bigger victories farther West.[41] This was possible because few voters were well informed about or committed to any of the many Democratic candidates. During the same period the media exaggerated the significance of President Gerald R. Ford's early primary victories without noticeably influencing the public's feelings about him or his challenger, then-governor of California Reagan.[42] It is much more difficult to influence voters who have well-informed preferences.

The "winner-take-all" commentary on the presidential primaries has been replaced in recent years by commentary on "unexpected" winners and losers. Attention focuses on who does much better or much worse than expected, regardless of the number of votes they receive. The most favorable coverage may be given to a second- or third-place finisher, and the real winner in terms of numbers of votes may be treated as a loser if he or she has not won big enough. The irony of this type of commentary is that it essentially converts the errors in the media's preelection coverage into newsworthy political change. With the front-loading of the primaries, however, media coverage becomes irrelevant after the first few primaries.

Inequality in the resources available to candidates in presidential primary campaigns has an effect and is likely to be greater than in the presidential general election in which an equal amount of public financing is available to both major-party candidates. Forbes's ability to pour massive amounts of personal funds into a few early primaries allowed him to win victories over Dole in South Carolina and Arizona in 1996. Forbes's similar strategy in 2000 failed, no doubt because the voters were more familiar with him after four years and thus less able to be impressed by an expensive television advertising campaign.

In the 2000 election campaign, George W. Bush raised more than $100 million, more money by far than any of the other candidates and more than twice as much as any previous candidates for president. He also raised his money early. Six months before the first primary, he had raised more than half his eventual total. This enormous war chest served both to discourage other potential candidates and to defeat his most serious rival for the nomination, John McCain. In contrast, in 2004, Howard Dean raised a large amount of money early, but ultimately it did him no good.

Campaign Strategy

Those attempting to communicate with the American public on political matters face an awkward dilemma. The attentive members of the public, the individuals most likely to receive political messages, are least likely to be influenced by one or a few items of information. Meanwhile, the individuals who are open to persuasion are uninterested in politics and not likely to pay attention to politics in the media.

In conclusion, we can use material from this chapter as a basis for generalizing about political communication and campaign effects from the perspective of a candidate. In political campaigns, candidates stand little chance of altering the electorate's issue preferences on policies that are sufficiently prominent to affect their vote choices. In the short run, to change individuals' preferences on issues that they care about is difficult by any means, and it is particularly difficult through the impersonal content of mass media. To change an individual's preferences or pattern of behavior, personal contact is more effective than the media. Therefore, vote choice or turnout is likely to be influenced, if at all, by an acquaintance of the individual.

To a limited degree, candidates can alter the prominence of a few issues for some segments of the public, but their capacity to increase or decrease the importance of issues is slight compared with what will happen in the ordinary course of events. For example, a candidate cannot make corruption in government a salient issue solely through his or her campaign, but a major scandal can make it an issue whether the candidates want it to be or not. Nevertheless, it is worth some effort to increase the visibility of issues that are expected to benefit the candidate, even though that effort will probably fail. It is also worth some effort to attempt to reduce the salience of issues that hurt a candidate, though, again, this strategy is not likely to succeed.

The public's perceptions of candidates' positions on issues are much more susceptible to change. News and advertising through the mass media can convey a considerable amount of information on issue stands and dramatize the differences between candidates. The more factual the information and the more the candidates agree on the respective characterizations, the more fully the information is absorbed by the public. This is the area of attitude change and public awareness in which candidates can accomplish the most.

In the final analysis, candidates are most interested in winning votes, regardless of how strong a preference each vote represents. But there are grounds for wanting large numbers of supporters with very strong preferences. Individuals with an overwhelming preference, holding no significant conflicting views, form the base of support for a candidate that yields campaign contributions and workers. These are the individuals all through society who casually influence the people around them to hold views favorable to a candidate. These are the opinion leaders who interpret and misinterpret the news on behalf of their candidate.

The more obviously partisan or one-sided the content of either media message or personal contact, the less likely it is to influence the uncommitted, not to mention the hostile. This poses a problem for the campaigner. Even though extreme messages are most likely to attract the attention of the relatively apathetic uncommitted voter, those same messages are least likely to get results. For this reason, in part, events dramatizing an issue can be valuable or damaging to a candidate. Events that affect a candidate's personal image are especially important because these perceptions are the most difficult to change through direct appeals in campaign advertising.

The overall implications of this discussion are several. A long time and probably noncampaign periods of low intensity are needed to switch individual issue stands or party loyalties. The media presentation and personal discussion of political and social conditions or events have a greater impact on attitudes than advertising or party contacts.

To a considerable degree, these generalizations about political influence and communication imply that, by the time a candidate wins nomination, he or she faces a constituency whose basic values and preferences can be changed only by events over which the candidate probably has little or no control. The only impact the candidate can have through campaigning is to make issue positions known as dramatically as possible and to contrast those positions with the opponents'. No candidate will know in advance what the net effect of these efforts will be, and most will never know. But most elections are contested under conditions that give one candidate a great initial advantage in the partisan loyalty and issue preferences of the constituency. The best chance for candidates is to exploit what they believe are their advantages, but in most cases the stable party loyalties and unchanging issue preferences of a constituency impose significant constraints on how much difference campaign strategies can make.

Speculation on the nature of political communication has ranged from alarm over the vulnerability of the mass public to manipulation through the media to annoyance at the difficulty of reaching the public. The American people make use of the mass media to inform themselves on matters of interest, but this does not mean that the public pays attention to everything in the media. Individuals have a remarkable ability to ignore information—a capacity as fully developed as the ability to absorb information. Influencing individuals on a subject about which they feel strongly is extremely difficult because they reject the media content, and influencing individuals on a subject about which they are indifferent offers problems because they ignore the media content.

Also, the media are difficult to use for manipulation because so many different points of view are found within the media. An extremely wide range of political perspectives is available to some degree in the mass media, although some perspectives are much more frequently available and more persuasively presented than others. The media in American society allow all views to enjoy some expression, although media coverage of many topics may be expressed in a manner favorable to some viewpoints and unfavorable to others. Disentangling the bias associated with the news and commentary in the media from the distortion found in the individual's reception of political information would be difficult. The public has a considerable capacity for ignoring media content or misinterpreting that content. Either of these conditions would be adequate to account for considerable discrepancy between political reality and the public image of that reality.

Notes

1. The classic statement on cognitive dissonance was Leon Festinger, *A Theory of Cognitive Dissonance* (Evanston, Ill.: Row, Peterson, 1957). For some of the most interesting experimental work in this field, see Milton J. Rosenberg, Carl I. Hovland, William J. McQuire, Robert P. Abelson, and Jack W. Brehm, *Attitude Organization and Change* (New Haven: Yale University Press, 1960).
2. Elihu Katz and Paul F. Lazarsfeld, *Personal Influence: The Part Played by People in the Flow of Mass Communications* (New York: Free Press, 1964).
3. Elisabeth Noelle-Neumann, *The Spiral of Silence* (Chicago: University of Chicago Press, 1984).
4. This well-known example is supported by remarkably little evidence. Seemingly the only data on the separate television and radio audiences are in an obscure report on surveys by Sindlinger and Co. of Philadelphia in *Broadcasting*, November 7, 1960, 28–30.
5. Pew Research Center for the People and the Press, "2004 Biennial Media Consumption Survey," April/May 2004, available at www.people-press.org.
6. Pew Research Center for the People and the Press, "2004 Biennial Media Consumption Survey."
7. Everette E. Dennis, *The Media Society* (Dubuque, Iowa: Wm. C. Brown, 1978), 37–41.
8. Michael B. MacKuen and Steven L. Coombs, *More Than News* (Beverly Hills, Calif.: Sage Publications, 1981).
9. Kathleen Hall Jamieson, *Dirty Politics: Deception, Distraction, and Democracy* (New York: Oxford University Press, 1992).
10. Pew Research Center for the People and the Press, "2004 Biennial Media Consumption Survey."
11. For an early statement of this point, see Bernard C. Cohen, *The Press and Foreign Policy* (Princeton: Princeton University Press, 1963).
12. Times Mirror Center for the People and the Press, "The People, The Press, and The War in the Gulf," January 31, 1991, available at people-press.org/reports/display.php3?ReportID=19919131.
13. Pew Research Center for the People and the Press, early April 2003 War Tracking Poll, available at people-press.org/reports/print.php3?PagesssID=699.
14. CBS News/*New York Times* Poll, press release, January 17, 1991, and CNN/*USA Today*/Gallup Poll, March, April, 2003, available at www.pollingreport.com.
15. See Dennis, *The Media Society*, chaps. 5, 7.
16. A variety of publications, including monthly reports, is available on the Web site of the Pew Research Center for the People and the Press at www.people-press.org.
17. These data on attention to news stories can be found in the "Hurricane Katrina Survey," September 6–7, 2005, at www.people-press.org.

18. Anthony Downs, *An Economic Theory of Democracy* (New York: Harper and Brothers, 1957).
19. Samuel Popkin, *The Reasoning Voter* (Chicago: University of Chicago Press, 1991), 47–49.
20. Thomas E. Patterson, *The Mass Media Election* (New York: Praeger, 1980), 14–15.
21. Philip Converse, "Information Flow and the Stability of Partisan Attitudes," *Public Opinion Quarterly* 26 (winter 1962): 578–599.
22. "Misperception, the Media, and the Iraq War," Steven Kull, principal investigator, Program on International Policy Attitudes and Knowledge Networks, October 2, 2003, available at www.pipa.org.
23. Pew Research Center for the People and the Press, "2004 Biennial Media Consumption Survey."
24. "The State of the News Media 2005," Project for Excellence in Journalism, available at www.stateofthemedia.org.
25. Pew Research Center for the People and the Press, "Modest Bush Approval Rating Boost at War's End, Economy Now Top National Issue," April 18, 2003, available at people-press.org/reports/display.php3?report ID=182.
26. CBS News Poll, July 30, 1998. Data provided by the Inter-university Consortium for Political and Social Research.
27. Andrew Gelman and Gary King, *Why Do Presidential Election Campaign Polls Vary So Much When the Vote Is So Predictable?* (Cambridge, Mass.: Littauer Center, 1992).
28. Michael S. Lewis-Beck and Tom W. Rice, *Forecasting Elections* (Washington, D.C.: CQ Press, 1992). These economic forecasts limit themselves to two-party races and cannot accommodate third-party candidates such as Ross Perot.
29. Recomputed from Elihu Katz and Jacob J. Feldman, "The Debates in the Light of Research: A Survey of Surveys," in *The Great Debates: Background, Perspective, Effects,* ed. Sidney Kraus (Bloomington: Indiana University Press, 1962), 212.
30. James E. Campbell, Lynna L. Cherry, and Kenneth A. Wink, "The Convention Bump," *American Politics Quarterly* 20 (July 1992): 287–307.
31. Thomas E. Patterson and Robert D. McClure, "Television News and Televised Political Advertising: Their Impact on the Voter," paper presented at the National Conference on Money and Politics, Washington, D.C., 1974; and Thomas E. Patterson and Robert D. McClure, *Political Advertising: Voter Reaction to Televised Political Commercials* (Princeton: Citizens' Research Foundation, 1973).
32. Thomas E. Patterson, "Vote Choice in the 1976 Presidential Primary Elections," paper presented at the annual meeting of the Southern Political Science Association, New Orleans, 1977.
33. Popkin, *The Reasoning Voter,* 73.
34. *Gallup Opinion Index* 183 (December 1980): 51.
35. "Opinion Roundup," *Public Opinion* 3 (April/May 1980): 38.
36. Joe McGinniss, *The Selling of the President* (New York: Trident Press, 1969).
37. Jamieson, *Dirty Politics,* chap. 1.
38. Whether this interpretation will change under the ruling in *McConnell v. FEC* is unclear as of late summer 2005.
39. Marion R. Just, Ann N. Crigler, Dean E. Alger, Timothy E. Cook, Montague Kern, and Darrell M. West, *Crosstalk: Citizens, Candidates, and the Media in a Presidential Campaign* (Chicago: University of Chicago Press, 1996).
40. Thomas E. Patterson, "Press Coverage and Candidate Success in Presidential Primaries: The 1976 Democratic Race," paper presented at the annual meeting of the American Political Science Association, Washington, D.C., 1977.
41. James D. Barber, ed., *Race for the Presidency* (Englewood Cliffs, N.J.: Prentice-Hall, 1978), chap. 2.
42. Patterson, *The Mass Media Election,* 130–132.

Suggested Readings

Graber, Doris. *Processing the News*. New York: Longman, 1988. An in-depth study of a few respondents on the handling of political information from the media.

Jamieson, Kathleen Hall. *Dirty Politics: Deception, Distraction, and Democracy*. New York: Oxford University Press, 1992. A blistering commentary on political advertising strategies and the interaction between advertising and news coverage.

Just, Marion R., Ann N. Crigler, Dean E. Alger, Timothy E. Cook, Montague Kern, and Darrell M. West. *Crosstalk: Citizens, Candidates, and the Media in a Presidential Campaign*. Chicago: University of Chicago Press, 1996. A multimethod study of the 1992 presidential election campaign.

Neuman, W. Russell, Marion R. Just, and Ann N. Crigler. *Common Knowledge*. Chicago: University of Chicago Press, 1992. An interesting analysis of mass media and political attitudes.

Patterson, Thomas E. *The Mass Media Election*. New York: Praeger, 1980. A major study of the impact of mass media on public opinion and voting behavior.

Popkin, Samuel L. *The Reasoning Voter*. Chicago: University of Chicago Press, 1991. A wide-ranging discussion of campaigning and presidential vote choice.

West, Darrell M. *Airwars: Television Advertising in Election Campaigns, 1952–2000*, 3d ed. Washington, D.C.: CQ Press, 2001. An interesting survey of political advertising over the years.

Internet Resources

The Web site for the Pew Research Center for the People and the Press, www.people-press.org, has both data and analysis of many topics covered in this chapter. For information, click on "Commentary," "Survey Reports," and "News Interest Index." Data are available for the most important items from past surveys.

During election years most major news organizations have Web sites with survey data on many political items.

Vote Choice and Electoral Decisions

THE CENTRAL FOCUS of research on American political behavior is vote choice, especially presidential vote choice. No other single form of mass political activity has the popular interest or analytic significance that surrounds the selection of a president every four years. Most Americans follow presidential campaigns with greater attention than they give other elections, and eventually about 50 percent of the electorate expresses a preference by voting. The results of presidential balloting are reported and analyzed far more extensively than any others. This chapter will explore the main determinants of vote choice and the interpretation of election outcomes in light of these determinants. We will attempt to generalize the discussion beyond presidential choice, but inevitably most of the illustrations are drawn from recent presidential election studies.

As seen in earlier chapters, party loyalty is a basic characteristic that influences many aspects of an individual's political behavior. In regard to vote choice, an individual's partisanship can be construed as a long-term predisposition to vote for one party or another, other things being equal. In other words, in the absence of any information about candidates and issues or other short-term forces in an election, individuals can be expected to vote according to their partisanship. However, to the extent that such short-term forces have an impact on them, they may be deflected away from their usual party loyalty toward some other action. The more short-term forces there are in an election—or the more a voter is aware of them—the less will be the impact of partisanship. This idea is crucial for understanding the relative impact of partisanship in different types of elections. In highly visible presidential elections, when information about candidates and at least some issues is widely available, partisanship will typically be less important to the voter's decision than in less visible races down the ticket. Furthermore, more potent short-term forces would be required to cause a very strong partisan to vote for another party than would be necessary to prompt a weak partisan to defect. An individual's vote in an election can be viewed as the product of the strength of partisanship and the impact of the short-term forces on the individual.

In most elections, both candidates and political commentators give their attention to short-term forces, such as the personalities of the candidates, issues, and the parties' records, because these elements might be modified by the actions of candidates and campaign strategies. Although in many respects partisanship is the most important element, it is taken as a constant because, in the short run, it is not likely to change. This chapter will consider the impact of the short-term forces of candidate image, current party images, and issues within a setting of stable party loyalties.

Candidate Image

The appeal of candidates has been given more attention in recent elections than any other short-term influence. During the past fifty years national samples have been extensively questioned about likes and dislikes concerning the presidential candidates. During this period several very popular candidates had extremely favorable images, and several others were rejected by the electorate largely on the basis of their personal attributes.

The specific content of candidates' images has varied greatly, and, as can be seen in Figure 8-1, no single pattern appears associated with either party. Perhaps the most prominent feature of this series is its downward trend. Presidential candidates of both parties are viewed far less favorably now than in the past. The disenchantment with government and politics, catalogued in Chapter 1, clearly extends to the personal images of the presidential candidates.

The form of analysis shown in Figure 8-1, which counts the number of positive and negative comments about the candidates in response to open-ended questions in the National Election Studies (NES) surveys, should be viewed cautiously because the relative seriousness of the complaints—for example, being too old versus being unprincipled—is not taken into account. In addition, the comments about the candidates are in response to a question about what the respondent likes and dislikes about the candidate. They range from comments on personal traits ("He's dishonest") to those removed from the personality of the candidate ("I like what he's saying about health care"). Although both are

FIGURE 8-1   Images of Presidential Candidates, 1952–2004

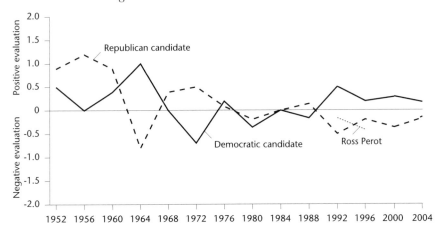

Source: Warren E. Miller and Santa Traugott, *American National Election Studies Data Source-book, 1952–1986* (Cambridge: Harvard University Press, 1989), 113, 115; and National Election Studies, available at www.umich.edu/~nes.

counted as reflecting feelings about the candidate's image, they are different in tone. Given the unusually high number of domestic issue–related comments about the Democratic candidates in recent elections, or the Iraq war mentions about Bush in 2004, care needs to be taken not to interpret candidate image as reflecting only personality traits.

Dwight D. Eisenhower in 1952 and 1956 and Lyndon B. Johnson in 1964 had positive images. Richard M. Nixon enjoyed a more favorable image than his opponents in 1960, 1968, and 1972. Although most American voters would ultimately revise their evaluations, Nixon in 1960 was more favorably perceived in personal terms than John F. Kennedy; his personal image rivaled Eisenhower's. Kennedy's image improved during his presidency, but his extraordinary popularity came after his assassination. Sometimes a candidate enjoys an advantage because the opponent is extremely unpopular. Johnson had such an advantage over Barry Goldwater in 1964, as did Nixon over George McGovern in 1972.

Despite his presumed personal popularity, Ronald Reagan received more negative than positive comments in 1980 and 1984. In both years a large share of the negative comments referred to his age. Although many people mentioned this point, it does not seem to have been an intensely unfavorable evaluation. Fortunately for Reagan, his opponents were viewed even more negatively.

In 1988 the images of George Bush and Michael S. Dukakis were evenly balanced, with Bush holding a slight advantage. By 1992 Bush's image had deteriorated to one of the worst in forty years; only Goldwater and McGovern had been viewed more unfavorably. Bush's reneging on his campaign promise of "read my lips, no new taxes" and his perceived responsibility for the bad state of the economy were the most damaging contributors to his image problem.

By contrast, Bill Clinton had, on balance, a positive image in 1992. He was not viewed so favorably in personality terms (for example, on traits such as honesty and experience or for his avoidance of military service during Vietnam), but this perception was more than offset by positive comments about his views on a wide range of issues. Respondents mentioned Clinton's positions on health care or the deficit as things they liked about him. By any standards, Clinton's image in 1992 was unusually issue-based.

In 1996 Clinton still enjoyed a favorable image, although not as favorable as in 1992. Positive comments about Clinton continued to focus on issues. His integrity was still questioned by significant numbers of respondents, and negative comments about first lady Hillary Rodham Clinton increased dramatically between 1992 and 1996. Bob Dole, Clinton's challenger in 1996, had a better image than Bush in 1992, but Dole was still seen more negatively than positively. Dole was seen as honest and experienced but, like Reagan, received many negative comments about his age.

Ross Perot was a significant factor in the election of 1992, less so in 1996, but he did not have a positive image in either election. In 1992 he was not particularly well known. He received positive comments about being a successful businessperson, but these were offset by negative comments about his lack of governmental experience. In 1996 he received almost no positive issue or governmental policy references, and comments about his personal characteristics were strongly negative. His temporary withdrawal from the race in 1992 continued to draw unfavorable comment in 1996.

In 2000 the public's overall evaluation of George W. Bush was balanced between positive and negative mentions of both personal qualities and issue positions. The slight negative balance overall resulted from the criticism that he favored big business and the rich. As his campaign intended, the positive issue responses were focused on taxes, abortion, and gun control. Al Gore was viewed more negatively than positively in personal terms, but, on issues, he was viewed much more positively than negatively. The favorable response to his issue stands on Social Security, health, and education more than offset his unfavorable personal image.

Bush's image improved slightly in 2004 but remained, on balance, negative. By far the most unfavorable mentions were about the war in Iraq. The reasons for liking Bush were mainly leadership qualities, such as strong and decisive, sincere, and principled. John Kerry's image was evenly balanced between positive and negative comments. The most frequent mentions were personal characteristics, not issue-related. It is indicative of the extent to which the 2004 election was a referendum on Bush that the single most frequent reason given for liking Kerry was a dislike of Bush. Kerry was frequently described as weak and indecisive in comparison with Bush. Reaction to Kerry's war record was evenly balanced between positive and negative.

A good deal of nonsense has been written in recent years about winning elections by manipulating the images of the candidates, mainly through the mass media. The implication has been that the images of candidates are easily created and altered, but, as discussed in Chapter 7, to do either is difficult, particularly with well-established candidates about whom voters are reasonably well informed. Campaigns do have some choices about raising particular issues, as, for example, the Kennedy campaign in 1960 had to decide whether to raise or not raise the issue of Kennedy's Catholicism—a factor that would generate both positive and negative reactions. But once such a decision is made, less leeway exists in controlling the impact of the issue. In most other cases, candidates have little control in deciding whether to raise certain topics, for often the opponent or the media will do so anyway.

An incumbent candidate or a former vice president benefits from a perception of being experienced, which is not purely a result of campaign advertising. Also, negative reactions aroused by being involved in an unpopular administration cannot be avoided. The public's impressions of candidates for major office seem to be realistic, gained primarily through ordinary news coverage. This is not to say that these images are accurate or fair or sophisticated, but they are not fictitious pictures created by public relations personnel. The Gore campaign's attempt in 2000 to redesign his personality throughout the campaign and especially before each debate failed utterly—but not disastrously. After eight years in the public eye, Gore's image as wooden and a bore could not be changed, but neither could the perception that he was smart and issue-oriented.

Unlike incumbents and established candidates, presidential candidates who are less well known have a greater opportunity to create a favorable image during the relatively brief period of the campaign. Conversely, such candidates are also more vulnerable to an attempt by an opponent to pin an unattractive image on them. In 2004 the Bush campaign was reasonably successful in creating an image of Kerry as flip-flopping on issues. Skillful manipulation of images was part of this success, but this was possible only because Kerry was not particularly well known.

Few candidates for other offices are as well known or as well publicized as candidates for the presidency. Most candidates in most elections are unknown quantities for the average voter. Typically, voters will be aware of the candidate's party affiliation and whether he or she is an incumbent, but not much more. In fact, these pieces of information may come to the attention of the voter only if they are indicated on the ballot.

Normally, the impact of candidate image on vote choice declines as one goes farther down the ticket to less visible and less well known offices. This does not mean that the candidate's personal qualities are unimportant in winning election to these offices. They may be of paramount importance in obtaining the nomination or endorsement of the party organization, in raising financial support, in putting together a campaign staff, and in gaining backing from the leadership of influential organizations. But these personal attributes are unlikely to influence the decisions of the average voter simply because the voter is unlikely to be aware of them.

Party Image

The images of the parties are another factor that can influence the voting decisions of the electorate. Even though party images are strongly colored by long-standing party loyalties, the focus of this analysis is a set of potentially variable attitudes toward the parties that can be viewed as short-run forces at work in an election. These attitudes usually have to do with the ability of the parties to manage government, to keep the economy healthy, and to keep the country out of war. Party images also affect and are affected by the images of the candidates running under the party label and by the attitudes toward issues espoused by the candidates or the party platforms. These factors can be kept distinct conceptually, though disentangling the effects may be impossible in any actual situation.

Traditionally, the Republican Party has been viewed as the party best able to keep the country out of war; the Democratic Party held a similar advantage as the party of prosperity. Figure 8-2 shows the trends in these party images in recent years. The Democrats briefly lost their traditional advantage as the party best able to handle the economy in 1994; the Republicans lost their foreign affairs advantage in 2000 and beyond. The post–September 11 atmosphere has created a paradox. The Republican Party is seen as best able to handle the threat of terrorism, even as it is seen as less able to keep the country out of war. However, a large proportion of the electorate does not perceive a difference between the parties on these items.

The role of party images in vote choice has been labeled "retrospective voting" by Morris P. Fiorina, who argued that voters continuously evaluate the performance of the political parties, especially the

FIGURE 8-2   Party Better Able to Handle the Nation's Economy and Keep the Country out of War, 1988–2004

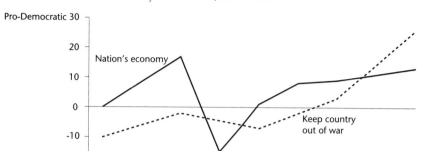

Source: National Election Studies, available at www.umich.edu/~nes.

Note: The data points in the figure represent the percentage of respondents answering "Democrats" minus the percentage answering "Republicans."

president's party.[1] Voters use the evaluation of past performance as an indicator of future performance, and they take this retrospective assessment into account in making their vote choices. Because these assessments are likely to involve the performance of the current administration, questions about the incumbent president's handling of certain policy areas have been used as indicators of the extent of retrospective voting. In a sophisticated analysis of presidential voting in 1988, J. Merrill Shanks and Warren Miller demonstrated that voters' approval or disapproval of Reagan's performance as president had a noticeable impact on the choice between Bush and Dukakis.[2] In both 1992 and 1996 there was an incumbent president to be evaluated as he ran for reelection. President Bush had very low evaluations in 1992, which had a disastrous impact on his reelection prospects. It was just the opposite in 1996 for President Clinton, who came into the race with fairly positive evaluations. In 2004 George W. Bush's approval ratings offered a mixed bag. His negative ratings on handling the economy and the war in Iraq were offset by positive evaluations of his handling of the threat of terrorism (as will be seen in Table 8-6).

Party images and presidential evaluations are strongly related to partisanship, with partisans more likely to embrace positive images of their party and to reject negative ones than independents or partisans of the opposition. Partisanship and party image, however, are not synonymous, because individuals often hold unfavorable perceptions of their party without changing party identification. Yet, at some point, negative images of one's own party or positive perceptions of the other party undoubtedly lead to partisan change.

The images of local or state parties may be considerably different from and independent of those of their national counterpart. A state or local party organization may be perceived in different terms from the national party, and many a local or state party has gained a reputation for ineptitude or corruption that did not influence voting decisions for national offices. At the same time, such local images may become increasingly important in voting for offices at lower levels because party labels become a more important identifying characteristic in those races.

Issue Impact

Candidate images and party images may be closely related to issues, and under some circumstances they are indistinguishable. The perception of the stands of candidates and parties on issues is a basis for making vote choices, a basis usually distinct from either personality characteristics or long-standing symbolism. Most significant, candidates can establish issue positions or alter their appeals through their presentation of issues in ways that are not applicable to personal images or party characteristics. In the short run, candidates cannot change their job experience or religion or party, but they can take new stands on issues or attempt to change the salience of issues. Therefore, candidates can attempt to appeal for votes on the basis of issues.

Over the years, considerable commentary has focused on the rise of single-issue voting. Collections of voters, caring intensely about a particular issue, vote for whichever candidate is closest to their views on that issue, regardless of the candidate's party, personal characteristics, or positions on other issues. There is nothing new about this phenomenon. The classic example of single-issue voting in American politics was abolition, an issue of such intensity that it destroyed the Whig Party, launched several new parties including the Republican Party, and was a major contributing factor to the Civil War. Abortion is currently an issue that determines the way many people will vote.

Although organizational sophistication and increased opportunities for dissemination of information make single-issue groups a potent force in American politics today, politically ambitious candidates have always searched for issues of this type to help them gain a following. At the same time, incumbent candidates and the broadly based political parties have seen advantages in avoiding or glossing over such issues. Intense concentration on a single issue is potentially divisive and damaging to parties that must appeal to a broad range of voters or to those in office who must cast votes on a wide range of issues. Nevertheless, the political opportunity for the candidate who can capture a group of vot-ers willing to vote on the basis of a single issue or cluster of issues is so great that it is unlikely that any intense concern in the electorate will be long ignored.

Several characteristics of electoral behavior conflict with this de-scription of the role of issues in influencing vote choice. For one thing, in most elections many voters are unaware of the stands taken by candi-dates on issues. Voters commonly believe that the candidates they sup-port agree with them on issues. This suggests that voters may project their issue positions onto their favorite candidate more often than they decide to vote for candidates on the basis of their position on issues. Fur-thermore, when voters agree on issues with the candidate they support, they may have adopted this position merely to agree with their candidate. Candidates and other political leaders frequently perform this function for members of the electorate; they provide issue leadership for their fol-lowing. Within the enormous range of possible issues at any given time, complete indifference to many is common. Most issues important to po-litical leaders remain in this category for the general public.

The extent to which voters are concerned with issues in making vote choices is a subject of considerable debate. Several prominent scholarly efforts were designed to rescue the voter from an undeserved reputation for not being issue-oriented.[3] *The Changing American Voter,* by Norman H. Nie, Sidney Verba, and John R. Petrocik, documents a rise in issue voting associated with the election of 1964.[4] According to their data, the correlation between attitudes on issues and vote choice peaked in the ideological Johnson-Goldwater campaign but remained through 1972 at a considerably higher level than in the "issueless" 1950s. More recently, in a thorough assessment of the impact of issues in the elec-tions of 1988 and 1992, J. Merrill Shanks and Warren E. Miller found relatively low levels of issue impact.[5]

TABLE 8-1   Presidential Vote and Attitude toward Government
             Services, 2004

	Decrease government services	←	Neutral	→	Increase government services
John Kerry	14%	28%	43%	70%	78%
George W. Bush	86	72	57	30	22
Total	100%	100%	100%	100%	100%
(*N*)	(88)	(114)	(238)	(156)	(106)

Source: 2004 National Election Study, available at www.umich.edu/~nes.

TABLE 8-2   Presidential Vote and Attitude toward Government Help for Blacks, 2004

	Government help for blacks	←	Neutral	→	Let blacks help themselves
John Kerry	89%	76%	60%	39%	28%
George W. Bush	11	24	40	61	72
Total	100%	100%	100%	100%	100%
(N)	(90)	(67)	(177)	(126)	(245)

Source: 2004 National Election Study, available at www.umich.edu/~nes.

In 2004, as in most years, a fairly strong relationship existed between a domestic issue such as increasing or decreasing government services and the vote for president. As can be seen in Table 8-1, those who favored decreasing governmental services and spending voted overwhelmingly for Bush over Kerry. Those voters who favored increasing services and spending preferred Kerry over Bush by a sizable margin.

On another domestic issue—whether the government should help blacks versus letting blacks help themselves, shown in Table 8-2—a similar liberal-conservative relationship exists. Those people who favor government programs to help blacks voted overwhelmingly for Kerry over Bush 89 to 11 percent. The voters who said blacks should help themselves favored Bush 72 to 28 percent.

Because both these issues deal with themes that have long divided the parties, it is not surprising that substantial relationships exist between holding a certain view and supporting a particular candidate. The issue of abortion has not always been so closely related to vote choice. The strong relationship found in 2004 and shown in Table 8-3, also true

TABLE 8-3   Presidential Vote and Attitude toward Abortion, 2004

	Pro-life ←		→ Pro-choice	
John Kerry	33%	41%	42%	68%
George W. Bush	67	59	58	33
Total	100%	100%	100%	101%
(N)	(96)	(249)	(138)	(289)

Source: 2004 National Election Study, available at www.umich.edu/~nes.

TABLE 8-4   Presidential Vote and Attitude toward the War in Iraq, 2004

	War in Iraq increased threat of terrorism	Same	War in Iraq decreased threat of terrorism
John Kerry	75%	48%	16%
George W. Bush	25	52	85
Total	100%	100%	101%
(*N*)	(307)	(268)	(207)

Source: 2004 National Election Study, available at www.umich.edu/~nes.

in 2000, suggests increasing polarization between the major parties on social issues. Bush's support was higher on the pro-life side of the issue; Kerry drew more votes from the pro-choice side. Respondents taking the two moderate positions on the abortion issue show no difference in their vote choice for president.

One of the questions asked in the 2004 National Election Study was whether people thought the war in Iraq increased or decreased the threat of terrorism. Table 8-4 shows a strong relationship between people's perceptions of the Iraq war and their vote for president. Those who saw the war as increasing the risk of terrorism voted solidly for Kerry; those who saw Iraq as decreasing the threat of terrorism voted overwhelmingly for Bush.

Figure 8-3 looks at vote choice in a somewhat different manner by illustrating the electorate's perceptions of the ideological positions of Bush and Kerry, as well as the relationship between the voters' own ideological positions and their vote choices between the two candidates. In the 2004 National Election Study survey, voters were asked to locate each candidate on a seven-point scale ranging from "extremely liberal" to "extremely conservative." In Figure 8-3 the frequency distributions in the lower half of the chart illustrate the voters' perceptions of the two candidates' ideological positions. For example, 17 percent of the respondents labeled Kerry as extremely liberal, and only 3 percent labeled him extremely conservative. Twenty-one percent placed Bush in the most extreme conservative position. (This is an increase from just 9 percent who labeled him extremely conservative in 2000.) Most voters placed Kerry on the liberal end of the scale and placed Bush on the conservative side.

Voters were also asked about their own ideological position using the same seven-point scale. The distributions in the upper half of Figure 8-3 indicate the self-placements of those who voted for Bush and Kerry. They show that Bush drew most of his support from conservative voters,

FIGURE 8-3   Vote for President according to Voters' Ideological
                        Identification and Perceptions of Candidates' Ideology, 2004

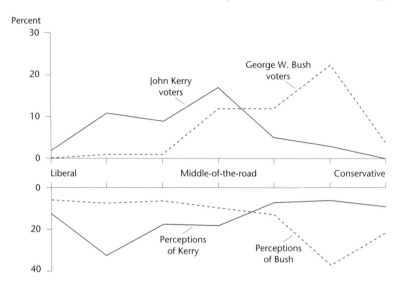

Source: 2004 National Election Study, available at www.umich.edu/~nes.

and Kerry received most of his from liberals. Kerry also gained a greater share of the votes of those in the middle of the ideological spectrum. Figure 8-3 also reinforces a point made earlier. The electorate sees itself as more middle-of-the-road than they see the leaders of the respective parties. The parties may be polarized, but the electorate is not.

A number of factors must be present for issues to have an impact on vote choice. First, voters must be informed and concerned about an issue; second, candidates must take distinguishable stands on an issue; and third, voters must perceive the candidates' stands in relation to their own. These conditions often are not achieved. Voters may be unable to locate themselves or the candidates on one or more issues. In 2004, 14 percent of the electorate had no opinion on the issue of cutting government services and spending versus increasing government spending and services. An additional 6 percent were unable to locate the position of either Bush or Kerry on this issue. Similar proportions of the electorate could not locate themselves or the candidates on the issue of defense spending. Voters may misperceive the candidates' positions. For example, a few voters viewed Kerry as an extreme conservative or Bush as an extreme liberal, although most perceptions appeared accurate.

A weak relationship between an individual's issue positions and vote choice may result from the fact that the analyst chooses the issues for analysis, and these might be issues that are not important to the individual. If the voter is allowed to define what he or she sees as the most important issue, a somewhat stronger relationship between his or her position on issues and voting decisions is found.[6] Others have argued that a rational and issue-oriented voter judges the past performance of the candidates instead of simply comparing the candidates' promises for the future.[7]

This analysis also does not reveal what causes these relationships. Perception of issues may cause an individual's vote choice. Alternatively, a preference for a candidate on other grounds may lead individuals to adjust their perceptions of issues in support of their vote choice. No data are available that would conclusively resolve this question. Regardless of the causal relationship, it is significant that, although many voters lack opinions on issues or on the candidates' positions, those who do have opinions show considerable consistency between issue positions and vote choice.

Determinants of Vote Choice

The preceding sections considered candidate images, party images, and issues as short-term forces that either reinforce or deflect voters from their long-term party loyalty. An interesting, but far more difficult, question is the relative impact of these factors on vote choice. Because all these factors are strongly interrelated and almost certainly all influence each other, disentangling their effects with the kind of data available in nationwide surveys is virtually impossible. If one assumes that issues are all-important in determining vote choice, most voting behavior can be accounted for by issues alone, ignoring other factors. However, if one assumes that party identification and a few social characteristics are all-important, most voting behavior can be accounted for with these variables, ignoring issues. The conflicting conclusions that are reached are largely a matter of the theoretical assumptions with which one starts.

In light of these difficulties, some analysis of the impact of short-term forces has focused on the unique impact of each element in the presence of others. One of the best examples of this mode of analysis is Donald E. Stokes's effort to measure attitudinal forces influencing presidential vote choices.[8] Following Stokes's method, Arthur H. Miller and Martin P. Wattenberg have analyzed the nine presidential elections from 1952 to 1984 (see Table 8-5).[9] Negative values indicate a factor that helped the Democratic candidate; positive values indicate a benefit to the Republican candidate. The perception of group benefits is a consistently large pro-Democratic element in all nine elections. Foreign policy matters have almost always helped the Republican candidate, with the exception of Goldwater in 1964 and Reagan in 1984. The impact of foreign affairs and domestic policies was unusually strong and pro-

TABLE 8-5   Net Impact of Six Attitudinal Components in Determining Vote Choice, 1952–1984

	1952	1956	1960	1964	1968	1972	1976	1980	1984
Domestic policy	-1.3	-0.9	-0.5	-2.4	1.1	1.4	-0.7	3.1	1.5
Foreign policy	3.3	2.5	1.8	-0.3	1.0	3.2	0.4	2.8	-0.3
Party management	5.4	1.2	1.2	-0.3	1.5	0.0	0.2	0.6	0.5
Group benefits	-4.3	-5.5	-4.0	-2.6	-3.6	-4.6	-4.5	-4.5	-5.6
Democratic candidate	-1.2	0.2	-2.0	-4.0	0.9	4.3	-0.1	-0.4	1.3
Republican candidate	4.4	7.6	5.7	-2.6	1.6	4.0	2.2	-0.5	1.5

Sources: For 1952–1980, Arthur H. Miller and Martin P. Wattenberg, "Policy and Performance Voting in the 1980 Election," cited in *Controversies in Voting Behavior*, 2d ed., ed. Richard Niemi and Herbert Weisberg (Washington, D.C.: CQ Press, 1984), 91; for 1984, Martin P. Wattenberg (personal communication).

Note: Positive values are pro-Republican effects; negative values indicate a Democratic advantage. The values can be interpreted as the percentage of the vote moved in one partisan direction or the other.

Republican in 1980. This reflected the strongly unfavorable reactions to Jimmy Carter's handling of the economy and the Iranian hostage crisis. At the same time, the candidates' personalities had an unusually weak influence on vote choice in 1980. In contrast, in 1984 foreign and domestic policy considerations had declined in importance, but the personalities of the candidates had become significantly pro-Republican factors.

Shanks and Miller published a much more complex analysis of the 1988 and 1992 presidential elections in *The New American Voter*. Their results cannot easily be compared with the work of Stokes and others in Table 8-5, but overall they argue for the importance of long-standing predispositions and retrospective evaluations in contrast to issues and personality traits.

In Table 8-6 we offer an analysis of the determinants of the choice between George W. Bush and John Kerry in 2004. For simplicity, we consider only seven possible determinants of vote choice. The first column of the table shows the strength of the relationship between the variable and vote choice. The higher the coefficient is, the greater the impact on the individual's choice. The other columns are the net benefits of that variable to a candidate, similar to the estimates given for earlier elections in Table 8-5.

As can be seen in Table 8-6, party identification is the factor most strongly related to the choice between Bush and Kerry, indicating a high degree of party loyalty at work in the 2004 election. At the same time,

TABLE 8-6   Determinants of Presidential Vote Choice, John Kerry versus George W. Bush, 2004

	Strength of relationship	Net shift of votes	
		Pro-Kerry	Pro-Bush
Party identification	0.28		2%
Ideological identification	0.00		
Bush's handling of the economy	0.23	1%	
Bush's handling of Iraq	0.26	2	
Bush's handling of the war on terror	0.16		3
Policy positions			
Government services and spending	0.08	1	
Gay marriage	0.05		1

Source: 2004 National Election Study, available at www.umich.edu/~nes.

Note: Standardized partial regression coefficients are used to represent the strength of relationship between each variable and presidential vote choice controlling for the other variables. Multiple R-squared is 0.78. These variables correctly predict 95 percent of the votes.

because party identification is so evenly balanced, it produced only a small net gain for Bush. More noteworthy than the size of the net gain is that it benefited the Republican candidate. In similar analysis in previous years, party has always benefited the Democratic candidate.

The three assessments of Bush's handling of his job as president account for most of the remaining impact on vote choice in 2004. The second strongest determinant is the impact of attitudes toward Bush's handling of Iraq. Although, on balance, this favored the Democratic candidate, here again, the issue cut both ways and the net advantage to Kerry was small. In contrast, attitudes toward Bush's handling of the war on terror contributed more toward Bush's victory, even though it was less strongly related to vote choice, because reactions to Bush's handling of the threat of terror where more uniformly positive toward him.

During the conventions and the brief period of the general election campaign, political parties cannot do much about the basic strength each party commands. Therefore, they concentrate on presenting candidate images and issue positions calculated to have greatest appeal to the uncommitted voters. Even if the outcome of an election is not substantially affected by party strategies, the content of the campaign and the meaning the election comes to have for leaders and the public are created by these strategies. The information in Tables 8-5 and 8-6 can be viewed as measures of the content of the campaign and its meaning for voters.

Who Switched Their Votes between 2000 and 2004?

The presidential elections of 2000 and 2004 were exceedingly close but with different results in the popular vote. In 2000 the Democratic candidate won the popular vote by about 500,000 votes (and lost the electoral college by four votes). In 2004 George W. Bush won the popular vote by three million votes (and the electoral college by thirty-five votes). The inevitable question is: Who switched?

The 2000 and 2004 representative national samples surveyed by the NES contained within them a panel study, in which respondents from 2000 were reinterviewed in 2004. Ninety percent of those who voted in both 2000 and 2004 supported the same party for president in each election. Half of these party loyal voters voted for Bush twice, the other half voted for Al Gore in 2000 and Kerry in 2004. This is a high degree of party loyalty in presidential voting, probably the highest in more than a half century.[10]

While the voters who switched sides are not a large group to study, it is fairly easy to characterize them. As might be expected, those who switched were much more likely to be independents than partisans. The switchers were also nonideological. Those who switched away from Bush between 2000 and 2004 strongly disapproved of the job he was doing as president and also disapproved of his handling of the war in Iraq. Those who switched to Bush after having voted for Gore in 2000 were overwhelmingly approving of Bush on both counts. In other words, the switchers were moderate independents who treated the 2004 election as a referendum on Bush's performance. The number of switchers was small, but about twice as many voters switched from Gore to Bush as switched from Bush to Kerry. Oddly, most of the switchers were in safe Democratic and Republican states, not the battleground states that were so heavily targeted by the candidates' campaigns.

People who switched their votes were not the only source of change between the two elections. Both parties tried to mobilize voters who had failed to vote in 2000. Some of this occurred and slightly favored Bush. In particular, Bush campaign officials believed he lost the popular vote in 2000 because white fundamentalist and evangelical Protestants did not fully support him. In 2004 great efforts were made to turn out those voters and win their support. The efforts were successful on both counts. Turnout among white fundamentalist and evangelical Protestants was up 10 percent over 2000 and support for Bush in this group increased from 65 percent to 78 percent. Over half of this group is found in safe Republican states in the South, so the strategy was designed to increase the popular vote, not the electoral college vote.

Young voters who were able to vote for the first time are another source of new votes, and Kerry had a slight edge among this group. Another possibility is to demobilize one's opponent's voters. This may have been attempted in 2004, but no evidence of it appears in the National Election Study. Virtually no participant in the 2000 election sat out in 2004.

The Popular Vote and the Electoral College

In 2000, for the first time in more than one hundred years, the electoral college chose a president who was not the winner of the popular vote. In 2004 the possibility loomed again, although it did not happen — in part because of Republican strategists' efforts to mobilize extra voters in safe Republican states to prevent a second popular vote loss for Bush. In a system that purports to be a democracy, it is a significant occurrence when the candidate with fewer votes is declared the winner. How did this happen in 2000? What, if anything, is likely to be done to change the system so that it does not happen in the future?

Under the constitutional system adopted in 1787 and amended in 1804, the president is selected by the electoral college, with each state having electoral votes equal to the combined seats that it has in the U.S. House of Representatives and Senate. Voters cast a ballot for one or the other party's presidential and vice presidential nominees. Legally, however, the voter is casting a ballot for that party's slate of electors, which was certified months before by the party's formal submission of the slate to a state official. The electors of the winning party in each state meet in their respective state capitals on the Monday following the second Wednesday in December and cast their votes for president and vice president. Almost without exception they respect their pledge and vote for their party's nominees. A majority of the electoral votes is required to elect a president—270 electoral votes at this time.

To understand how the electoral college could produce a winner who is not the popular vote winner, it is important to remember that all states (except Maine and Nebraska) use a winner-take-all procedure for deciding who wins the states' electoral votes. In other words it does not matter whether a candidate wins the state narrowly or by a wide margin, all of the electoral votes go to the winner. If one candidate wins many states narrowly and the other candidate wins states by a wide margin, the first candidate can win in the electoral college while the second candidate can have more popular votes. Usually the second candidate is said to have wasted votes by winning by a larger margin than needed to carry the state.

In 2000 Gore won by large margins in a number of big states such as California and New York, accumulating a huge number of popular votes, while George W. Bush won some big states, such as Florida, narrowly. In 2000 another factor was at work to a degree. Bush won a large share of the small states, in which the two electoral votes assigned to every state to represent their seats in the U.S. Senate create something of a bonus. If turnout is comparable, each electoral vote in a small state represents fewer voters than in a large state. In 2000 each electoral vote in Wyoming represented 70,000 popular votes and in California each electoral vote represented more than 200,000 popular votes.

Although only rarely does the electoral college produce a winner who has not won the popular vote, the consequences of a winner-take-all system are well known to campaign strategists in presidential elections. The electoral college arrangement strongly influences presidential campaign strategy. The closer the expected margin in a state and the larger the number of electoral votes available, the more resources the campaigns will put in the state and the more aggressively the candidates will attempt to respond to the political interests in the state. These are the battleground states, where both candidates have a chance to win and much is at stake. In contrast, safe states are relatively unimportant to both candidates in a general election campaign—taken for granted by one and written off by the other—although they may be visited by one or both candidates to raise funds to spend in competitive states. The

2000 presidential election was deceptive in making every state appear crucial because the result was so close, but, in fact, a winning strategy in this and other presidential elections calls for slighting most states.

In retrospect, it may seem odd that the founders created such a peculiar scheme for selecting a president. Their main concern was to devise a method for selecting the president that would result in the selection of George Washington as the first president. The allocation of electoral votes simply combined the state representation in the Senate and the House of Representatives, an easy decision after the Great Compromise had been reached. In the context of the Constitutional Convention, the electoral college had another virtue: It treated the states as they viewed themselves—as sovereign entities. In the current climate, retaining the states as meaningful units in a federal system is one rationale for maintaining the electoral college.

The fact that the electoral college was extremely indirect democracy was not a concern for the founders. Most of the founders were wary of too much democracy, thus having state legislatures select the electors had appeal. The founders did not anticipate the emergence of political parties that quickly changed the process of selecting electors into intense partisan conflict. By 1824 most state legislatures had turned the selection process over to the public to avoid the political hassle.

Over the years, proposals have been put forth to change or abandon the electoral college.[11] Some proposals are modest, such as getting rid of the slate of electors (who occasionally do not vote the way they are pledged) and have the secretary of state simply certify each state's electoral votes. Proponents of greater change have resisted this proposal, though in itself noncontroversial, for fear that adopting it would reduce the incentive to make more substantial changes in the system.

The most sweeping proposal, and the one most commonly discussed by political commentators, would be the substitution of a nationwide popular election for the electoral college. This is an obvious alternative method of selecting the president, answering the main criticism of the electoral college—the potential (which was realized in 2000) that the popular vote winner is not the electoral college winner. A nationwide popular election, however, has problems of its own. It is generally believed that a national popular election would attract more and more candidates—third-party candidates, independent candidates, and major-party candidates who failed to get their party's nomination. Candidates with a small but crucial constituency could threaten to take votes away from the major-party nominees as a way to win concessions. But presumably more candidates would stay in the race to demonstrate their strength. So gradually the percentage of the vote needed to win would shrink. The popular vote winner could have 35 or 25 percent of the total vote, and arguably, this would undermine the legitimacy of the winner. As a consequence, most proposals for a national popular election have included provisions for a runoff election if the winner's percentage was below, say, 40 percent. The prospect of two presidential elections and the political maneuvering associated with runoff elections has reduced enthusiasm for the change.

Two other proposals have been advanced that would not require a constitutional amendment, although a constitutional amendment would be required to adopt them uniformly across the country. The district method, now used in Maine and Nebraska, allows two electors to be selected statewide and the remainder to be selected within congressional districts. The proposal does not eliminate the winner-take-all characteristic, but it does reduce the magnitude of the distortions that can occur. The proportional method would allocate all of the electoral votes on a statewide basis, but through proportional representation instead of to the plurality winner. Given the typical margin of victory in the popular vote in a state, a winning candidate would be unlikely to gain more than a one-vote electoral margin from a state using proportional representation. No individual state is likely to adopt this method because, with only one electoral vote at stake, it would become the least attractive state in the nation for presidential candidates to campaign in.

For years, political scientists and some political commentators have predicted that the electoral college would be immediately abandoned if, in the modern age, it produced a nonpopular vote winner. Why, then, has so little happened to jettison the electoral college since the 2000 election? There are probably a number of reasons that a movement to change the college has not materialized. One is that the 2000 election produced new, more pressing issues for reform—notably ballot type and vote-counting procedures. The nationwide popular vote alternative also appears less attractive after the Florida recount, as the possibility of a nationwide recount is contemplated. Most important, perhaps, is the realization on the part of Republicans (in the majority in the House and Senate for most of the time since 2000) that the presence of the electoral college produced a Republican president. When a substantial part of the political elite senses a benefit in current arrangements, little likelihood exists that the extraordinary majority needed to change the Constitution could be assembled. Much more likely is the possibility that some individual states will decide to follow the example of Maine and Nebraska and adopt the district method of apportioning electors.

Vote Choice in Other Types of Elections

Vote choice can be thought of as the product of a voter's long-term partisanship and the impact of the campaign's short-term forces of candidate characteristics, issue positions, and evaluation of the party's performance. In presidential elections, in which information about the candidates and issues is widespread and easily available, short-term forces often overcome partisanship and cause substantial numbers of voters to defect from a party. In less prominent races, voters make choices with less information and fewer factors influencing their decisions.

In voting for members of Congress, most of the electorate has relatively little information about the candidates, especially candidates challenging incumbents. Party-line voting becomes stronger for less visible offices, including Congress, because issues and personal attributes of the candidates are less likely to have an impact on the voter in less publicized races.

Another significant factor in congressional elections is incumbency. Studies have shown that voters are about twice as likely to be able to identify the incumbent as the challenger in congressional races, and almost all the defections from partisanship are in favor of the more familiar incumbent.[12] Both Republicans and Democrats seem strongly susceptible to voting for incumbents, with more than one-third typically abandoning their usual party for an incumbent representative of the other party. Strong partisans of both parties frequently defect to incumbents of the other party but, on balance, support the challengers from their own party more often than not. Both Democratic and Republican weak partisans, in contrast, are more likely to defect for incumbents than to vote for challengers from their own party.

The advantage that incumbents have does not mean that congressional districts are invariably safe for one party, though many are. Instead, it suggests that even in those districts in which the outcome is virtually a toss-up when two nonincumbents face each other, the representatives who manage to survive a term or two find reelection almost ensured. This tendency becomes accentuated as the opposition party finds it increasingly difficult to field an attractive candidate to challenge a secure incumbent. Thus, many incumbent representatives are elected again and again by safe margins from districts that may fall to the other party once the incumbent no longer seeks reelection. Put another way, the existence of a safe incumbent in a district may say little about the underlying partisan division in that district. It may simply reflect short-term forces that were at work in the last election in which two nonincumbents faced each other.

A Senate election has relatively high visibility and, unlike most congressional races, is amenable to a mass media campaign using television. The more information about the election that gets through to the voters, the less they rely on either partisanship or the familiarity of the incumbent's name. The visibility of a Senate race makes an incumbent senator vulnerable to a well-financed campaign by an attractive opponent. Incumbency may even become a disadvantage in such circumstances because the incumbent has a voting record to defend.

In our companion volume *Political Behavior in Midterm Elections,* we analyze voting in congressional elections at length. Here we simply update that analysis with a discussion of the 2004 elections. The Republicans gained a comfortable majority of fifty-five seats in the Senate as a result of the 2004 elections. Almost all of the Republican pick-ups of previously Democratic seats came in safe Republican states. Only their win in Florida came in a battleground state. Two of the Republican wins in safe states were, nonetheless, close. John Thune's victory over Democratic minority leader Tom Daschle in South Dakota was very competitive as was Richard Burr's win over Erskine Bowles in North Carolina. In Colorado the Democrats managed to win a Republican-held seat with Ken Salazar's narrow victory over Peter Coors. Most of the Senate races were one-sided and none more so than new Democratic senator Barack Obama's win over Alan Keyes.

By most reckoning, the 2004 House races were the least competitive in history. The only challenger to this distinction would be 2002.[13] Only five House incumbents lost a bid for reelection and two of those losses came in Texas as a result of the Republican-controlled redistricting of the 2001 redistricting. In only 23 out of 435 races was the margin of victory as small as 10 percent. Over 80 percent of the races were won by margins greater than 20 percent. Almost half of the House seats that changed from one party to another were in Texas, and these supplied the Republicans with a net gain of six seats. The increase in the size of the Republican majority in the House of Representatives was basically the result of changes in Texas.

The Meaning of an Election

Politicians and news commentators spend much time and energy interpreting and explaining the outcome of an election. The difficulties in assigning meaning to election results are easy to exaggerate. The most important element is usually clear—the winner. Elections are primarily a mechanism for selecting certain governmental leaders and, just as important, for removing leaders from office and preventing others from gaining office. Nevertheless, an effort is often made to discover the policy implications of patterns of voting and to read meaning into the outcome of elections. This effort raises two problems for analysis: first, the policy implications of the winning and losing candidates' issue stands and, second, the issue content of the voters' decisions.

In both 1980 and 1984 Ronald Reagan articulated an unusually clear set of ideological and policy alternatives. Not all elections offer voters a clear choice between a conservative and a liberal candidate, but the 1980 and 1984 races between Reagan and his opponents—Jimmy Carter and Walter F. Mondale, respectively—were widely perceived as doing so. Because Reagan won both elections by wide margins, his administration understandably claimed a popular mandate for a wide range of policies. Similarly, the victory of the House Republicans in 1994 made it easy for them to claim a popular mandate for their Contract with America.

It is perfectly appropriate to attribute policy significance to an election on the basis of the policy preferences of the winning candidates, so long as it is not implied that the voters had these policy implications in mind when they voted. In other words, it is appropriate to observe, particularly in presidential elections, that the election outcome means lower taxes or expanded programs because the victor has pledged to implement lower taxes or to expand programs. But it is very difficult to establish that the voters' preferences have certain policy meaning or that the votes for a particular candidate provide a policy mandate. Several obstacles lie in the way of stating simply what policies are implied by the behavior of the voters. In many elections, the voters are unaware of the stands of candidates on issues, and sometimes the voters are mistaken in their perceptions.

Furthermore, many voters are not concerned with issues as such in a campaign but vote according to their party loyalty or a candidate's personality. Their votes have no particular policy significance but reflect a general preference for one candidate. Voters who supported Reagan in 1980 had an unfavorable view of Carter's performance as president, especially his handling of the Iranian hostage crisis. The dissatisfaction with Carter was clear enough. However, the expectations about Reagan were vague and perhaps limited to the hope that he would strengthen national defense and balance the budget. In 1992 many voters cast a ballot against the elder Bush because of dissatisfaction over the state of the economy, though not for any particular policies. This characteristic of the vote, added to Clinton's low percentage (well below 50 percent) of the overall vote, made it difficult for Clinton to claim any clear mandate. In 1996 the reelection of Clinton, simultaneously with the election of Republican majorities in both the House and Senate, was interpreted, on both sides, as a mandate for bipartisan cooperation. The 2000 election was so close and featured such conflicting signals that no serious claim of a mandate has emerged. The policy significance is undeniable, however, as George W. Bush succeeded in his goal of cutting tax rates (and thereby, by design or inadvertently, eliminating the budget surplus he had inherited). After his victory in 2004, Bush's claim to have received affirmation of his policies in Iraq and in the war against terror needs to be taken seriously. However, little time passed before the administration discovered that a mandate to privatize Social Security is not what the voters had in mind when they reelected him.

Occasionally in a congressional election an incumbent's loss can be traced to a position or action at odds with majority sentiment among the district's constituents. More commonly, election victories say more about the incumbent's attention to constituent service and the advantages of incumbency than about the policy views of the candidates or voters.

A candidate has considerable freedom under most circumstances to interpret a victory with respect to the issues. President Reagan, for example, felt free to interpret his mandate as requiring a massive tax cut but not dictating a balanced budget. There was no more basis for this distinction in public opinion than a mandate to reduce social programs drastically. Conversely, Clinton chose to interpret his election in 1992 as a mandate for health care reform. As it turned out, the public was not as committed to the idea as he was.

Most election outcomes are just as vague and conflicting with respect to most issues, which partially explains the failure of the American political system to impose policy stands on elected officials. This situation illustrates as well the opportunities for leadership afforded to electoral victors. If they are perceived as successful in handling their job, political leaders can convert their following to support their policies, and subsequently it will appear as if the public had demanded the policies in the first place.

The supporters of a candidate usually do not intensely or widely oppose his or her stands. Voters will often vote for candidates who hold views they do not share, but these views are on matters of little interest to the voters. Presumably, voters seldom support candidates who hold views with which they disagree intensely.

On the one hand, American elections are hardly a classic model of democracy with rational, well-informed voters making dispassionate decisions. On the other hand, American elections provide an acceptable opportunity for parties and candidates to attempt to win or hold public office. Although the electorate is capable on occasion of responding to issue appeals both positively and negatively, the electorate does not appear easily moved by most appeals. The electorate offers the parties modest opportunities to gain voters without offering extreme temptations to reckless appeals.

Notes

1. Morris P. Fiorina, *Retrospective Voting in American National Elections* (New Haven: Yale University Press, 1981).
2. J. Merrill Shanks and Warren Miller, "Partisanship, Policy, and Performance: The Reagan Legacy in the 1988 Election," *British Journal of Political Science* 21 (1991): 129–197.

3. A good discussion of this topic in a single source is the collection of articles and commentary by Gerald Pomper, Richard Boyd, Richard Brody, Benjamin Page, and John Kessel in *American Political Science Review* 66 (June 1972): 415–470. See also Benjamin I. Page, *Choices and Echoes in Presidential Elections* (Chicago: University of Chicago Press, 1978).

4. Norman H. Nie, Sidney Verba, and John R. Petrocik, *The Changing American Voter* (Cambridge: Harvard University Press, 1976), chap. 10.

5. J. Merrill Shanks and Warren E. Miller, *The New American Voter* (Cambridge: Harvard University Press, 1996).

6. David RePass, "Issue Salience and Party Choice," *American Political Science Review* 65 (June 1971): 368–400.

7. Fiorina, *Retrospective Voting in American National Elections*.

8. Angus Campbell, Philip E. Converse, Warren E. Miller, and Donald E. Stokes, *The American Voter* (New York: Wiley, 1960), 524–531; and Donald E. Stokes, "Some Dynamic Elements of Contests for the Presidency," *American Political Science Review* 62 (1966): 19–28.

9. Arthur H. Miller and Martin P. Wattenberg, "Policy and Performance Voting in the 1980 Election," paper presented at the annual meeting of the American Political Science Association, New York, 1981, cited in *Controversies in Voting Behavior*, 2d ed., ed. Richard Niemi and Herbert Weisberg (Washington, D.C.: CQ Press, 1984), 91.

10. There are relatively few panel studies of the national electorate over two presidential elections. The National Election Studies conducted panels for 1956–1960, 1972–1976, and 1992–1996. The 2000–2004 loyalty is greater than any of those years.

11. See Lawrence D. Longley and Alan G. Braun, *The Politics of Electoral College Reform* (New Haven: Yale University Press, 1972), for a survey of the proposals for electoral college reform.

12. Donald E. Stokes and Warren E. Miller, "Party Government and the Saliency of Congress," *Public Opinion Quarterly* 26 (winter 1962): 531–546.

13. This discussion is drawn from information found in "Dubious Democracy" on the Web site of the Center for Voting in Democracy, www.fairvote.org.

Suggested Readings

Abramowitz, Alan I., and Jeffrey A. Segal. *Senate Elections.* Ann Arbor: University of Michigan Press, 1992. An extensive analysis of the factors contributing to election outcomes in Senate races.

Bartels, Larry M. *Presidential Primaries and the Dynamics of Public Choice.* Princeton: Princeton University Press, 1988. The best available analysis of public opinion and vote choice during presidential primaries.

Fiorina, Morris P. *Retrospective Voting in American National Elections.* New Haven: Yale University Press, 1981. An important conceptual argument for viewing vote choice as judgments about the past.

Jacobson, Gary C. *The Politics of Congressional Elections,* 4th ed. New York: Addison Wesley Longman, 1996. An authoritative survey of a broad topic and the literature surrounding it.

Niemi, Richard G., and Herbert F. Weisberg. *Classics in Voting Behavior.* Washington, D.C.: CQ Press, 1993. Niemi, Richard G., and Herbert F. Weisberg. *Controversies in Voting Behavior,* 4th ed. Washington, D.C.: CQ Press, 2001. These two collections offer the best readings from decades of research on public opinion and voting behavior.

Shanks, J. Merrill, and Warren E. Miller. *The New American Voter.* Cambridge: Harvard University Press, 1996. A sophisticated analysis of an elaborate model of vote choice.

Internet Resources

The Web site of the National Election Studies, www.umich.edu/~nes, has extensive data on topics covered in this chapter. Click on "Vote Choice," "Evaluation of the Presidential Candidates," and "Evaluation of Congressional Candidates" for a variety of political items from 1952 to the present. In addition, all of these political items are broken down by social characteristics.

The Elections U.S.A. Web site, at www.geocities.com/CapitolHill/6228, has current political information on elections as well as public opinion data. Major news organizations will post results of exit polls on their Web sites. Candidates for office, like the political parties, have Web sites that can be located with search engines.

a p p e n d i x

Survey Research Methods

MANY OF THE DATA in this book have come from survey research, and most of the analysis cited has been based on findings from survey research. For more than forty years the data from the National Election Studies (NES), as well as from other major survey projects in political science, have been available through the Inter-university Consortium for Political and Social Research and have formed the basis for countless research projects in many fields by scholars, graduate students, and undergraduates. Given this widespread use of survey data, it is appropriate to give some description of the data collection methods that underlie them.

During the past seventy years, social scientists have developed an impressive array of techniques for discovering and measuring individual attitudes and behavior. Basically, survey research relies on giving a standard questionnaire to the individuals to be studied. In most major studies of the national electorate over the years, trained interviewers ask the questions and record the responses in a face-to-face interview with each respondent. A few studies depend on the respondents themselves filling out the questionnaires. Recently, the rising costs of survey research, the pressure for quick results, and the availability of random-digit telephone dialing have led both commercial and academic pollsters to rely increasingly on telephone interviewing. The NES used both face-to-face and telephone interviewing in 2000 but returned to using face-to-face interviews exclusively in 2004.

The development of the Internet has allowed a different form of survey research, with respondents filling out questionnaires on a survey organization's Web site. Also, for several decades news organizations have conducted exit polls on election day to provide an early estimate of the outcome and provide additional information about voters that election statistics do not provide.

Survey Data Collection

We will describe four data-collection phases in the survey research process, noting the way these steps vary depending on whether the surveys are face to face, telephone, Internet, or an exit poll. The four phases are sampling, questionnaire constructing, interviewing, and coding.

Sampling

The key to survey research is probability sampling. It may seem inappropriate to analyze the entire American electorate using studies composed of fewer than two thousand individuals, which is about the average number of respondents in the studies used in this book. But it would be prohibitively expensive to interview the entire electorate, and the only way to study public opinion nationally is by interviewing relatively few individuals who accurately represent the entire electorate. Probability sampling is the method used to ensure that the individuals selected for interviewing will be representative of the total population. Probability sampling attempts to select respondents in such a way that every individual in the population has an equal chance of being selected for interviewing. If the respondents are selected in this way, the analyst can be confident that the characteristics of the sample are approximately the same as those of the whole population.

It would be impossible to make a list of every adult in the United States and then draw names from the list randomly. All survey organizations depart from such strict random procedures in some way. The National Election Studies, General Social Survey, and other high-quality surveys using face-to-face interviews employ stratified cluster samples, based on households.

Stratification means that random selection occurs within subpopulations. In the United States the sample is customarily selected within regions to guarantee that all sections are represented and within communities of different sizes as well. *Clustering* means that relatively small geographical areas, called primary sampling units, are randomly selected within the stratified categories so that many interviews are concentrated within a small area to reduce the costs and inconvenience for interviewers. Finally, the Survey Research Center samples *households* instead of individuals (although within households individuals are randomly selected and interviewed), which means that within sampling areas households are enumerated and selected at random. (This sampling procedure means that no respondents are selected on military bases, in hospitals, hotels, and prisons, or in other places where people do not live in households. However, after the enfranchisement of eighteen-year-olds the Survey Research Center began to include college dormitories as residences to be sampled.)

Increasingly, the commercial polling organizations have turned to telephone interviewing as a faster and cheaper alternative to field interviewing. Random-digit dialing is typically used by these polling operations to select both listed and unlisted numbers and to give each residential number the same chance of being called. Telephone sampling has an advantage over field surveys because it does not require clustering.

Telephone sampling ignores individuals without telephones and it also misses cell phone-only households. Otherwise, no major obstacles prevent drawing an excellent sample of telephone numbers. The problems begin at that point. Success in finding someone at home and completing a telephone interview is uneven, and failures may run as high as 50 percent. Some polling organizations make repeated callbacks, as the chances of getting an answer increase with the number of callbacks. Repeated callbacks, however, slow the data collection and increase the costs. Because an important reason for using the telephone is speed and low costs, most polling organizations do not call back.

Once the telephone is answered, or the household is contacted for a face-to-face interview, a respondent from the household must be selected. Some randomizing procedure is typically used to select the respondent. There are two methods for selecting respondents, and they have different consequences. The best sampling procedure, but a costly and time-consuming one, is to identify all the eligible members of the household and select one at random. If the respondent selected is not at home, an appointment is arranged for a callback. In a high-quality survey such as the National Election Study, many attempts are made to interview the individual randomly selected, but no substitutions are made. Telephone surveys, typically, allow a huge proportion of their respondents to be substitutes for the respondents who should have been interviewed. The alternative, and more common, method of selection identifies the respondent among those eligible who are at home and the interview is conducted immediately. This further compromises the sample, making it a selection among those people who happen to be at home when the interviewer calls.

The more often the randomly selected respondents cannot be contacted or refuse to be interviewed, the more the sample departs from its original design. Probability samples, with either face-to-face or telephone interviews, can result in unrepresentative samples if the *nonresponse rate* is high. The nonresponse rate refers to the number of respondents originally selected who, for whatever reason, are not interviewed and thus do not appear in the sample.[1] Should these nonrespondents share some characteristic disproportionately, the resulting sample will underrepresent that type of person. For example, if residents of high-crime neighborhoods, the elderly, or busy people refuse to be interviewed at higher rates than others, the sample will have fewer of these people than occur in the population and thus the sample will be biased. All the polling organizations take steps to counter these tendencies by weighting the results to compensate for various demographic biases.[2] This is a difficult problem to solve, however. Currently, survey organizations have the greatest difficulty getting interviews in the inner cities of the largest metropolitan areas. The likelihood is high that the people who consent to be interviewed in these areas are different from, and therefore not representative of, those who refuse. If this is the case, counting those who are interviewed more heavily (which is essentially what weighting the sample does) does not eliminate the bias.

Internet polls and exit polls have their own sampling problems. Self-administered Internet polls are new and still uncommon. Random-digit dialing is used to draw a sample of residential telephones, similar to a telephone poll, and create a "panel," a large group of individuals who agree to answer a questionnaire and participate in future studies. These individuals are provided with Internet access, if necessary, so the panel is not limited to those who already have such access. Each study draws a sample from the larger panel and these respondents are informed of the opportunity to go online to answer a questionnaire at a secure Web site. Although the sampling design initially produces a representative set of potential respondents, people who are willing to join the panel and participate in particular studies may be different from the rest of the public.

Internet polls have nothing in common with the self-selected "vote on the Internet" polls fancied by some television programs. When people take the initiative to respond, instead of being chosen to respond through a random selection procedure, there can be no claim that it is a representative sample of the public.

Exit polls involve random selection of polling places. Then interviewers go to each of the randomly selected polling places and are instructed to select, say, every tenth voter emerging from the polling place for an interview. At midday the interviewers call in the results of the first set of completed interviews and at this time the central office may adjust the interval of voters to speed up or slow down the pace of interviewing. A number of biases can be introduced in the sampling process, as busy voters refuse to be interviewed and other voters avoid interviewers on the basis of age or race.

Questionnaire Constructing

In survey questionnaires, several types of questions will ordinarily be used. Public opinion surveys began years ago with forced-choice questions that a respondent was asked to answer by choosing among a set of offered alternatives. For example, forced-choice questions frequently take the form of stating a position on public policy and asking the respondent to "agree" or "disagree" with the statement. The analysis in Chapter 6 was based in part on the answers to forced-choice questions on public policy that were used in NES questionnaires in which respondents were asked to "agree strongly," "agree," "disagree," or "disagree strongly." Some respondents either gave qualified answers that did not fit into these prearranged categories or had no opinions.

A major innovation associated with the Survey Research Center is the use of open-ended questioning. Open-ended questions give respondents the opportunity to express their opinions in their own way without being forced to select among categories provided by the questionnaire. Questions such as "Is there anything in particular you like about the Democratic Party?" or "What are the most important problems facing the country today?" permit the respondents to answer in their own terms. Interviewers encourage respondents to answer such questions as fully as they can with neutral "probes" such as "Could you tell me more about that?" or "Anything else?" or similar queries that draw forth more discussion. Open-ended questions are a superior method of eliciting accurate expressions of opinion.

Open-ended questioning has two major disadvantages: (1) it places more of a burden on interviewers to record the responses; and (2) the burden of reducing the many responses to a dimension that can be analyzed is left for the coders. For example, if Americans are asked, "Do you think of yourself as a Democrat, a Republican, or an independent?" almost all the responses will fit usefully into the designated categories:

1. Democrat
2. Independent
3. Republican
4. Other party
5. I'm nothing; apolitical
6. Don't know
7. Refused to say
8. Not ascertained

If a relatively unstructured, open-ended question is used, however— such as "How do you think of yourself politically?"—some people would answer with "Democrat," "Republican," and so forth, but many others might give answers that were substantially different, such as "liberal," "conservative," "radical," "moderate," "pragmatic," "apathetic"—and these could not easily be compared with the partisan categories. Analysts often intend to force responses into a single dimension, such as partisanship, whether the respondents would have volunteered an answer along that dimension or not. This is essential if researchers are to develop single dimensions for analytic purposes. Modern survey research includes questions and techniques considerably more complex than these examples for establishing dimensions.

Questionnaires differ a great deal in their complexity and sophistication. Face-to-face interviews with well-trained interviewers may have many open-ended questions or questions with branching, conditional on the responses to previous questions. Telephone interviews using Computer-Assisted Telephone Interview (CATI) technology and online Internet polls can also be complex, relying on computer branching to guide the respondent through the questionnaire. At the other extreme, exit polls are entirely forced-choice questions that can be completed quickly by the voter without instruction.

Interviewing

The selection of the sample depends in part on the interviewer, but even more important is the role of the interviewer in asking questions of the respondent and in recording the answers. Motivated, well-trained interviewers are crucial to the success of survey research. The interviewer has several major responsibilities. First, the interviewer must select the respondent according to sampling instructions. Second, the interviewer must develop rapport with the respondent so that he or she will be willing to go through with the interview, which may last an hour or more. Third, the interviewer must ask the questions in a friendly way and encourage the respondent to answer fully without leading the respondent to distort his or her views. Fourth, the interviewer must record the answers of the respondent fully and accurately. The best survey organizations keep a permanent staff of highly trained interviewers for this purpose.

A technological innovation used in telephone interviewing is the CATI system. The interviewer sits at the telephone, with the questionnaire appearing on a computer screen. As the interviewer moves through the questionnaire, responses are entered directly into the computer and automatically coded. Complicated branching to different questions, conditional on the responses given to preceding questions, is possible.

Telephone interviewing has some real advantages. The travel costs of a field staff are eliminated. Having interviewing conducted from a call-room allows for direct supervision of the interviewing staff, enhancing the uniformity of the administration of the questionnaires. Within-interview "experiments" are possible with the CATI system. Also, changing the content of the questionnaire during the course of the study is easy and inexpensive. The great disadvantage is that face-to-face interviews yield higher quality data.

In Internet polling, on the one hand, there are no interviewers, which is a great saving in cost. On the other hand, there is no interviewer to help the respondent navigate the questionnaire or to keep the respondent motivated—or to make judgments about the plausibility of the responses.

Exit polls generally use a combination of self-administered questionnaires with interviewers available to read the questionnaires and record responses for those voters who need assistance. Given that exit polls might provide one day of work every couple of years, exit poll interviewers are not seasoned professionals. They also work in scattered locations with no direct supervision. Errors in implementing the sampling technique or in administering the questionnaires would rarely be caught and unlikely to be corrected in the short time span of election day.

Coding

Once the interviewers administer the questionnaires to respondents, the verbal information is reduced to a numerical form, according to a code. Numeric information, unlike verbal information, can be processed and manipulated by high-speed, data-processing equipment. The coder's task may be simple or complex. For example, to code the respondent's gender requires a simple code: 1 = male, 2 = female. A data field that contains information on the respondent will have a location designated for indicating the respondent's gender. A value of 1 will indicate male, and a value of 2 will indicate female. The list of partisan categories above gives the coding numbers that would stand for various responses. Printed questionnaires for face-to-face interviews are precoded for many of the more straightforward questions, and the CATI system allows precoded categories to be assigned automatically as the interviewer records the respondent's answers.

Some coding is complicated, with elaborate arrays of categories. For example, coding the responses to a question such as "Is there anything in particular you like about the Democratic Party?" might include hundreds of categories covering such details as "I like the party's farm policies," "I like the party's tax program," and "I've just always been a Democrat." Some codes require coders to make judgments about the respondents' answers. In political surveys these codes have included judgments on the level of sophistication of the respondents' answers and judgments about the main reason for respondents' vote choices.

After the verbal information has been converted into numbers according to the coding instructions, the data are ready for analysis by computer. At this point, the survey research process ends; the political analysts take over to make what use of the data they can.

Validity of Survey Questions

A frequent set of criticisms directed at public opinion research questions the validity of the responses to survey items. *Validity* simply means the extent to which there is correspondence between the verbal response to a question and the attitude or behavior of the respondent

Advantages and Disadvantages of Different Types of Surveys

Face-to-face interviews with respondents drawn from a sample of households

Advantages	High-quality data
	Allows for longer, more in-depth interviews
Disadvantages	High cost
	Slow data collection and processing

Telephone interviews of respondents drawn from a sample of residential telephone numbers

Advantages	Lower cost
	Fast turnaround especially using a Computer-Assisted Telephone Interview system
	Allows direct supervision of interviewing process
Disadvantages	Cell phone- and no-phone households are excluded from the sample
	Call-screening and resistance to stranger calls further degrades the sample

Self-administered Internet polls

Advantages	Less expensive once the panel is set up
	Subsamples with particular characteristics can be drawn from the panel
Disadvantages	Those who agree to participate may be unrepresentative of the population

Exit polls

Advantages	Provides a large number of journalists with material for reporting and commentary immediately after an election
Disadvantages	Lack of training and supervision of interviewers
	With increase in absentee and mail-in voting, poll needs to be supplemented with telephone survey of voters who do not go to a polling place

that the question is designed to measure. There is no one answer to doubts about validity, because each item has a validity applicable to it alone. Some items are notoriously invalid; others have nearly perfect validity. Many survey items have not been independently tested for their validity, and for practical purposes, the researcher is forced to say that he or she is interested in analyzing the responses, whatever they mean to the respondent. In other instances the sample result can be compared with the known population value.

The items with the most questionable validity in political studies come from those situations in which respondents have some incentive to misrepresent the facts or when their memories may not be accurate. Questions about voter turnout or level of income are noteworthy in this regard. Validity checks reveal that respondents are about as likely to underestimate their income as overestimate it, and a noticeable percentage of respondents claim to have voted when they did not.[3]

Recall of past voting behavior falls victim to failing memories and intervening events. Changes in party identification, past votes cast, the party identification of one's parents—all may contain substantial error. For example, during November and December immediately after the 1960 election, respondents were asked how they had voted for president. Most remembered voting for either John F. Kennedy or Richard M. Nixon, and, as shown in Table A-1, they were divided about evenly between the two. (The slight deviation of 1 percent from the actual results is within sampling error by any reasonable standards.) The 1962 and 1964 sample estimates of the 1960 vote reveal increasing departures from the actual outcome. Granting that some change in the population over four years may affect vote-choice percentages, a substantial proportion of the 1964 sample gave responses to the question of 1960 presidential vote choice that misrepresented their vote. The validity of this

TABLE A-1   Recalled Vote for President in 1960, 1962, and 1964

Recalled vote	1960	1962	1964	Actual vote in 1960[a]
John F. Kennedy	49%	56%	64%	49.7%
Richard M. Nixon	51	43	36	49.5
Other	b	b	b	0.7
Total	100%	99%	100%	99.9%
(*N*)	(1,428)	(940)	(1,124)	

Sources: National Election Studies, available at www.umich.edu/~nes and from the U.S. House of Representatives, Office of the Clerk, clerk.house.gov.

[a] The 1960 popular vote can be tallied in a number of ways, including those that show Nixon with a slight popular vote majority. No matter how the votes are counted, the election was very close.
[b] Less than 0.5 percent.

item always declines over a four-year period, but President Kennedy's assassination in the intervening years created an unusually large distortion in recalled vote.

Validity versus Continuity

One of the important features of the NES is its continuity over a fifty-year time span. Samples of the American population have been asked the same questions during every national election campaign throughout this period, offering an extraordinary opportunity for studying trends in the attitudes of the American electorate. The development of this valuable, continuous series does have one unfortunate aspect, however. Because the value of the series depends on the comparability of the questions, researchers are reluctant to alter questions, even when doubts about their validity arise. Improving the questions undermines comparability. Therefore, a choice between continuity and validity must be made.

The NES questions concerning religious preference provide a recent example in which validity was chosen over continuity. For years, respondents were simply asked, "What is your religious preference?" Although a small percentage in each survey answered "None," it was clear that a significant number of those answering "Protestant," and fewer numbers citing other religions, had no meaningful religious affiliation. In the 1992 survey, the NES began asking the question differently. Respondents were first asked, "Do you ever attend religious services, apart from occasional weddings, baptisms, and funerals?" Those who answered "no" were asked an additional question about their religious preference: "Regardless of whether you now attend any religious services, do you ever think of yourself as part of a particular church or denomination?" Those who did not answer "yes" to one of these two screening questions were not asked the traditional question about religious affiliation that then followed. As a result, the percentage of the population categorized as having no religious affiliation increased dramatically. This new question more validly reflects the religious sentiments of the American public, but it is now impossible to compare these later results with those of previous years. We cannot infer a large drop in religious affiliation on the basis of the responses to these new and different questions. In this instance, continuity has been sacrificed in favor of validity.

Despite inevitable concerns about validity, survey research provides the best means of investigating the attitudes and behavior of large populations of individuals such as the American electorate.

Notes

1. See John Brehm, *The Phantom Respondents* (Ann Arbor: University of Michigan Press, 1993).
2. *Public Opinion* 4 (February/March 1981): 20.
3. Paul Abramson and William Claggett, "Race-Related Differences in Self-Reported and Validated Turnout," *Journal of Politics* 46 (August 1984): 719–738.

Suggested Readings

Asher, Herbert. *Polling and the Public,* 5th ed. Washington, D.C.: CQ Press, 2001. A good discussion of how polls are conducted and how they are used.

Backstrom, Charles H., and Gerald D. Hursh-Cesar. *Survey Research,* 2d ed. New York: Wiley, 1981. A good introduction to survey research methods.

Kish, Leslie. *Survey Sampling.* New York: Wiley, 1965. By far the most authoritative work on sampling.

Mann, Thomas E., and Gary R. Orren, eds. *Media Polls in American Politics.* Washington, D.C.: Brookings Institution, 1992. An excellent collection of essays on the use of polls in contemporary media analysis.

Survey Research Center. *Manual for Interviewers* and *Manual for Coders.* Ann Arbor: Survey Research Center, University of Michigan, n.d. A simple, thorough introduction to the interviewing and coding processes.

Weisberg, Herbert F., Jon Krosnick, and Bruce D. Bowen. *An Introduction to Survey Research and Data Analysis.* San Francisco: W. H. Freeman, 1989. A good, methodological textbook on survey research and the interpretation of statistical analysis.

Internet Resources

The Web site of the National Election Studies, at www.umich.edu/~nes, has extensive information on survey research methods. Click on "Studies, Data, and Other Resources" to examine NES questionnaires and codebooks for recent studies. The codebooks also have discussions of the NES sampling design and the selection of respondents.

Some other Web sites with methodological information are the Gallup Poll at www.gallup.com; the Pew Research Center for the People and the Press at www.people-press.org; the General Social Survey at www.icpsr.umich.edu/gss; and the Institute for Research in Social Science at www.irss.unc.edu/data-archive.

Index